HELP YOURSELF TO ESSENTIAL
SPANISH GRAMMAR

A grammar reference and workbook
GCSE/Standard Grade

Niobe O'Connor

Pearson Education Limited
Edinburgh Gate
Harlow
Essex
CM20 2JE
England and Associated Companies throughout the World

ISBN 0582 28747 2

First published 1998
Third impression 2004
Printed in China
SWTC/03

The Publisher's policy is to use paper manufactured from sustainable forests.

Acknowledgements

Sincere thanks to Mireille Ribière and Thalia Marriott for their comments on the
manuscript and to the O'Connor family for their constant support.

Contents

Introduction

Help Yourself to Essential Spanish Grammar is a combined grammar reference book with exercises. It is designed both for self-study and class-based learning at the elementary and intermediate stages of learning Spanish.

It is suitable for use as a one-year revision programme for Year 11 pupils at school and as a preparation for GCSE or Standard Grade. It is also aimed at adult learners taking intermediate Spanish or GCSE, and for individuals studying on their own.

Preparation for GCSE and Standard Grade (Scotland)

Using this book will enable students to reach the level required to obtain Foundation and Higher GCSE grades, and Standard Grade (Scotland).

Units 1–8 cover the main structures and grammar required. Unit 9 contains material which those aiming at the highest grades may need to use actively. Further points which normally require reading and listening recognition only are covered in the Appendix.

Presentation of grammar and vocabulary

The structures and exercises are carefully graded. Grammatical terms are explained when first used, and there is a quick reference guide in the Appendix.

The vocabulary used in the exercises covers topics which are appropriate to communicative language teaching and learning at this level: everyday activities, personal and social life, the world around us, the world of work, the international world.

All vocabulary has been carefully selected as being appropriate to the requirements of the GCSE syllabuses.

Contents of the units

Each unit contains three chapters. In units 1–8 every chapter starts with *What do you know?* exercises which are designed to identify problem areas and assess the particular needs of students.

These exercises are followed by the *grammar explanations*. They present in plain language the structures and grammar needed in order to speak and write simple but correct Spanish.

The final section contains the *What have you learnt?* exercises, enabling students to apply and practise the grammar covered in the chapter.

At the end of each unit, a *Revision Test* helps students check that they have understood and remembered the grammar explained in the last three chapters.

Unit 9 presents some more advanced points of grammar. Each of the three chapters contains grammatical explanations followed by simple practice exercises. The unit ends with a *Revision Test*.

Appendices

Appendices include verb tables with the regular and irregular verbs needed at this stage, and further information about language rules and usage which will be useful to students when doing the exercises and when communicating in Spanish.

Glossaries and grammar index

The Spanish-English and English-Spanish glossaries provide all the vocabulary needed to complete the exercises. The Grammar index enables both teacher and learner to find grammatical explanations for all grammar points covered in the book.

Key to exercises

Solutions to all exercises are given at the end of the book. These pages can be removed for class use.

Further advice to students learning on their own

You can use this book in three ways: as a workbook, as a grammar reference, or as both!

Using the book as a workbook

The exercises and language points covered in Units 1–9 are carefully graded to enable you to work systematically through the book. Use the *What do you know?* exercises to find out your strengths and weaknesses, read through the grammar explanations, and then do the *What have you learnt?* exercises to check your understanding. Finally, at the end of each unit, revise what you have learnt by doing the *Revision Test*.

Using the book as a grammar reference

To find out about a particular point of grammar, look up the chapter reference in the Grammar index at the back of the book. Read the explanations carefully and do the relevant exercises (*What do you know? What have you learnt?* and the *Revision Test*).

Before you begin ...

Here is some advice on how to tackle the exercises.

1 Remember that the vocabulary needed to understand the exercises and to complete them is provided at the back of the book.

2 Before starting each exercise, read through the instruction and example carefully to make sure you understand the point of the exercise and what you have to do. It may be helpful to write out your answers in full and check your work carefully for any spelling mistakes, necessary agreement of adjectives, verb endings etc.

3 Then, and only then, check your answers against the Key to exercises at the back of the book. Learn from any mistakes you made by re-reading the relevant grammar point again in the grammar explanations. Make a note of, and learn, any new vocabulary. Later on, you might like to tackle some of the exercises again to see if you can get all the answers right this time!

¡Buena suerte!

Niobe O'Connor

¿Dónde?

Before looking at the explanations in this unit, find out what you know by doing the following activities.

A Fun day at school seems to have been a bit of a disaster! Complete the Deputy Head's complaints by inserting **el**, **la**, **los** o **las** in the spaces provided.
e.g. ¡Hay papeles en … patio!   →   ¡Hay papeles en **el** patio!

¡Qué desastre!
1 ¡Hay papeles en … patio!
2 ¡Hay bolsas de patatas fritas en … cocinas!
3 ¡Hay coca-cola y limonada en … mesas!
4 ¡Hay mucha basura en … pasillos!
5 ¡Hay mesas en … entrada!
6 ¡Hay un montón de sillas en … gimnasio!
7 ¡Hay ropa de deporte y raquetas en … laboratorios!
8 ¡Hay un proyector en … campo de fútbol!
9 ¡Hay un elefante en … oficina de la directora!

B Compare the number of rooms in your flat with those in the Royal Palace in Madrid: rewrite the word underlined to show there's more than one of them.
e.g. hay una <u>cocina</u>   →   hay tres **cocinas**

Mi piso y el Palacio Real
1 hay una <u>cocina</u>   hay tres …
2 hay un <u>dormitorio</u>   hay cincuenta y dos …
3 hay un <u>pasillo</u>   hay miles de …
4 hay un <u>aseo</u>   hay cuarenta …
5 no hay <u>garaje</u>   hay treinta …
6 hay un <u>comedor</u>   hay cinco …
7 hay un <u>cuarto de baño</u>   hay veintidós …

Nouns

1 A NOUN is the name for a person, place or thing. *Teacher, school, book* are all nouns.

2 In English, people are *he* (masculine) or *she* (feminine) and objects are *it*.
   In Spanish, all nouns are MASCULINE or FEMININE. This is their GENDER.

3 Nouns can be SINGULAR (only one) or PLURAL (more than one).

Saying *a* and *some*

4 The Spanish **un** and **una** mean *a* or *one*; **unos** and **unas** mean *some*:

	SINGULAR	PLURAL
MASCULINE	**un** dormitorio *a/one bedroom*	**unos** dormitorios *some bedrooms*
FEMININE	**una** silla *a/one chair*	**unas** sillas *some chairs*

Saying *the*

5 In Spanish, **el**, **la**, **los** and **las** mean *the*:

	SINGULAR	PLURAL
MASCULINE	**el** laboratorio *the laboratory*	**los** laboratorios *the laboratories*
FEMININE	**la** oficina *the office*	**las** oficinas *the offices*

Gender of nouns

6 It is best to learn the gender of each noun as you meet it. However, in general, nouns
   ending in -**o** are masculine:

    un pis**o**   *a flat*
    un dormitori**o** *a bedroom*

Common exceptions:

    una man**o**   *a hand*
    una radi**o**   *a radio*
    una fot**o**   *a photo*

Words ending in -**ma** are often masculine. Common examples include:

el clima	*the climate*	el programa	*the programme*
el drama	*the drama*	el sistema	*the system*
el pijama	*the pyjamas*	el tema	*the theme, topic*

Help Yourself to Essential Spanish Grammar

7 In general, nouns ending in -**a** are feminine:

una casa   *a house*
una finca   *a farm*

Common exceptions:

un día   *a day*   un planeta   *a planet*
un sofá   *a sofa*   un tranvía   *a tram*
un mapa   *a map*   el yoga   *yoga*

8 Use *el* and *un* before feminine nouns which begin with *a-* or *ha-*. The noun still remains feminine but is easier to say:

quisiera **un** agua mineral fría   *I'd like a cold mineral water*
el hambre es terrible   *hunger is terrible*

9 Nouns ending in *-ista* can be masculine or feminine, depending on the gender of the person to which they refer:

Miguel es periodista y viaja mucho   *Miguel is a journalist and travels a lot*
¿la ciclista? se llama Marta   *the cyclist? She's called Marta*

10 Note, the noun **Correos** (*Post Office*) is used without **un**, **una**, **el**, **la** in front:

¿dónde está Correos?   *where is the Post Office?*

Plural of nouns

11 For nouns ending in a vowel (**a**, **e**, **i**, **o**, **u**) add -**s**; for those ending in a consonant (any other letter) add -**es**:

SINGULAR	una cocina *a kitchen*	un comedor *a dining-room*
PLURAL	dos cocinas *two kitchens*	dos comedores *two dining-rooms*

For nouns ending in -**z** in the singular, the -**z** changes to -**c** in the plural:

un lápi**z**   *one pencil*   dos lápi**c**es   *two pencils*

A vowel with an accent before the final consonant loses the accent in the plural:

una canci**ó**n   *a song*   dos canciones   *two songs*

12 In nouns made up of several words, the first word is given the plural ending:

un cuarto de baño   dos cuarto**s** de baño

CHAPTER 1   WHAT HAVE YOU LEARNT?

Now that you have studied the explanations on the previous pages, check that you have understood them by doing the following activities.

A Maite is on holiday in the grand Hotel Alfonso XIII. In this extract from a letter to her best friend, put the words in brackets into the plural.

e.g. Mis (*habitación*) preferidas   →   Mis **habitaciones** preferidas

El Hotel Alfonso XIII

Mis (*habitación*) preferidas son los (*salón*) en la planta baja. El más bonito tiene tres (*ventana*) grandes. Hay (*alfombra*) azules encima de la moqueta, y en las (*pared*) hay muchos (*cuadro*) antiguos. Tiene muchas (*butaca*) y muchos (*sofá*). Como es enorme, tiene dos (*televisor*), uno en el salón y otro cerca de las (*puerta*) principales. Está empapelado de azul claro con (*raya*) blancas. En los (*jardín*) hay (*flor*) y (*planta*), con muchos (*árbol*) y (*frutal*). Hay también tres (*patio*) bonitos, con (*fuente*) y (*terraza*) donde se puede tomar el sol.

B After the holidays, Maite looks at her school with new eyes. Complete her criticisms with **el**, **la**, **los** or **las**.

e.g. … edificios son muy antiguos   →   **Los** edificios son muy antiguos.

Mi instituto – lo bueno y lo malo

1 … edificios son muy antiguos.
2 … instalaciones deportivas son nuevas.
3 … aulas son viejas y pequeñas.
4 En … sala de profesores, se puede fumar: esto no es aceptable.
5 … gimnasio es grande y moderno.
6 … piscina es muy bonita.
7 … cantina es demasiado pequeña.
8 … campo de fútbol está lejos.
9 En general, … profes son simpáticos.
10 … clases prácticas son interesantes.

How positive or negative is Maite about her school? Decide whether each comment should go under the heading 'Lo bueno' (the good) or 'Lo malo' (the bad).
e.g. Lo malo: 1

Help Yourself to Essential Spanish Grammar

UNIT

1

A Señor Hernández is greeting visitors from Venezuela, with his class from an international school, at a town-twinning party in Barcelona. Work out whether he knows the people he talks to well or not by noting whether he uses **tú**, **vosotros**, **usted** or **ustedes**?

e.g. ¿De dónde eres, exactamente?   →   **tú**

La Reunión

1 ¿Qué tal estás? Oye, se me ha olvidado – ¿de dónde eres, exactamente?
2 Buenos días, Señora Ruiz! Mucho gusto! Es de Barcelona, ¿no?
3 Encantado, Señor Garai, Señora Garai. Son venezolanos, ¿verdad?
4 Chicos, ¡un poco de calma! ¡Estais un poco sobre-excitados!
5 Doña Carmen – ¡qué gusto verla! Es directora ahora, ¿no?
6 Marta, ¡eres imposible! ¡Cállate, por favor!

B In the twinning programme, letters from would-be pen-pals are brought to the international school in Barcelona. Choose the correct part of the verb **ser** (*to be*) in brackets in Rosario's letter.

La corresponsal

Hola, ¿qué tal? Me llamo Rosario y vivo en Venezuela con mi familia. En total, (*somos, soy*) cinco: mis padres, mis hermanos y yo. En realidad, yo (*soy, eres*) española, porque nací en Madrid en España. Pero Eduardo y Felipe (*son, somos*) venezolanos. Mi padre (*es, eres*) cartero – ¿qué hacen tus padres? Mi profe dice que vosotros vivís en Barcelona: ¿(*son, sois*) catalanes? Yo (*es, soy*) bastante alta y delgada y me encanta viajar. Y tú, ¿cómo (*soy, eres*)? ¡Un día quiero visitar tu país!

C At the international school, Milagros is waiting in the queue for lunch, listening to the snippets of conversation around her. Decide whether the sentences 1–3 need **el** or not, and whether the sentences 4–6 need **la** or not.

En la cola

1 Este año, aprendo … catalán también.
2 No, no hablo … español muy bien.
3 ¿El hombre grande? Es el director – … Señor Ruiz.
4 ¡Tengo hambre! ¿Qué hora es? ¿Es … una ya?
5 ¿Hay algo para vegetarianos? No me gusta … carne.
6 ¿Eres vegetariana? ¡A qué te dan … ensalada!

The verb **ser**: *to be*

1 A VERB is a word which describes an action. *To speak* and *to be* are verbs.

2 The PRESENT TENSE of a verb is used to explain:

what we are doing at the moment ***I'm reading*** *a new book*
what we usually do ***I read*** *a lot of science-fiction*
to emphasise what we do ***I do read*** *other things as well!*

3 There are two verbs *to be* in Spanish: **ser** and **estar** (page 10). The present tense of the verb **ser** is as follows:

yo	**soy**	*I am*	nosotros	**somos**	*we are*
tú	**eres**	*you are*	vosotros	**sois**	*you are*
él	**es**	*he is*	ellos	**son**	*they are*
ella	**es**	*she is*	ellas	**son**	*they are*
usted	**es**	*you are*	ustedes	**son**	*you are*

4 It is used to describe or identify people or things:

soy alta ***I'm tall***   **son** españoles ***they are*** *Spanish*

Saying *I, you* etc.

5 To show who is doing something in English, we use the subject pronouns *I, you, he* etc:

I'm *from Glasgow: where do* ***you*** *live?   John?* ***He*** *works very hard.* ***I*** *don't!*

In Spanish, these SUBJECT PRONOUNS (*yo, tú* etc.) are often left out. Subject pronouns are useful for emphasis:

Soy española ***I am*** *Spanish*
Toni y Marifé, **sois** muy habladores *Toni and Marifé,* ***you're*** *very chatty*
¡Pero **tú**, Marifé, **eres** la peor! *But* ***you****, Marifé,* ***are*** *the worst!*

6 There are four words for *you* in Spanish. With people you know well, use **tú** to one person, or **vosotros** to more than one person:

Carlos – ¡(**tú**) **eres** pesado! *Carlos – you're a pain!*
Chicos, ¡(**vosotros**) **sois** ruidosos! *Boys, you're noisy!*

7   With people you don't know well, use **usted** to one person, or **ustedes** to more than
   one person:

   ¿Señor Ruiz, (**usted**) **es** de Madrid?   *Mr. Ruiz, **are you** from Madrid?*
   ¿(**ustedes**) **son** de Barcelona?   ***are you** from Barcelona?*

Using **un** and **una**

8   **Un** and **una** are usually left out when describing someone's job:

   soy estudiante   *I'm **a** student*   es médico   *he's **a** doctor*

9   They are also omitted in front of the number **cien** (*100*), **mil** (*1000*):

   cien profes   *a hundred teachers*   **mil** alumnos   *a thousand pupils*

Using **el**, **la**, **los**, **las**

10 Spanish uses **el**, **la**, **los** and **las** where English does not use *the*:

   a   before languages, but not straight after **hablar** (*to speak*):

      el español es divertido   *Spanish is fun*   hablo español   *I speak Spanish*

   b   with time:

      es **la** una   *it's one o'clock*   son **las** dos   *it's two o'clock*

   c   with clothes and parts of the body, where English uses *my/your* etc:

      me lavo **la** cara   *I wash my face*   me pongo **el** abrigo   *I put on my coat*

   d   in general statements and with likes or dislikes:

      me gusta **el** café   *I like coffee*   **la** vida es difícil   *life is difficult*

   e   when using titles (*Mr.*, *Dr.*) and talking *about* someone:

      la Señora Ruiz me fastidia mucho   *Mrs. Ruiz gets on my nerves*

CHAPTER 2   WHAT HAVE YOU LEARNT?

A Señor Ruiz is a journalist, interviewing students in an international school. In his article, insert the correct part of **ser** from the list below.

e.g. El Instituto Mundial ... un ejemplo   →   El Instituto Mundial **es** un ejemplo

El Instituto Mundial

El Instituto Mundial ... un ejemplo maravilloso de una coexistencia alegre. Los estudiantes hablan español en las aulas, pero ... rusos, griegos, chinos, irlandeses – ¡una auténtica ensalada de nacionalidades! En el recreo, hablé con un chico, Ruani:

– ¿Y tú, Ruani, de qué nacionalidad ... ?
– ¿Yo? ¡... internacional!
– ¿Y cuántos ... en vuestra clase?
– Bueno, ... unos quince en total, pero todos de nacionalidades diferentes.
– ¿Y a veces, esto no ... un poco difícil?
– Claro hay dificultades en comunicarse, de vez en cuando, pero ¡nosotros ... muy pacientes!

somos   es   eres   soy   son   es   somos   sois

B Señor Ruiz spots Milagros in the foyer of the international school, waiting to go into lunch. Fill in the gaps in their conversation with one of **el**, **la**, **los**, **las** if necessary.
e.g. Hablo ... español.   →   Hablo español.

Milagros

SR. RUIZ   Eres de Perú, ¿verdad? ¿Qué idiomas hablas?
MILAGROS   Hablo ... español, claro.
SR. RUIZ   ¿Aprendes ... inglés?
MILAGROS   Sí. Y aprendo ... quechua también.
SR. RUIZ   ¿El idioma de ... indios?
MILAGROS   Sí. Mis amigos quechuas viven en el 'antiplano', es decir en ... sierra. Vamos allí durante ... vacaciones, a Quillabamba.
SR. RUIZ   Pero hablar ... quechua es muy difícil, ¿no?
MILAGROS   ¡Sí! Pero ... chicas del pueblo son simpáticas. Nos reímos mucho.
SR. RUIZ   ¿Te gusta ... vida allí?
MILAGROS   Sí, es muy diferente; ... ritmo de vida es más lento y relajado.
SR. RUIZ   Bueno, ya es ... una y media. ... Señor Martín nos llama. ¿Quieres comer?
MILAGROS   Sí. Pero primero, me lavo ... manos. Vuelvo en dos minutos.

UNIT

1

A Visitors to Madrid ask the tour guide how to get to the places of interest in their brochure. Use **¿Para ir a ...?** to form the questions.

e.g. el Museo del Prado   →   **¿Para ir al** Museo del Prado?

Lugares de interés

1 el Museo del Prado   – *pinturas muy famosas*
2 la Plaza de Cibeles   – *fuente y estatua bonita*
3 las tiendas en el Diagonal   – *compras de lujo*
4 el Rastro   – *mercadillo al aire libre*
5 las Ramblas   – *mercado de flores*

B None of the guests have returned for lunch! The guide, José Luis, receives a frantic phone-call. Fill the gaps with the correct part of the verb **estar** (*to be*) from the list below.

e.g. ¿Dónde ...?   →   ¿Dónde **estás**?

La llamada

JOSE LUIS ¡Claire! ¿Dónde ... ?
CLAIRE   En la Plaza Mayor. No ... muy bien: me duelen los pies.
JOSE LUIS ¿Y tu amiga Sasha? ¿ ... contigo?
CLAIRE   No. Yo ... un poco preocupada.
JOSE LUIS Tú y Claire – ¿no ... con los chicos Rob y James?
CLAIRE   ¡No sé dónde ... los chicos!
JOSE LUIS ¡Qué desastre!

estáis   estoy   estás   estoy   está   están

C José Luis arranges to pick up his guests from their different locations. Choose the correct place from the list below to complete the arrangements.

Si nos vemos ...

1 ¿Si nos vemos detrás del ...?
2 ¿Claire? ¿Nos encontramos delante de los ...?
3 Oye Sasha – ¿te espero en la entrada de la ...?
4 ¿Rob? Nos encontramos enfrente de ... – ¿vale?
5 ¿Me esperas en el parque cerca de las ...?

Correos   residencias   almacenes grandes   estación   Teatro Real

The verb **estar**:

1 The Spanish verb **estar** also means *to be*. The present tense is as follows:

yo	**estoy**	*I am*	nosotros	**estamos**	*we are*
tú	**estás**	*you are*	vosotros	**estáis**	*you are*
él	**está**	*he is*	ellos	**están**	*they are*
ella	**está**	*she is*	ellas	**están**	*they are*
usted	**está**	*you are*	ustedes	**están**	*you are*

2 **Estar** is used to:

  a say where someone or something is:

¿Dónde **está** la Oficina de Turismo?	*Where **is** the Tourist Office?*
¿Dónde **estamos**?	*Where **are** we?*

  b indicate a mood or state which is temporary:

Juan **está** enfermo	*Juan **is** ill (temporary)*
¿Qué tal **estás**? **Estoy** muy preocupado	*How **are** you? **I'm** very worried*
Esta sala **está** fría	*This room **is** cold (not always so)*

  but it is also used to talk about death and marital status:

El Rey **está** muerto	*The King **is** dead*
Mis padres **están** separados	*My parents **are** separated*

  Note that being single or widowed needs the verb **ser**:

  soy soltero pero mi hermana **es** viuda   *I'm single but my sister is a widow*

3 Some adjectives change meaning if used with **estar** instead of **ser**:

	estar	ser
aburrido	*bored*	*boring*
cansado	*tired*	*tiresome*
enfermo	*sick*	*sickly (unhealthy)*
listo	*ready*	*clever, sharp*
vivo	*alive*	*alert, lively*

Mi hermano **está** triste	*My brother **is** sad (temporarily)*
Mi hermano **es** triste	*My brother **is** gloomy (by nature)*

Help Yourself to Essential Spanish Grammar

Saying where things or people are

4 PREPOSITIONS explain where a person or object is.

a	to	en	in, at
de	*from*	**hasta**	*as far as*
desde	*from*	**entre**	*between*

Examples of PREPOSITIONS:

¿Vas **a** Ávila, o sólo **hasta** Madrid?   *You're going **to** Ávila, or only **as far as** Madrid?*

Está **entre** el bar y la farmacia   *It's **between** the bar and the chemist's*

5 a   When **a** is followed by the masculine singular **el** (*the*):

a + el = al

¿El museo? ¿Cómo se va **al** museo?   *The museum? How do you get **to the** museum?*

b   Similarly, when **de** is followed by the masculine singular **el** (*the*):

de + el = del

¿Para ir **del** banco al hotel?   *How do you get **from the** bank to the hotel?*

6   The following prepositions can be used on their own:

delante	*in front*	**detrás**	*behind*
al lado	*beside, next*	**enfrente**	*opposite*
encima	*above, on top*	**debajo**	*below, under*
cerca	*near*	**lejos**	*far*
dentro	*inside*	**fuera**	*outside*
al final	*at the end*	**alrededor**	*around*

Examples:

Hay un jardín **detrás**   *There is a garden behind*

¿La bolera está **lejos**?   *Is the bowling alley far?*

7   When used with a noun, these prepositions must be followed by **de**. In English, we often use *of*, *to* or nothing:

La cafetería está **al final de** la calle   *The café is **at the end of** the street*

Está **al lado de** los servicios   *It's **next to** the toilets*

Está **cerca de** la cafetería   *It's **near** the café*

See the Appendix, page 150 for a full list of common prepositions

CHAPTER 3   WHAT HAVE YOU LEARNT?

A Going to the park, Ana and Yoli explain to some tourists in the Calle Mayor where places are. Fill the gaps with the correct preposition and form of **de** (**de, del, de la, de los, de las**).

e.g. El mercado está ... Oficina de Turismo.

→ El mercado está **detrás de la** Oficina de Turismo.

En la calle

	M E R C A D O		
Cafetería	Farmacia	Oficina de Turismo	Servicios

---------------------------------- *Calle Mayor* ----------------------------------

| Discoteca | Correos | Banco de España | Parque |

1 El mercado está ... Oficina de Turismo.
2 ¿El Banco de España? Está ... Correos.
3 Vamos a ver. La discoteca está ... cafetería.
4 ¿Cerca? ¡No, qué va! La discoteca está ... servicios.
5 La farmacia está ... mercado.
6 No, no. No está lejos. El parque está ... banco.

B Ana and Yoli wander aimlessly through the park. Choose the correct verb *to be* (**ser/estar**) from the brackets.

Las vacaciones – ¡qué horror!

ANA ¡Es que (*soy/estoy*) aburrida!

YOLI Sí, es verdad que las vacaciones (*son/están*) muy aburridas.

ANA ¡A qué no haces nada, pero (*eres/estás*) cansada todo el día!

YOLI Sí, tienes razón. ¿Y tu hermana Isabel – qué tal (*es/está*)?

ANA Sabes que (*es/está*) viuda, ¿no? Mis padres (*son/están*) preocupados porque Isabel no quiere salir de casa, no quiere ponerse en contacto ...

YOLI Pobrecita. A lo mejor no (*es/está*) lista para hablar del accidente.

ANA Sí ... Y mi otra hermana y su marido (*son/están*) separados, así que ...

YOLI (*Es/está*) muy triste, todo eso.

ANA ¡Y mira las plantas! Incluso las plantas (*son/están*) muertas.

YOLI Falta agua. El parque no es nada bonito en verano. ¡Odio las vacaciones!

Revision test 1–3

A The Holiday Lets agent is checking through the contents list of the flat: put the words in brackets into the plural, if necessary.

e.g. hay dos (*sofá*) → hay dos **sofás**

El piso de alquiler

En el salón-comedor hay dos (*sofá*), tres (*sillón*), un (*televisor*), unas (*cortina*) azules, dos (*estante*) y dos (*alfombra*). Luego hay una (*mesa*) con seis (*silla*). En el dormitorio principal, hay dos (*cama*) individuales, dos (*armario*), y dos (*tocador*). Ah, hay dos (*mesilla de noche*) también. En el dormitorio de los niños hay dos (*litera*), y dos (*cómoda*).

B How good is your knowledge of geography and astronomy? Match up the words 1–6 with the correct definitions a–f, putting the correct word for *the* (**el** or **la**) in front of the underlined words.

eg. 1. El clima + d condiciones atmosféricos: **la** temperatura, **la** lluvia, **el** viento …

¿Qué sabes?

1	clima	a	cuerpo celeste que sólo brilla por <u>luz</u> que refleja del sol.
2	atmósfera	b	astro central en <u>sistema</u> planetario que produce calor.
3	planeta	c	astro satélite de <u>Tierra</u>.
4	luna	d	condiciones atmosféricos: <u>temperatura</u>, <u>lluvia</u>, <u>viento</u> …
5	sol	e	astro con <u>núcleo</u> poco denso y <u>cola</u> larga.
6	cometa	f	masa gaseosa que rodea <u>mundo</u>.

C Mum has arrived home to find it is strangely silent, and she is trying to find out where everyone is. Complete the gaps with the correct part of the verb *to be* **estar**.

e.g. Manolo – ¿dónde … ? → Manolo – ¿dónde **estás**?

¿Hay alguien en casa?

MAMA   Manolo – ¿dónde … ?

MANOLO   … en mi dormitorio.

MAMA   ¿Y tu papá?

MANOLO   Ni idea – ¿no … en el sótano?

MAMA   ¡Miguel y Juanjo! ¿Dónde … ?

MIGUEL   … en el desván, jugando con el ordenador.

MAMA   ¿Las chicas … con vosotros?

JUANJO   No – Clara … en casa de su amiga, y Ana – no sé.

MAMA   Pues, yo no voy a preparar la cena sóla – ¡si me necesitáis, … en el jardín con un Martini!

D Tere will try anything rather than finish her homework. Decide whether you need the
   verb **ser** or **estar**, then choose the correct part of that verb to fill the gaps.
   e.g. Es que … muy cansada.   →   **estar** : Es que **estoy** muy cansada.

   ¡Tramposa!
   TERE Es que … muy cansada – ¿puedo ir a la cama?
   PAPA Pero, son las siete de la tarde – ¿qué te pasa?
   TERE No me siento muy bien, papá – … enferma.
   PAPA ¿Sí? Voy a buscar el termómetro. ¡Dios mío – cuarenta y cuatro grados! No
         puedes … viva con una fiebre tan alta. ¡Qué lista …! ¡Has puesto el
         termómetro en tu taza de café!
   TERE Es que los deberes … aburridos – ¿no puedo ver la televisión un poco?
   PAPA ¡Ni hablar!

E Carmen is borrowing Marta's flat for a holiday. On arrival, she finds a note
   explaining where things are. Put the English expressions in brackets into Spanish.
   e.g. El vídeo está [inside the] armario   →   El vídeo está **dentro del** armario

   La carta
   ¡Hola, Carmen! Te dejo un poco de información útil …

   1 El vídeo está [inside the] armario, [behind the] puerta en el salón.
   2 Las cerillas están [in the] cajón, [under the] fregadero, en la cocina.
   3 Si tenéis frío, hay dos mantas más [beside the] cama, [on top of the] silla verde.
   4 La nevera está en el armario alto [between the] lavadora y el microondas.
   5 El lunes, ¿puedes bajar la basura [to the] calle? Vienen por la mañana a recogerla.
   6 Si quieres pan temprano, hay un supermercado pequeño [at the end of the] calle.

      ¡Espero que lo pases muy bien! Hasta la vista, Marta.

F The first day in a new college is always confusing as you find your way around.
   Complete the questions with **el**, **la**, **los** or **las** and the answers with **de**, **del**, **de la**, **de**
   los or **de las**.

   e.g. ¿Dónde está … oficina del director?   →   ¿Dónde está **la** oficina del director?
        Al final … pasillo.   →   Al final **del** pasillo.

   El primer día
   1 ¿Dónde está … oficina del director? – Al final … pasillo.
   2 ¿Dónde están … vestuarios?   – A la derecha … entrada.
   3 ¿ … servicios están por aquí?   – No, al lado … vestuarios.
   4 ¿… gimnasio está cerca?   – Enfrente … duchas.
   5 ¿Dónde están … cocinas?   – Detrás … salón de actos.
   6 ¿ … aulas de español y francés?   – Cerca … laboratorio.

Yo y los míos

A As part of her application for an exchange, Zeneida is being interviewed about her family. Complete the gaps with the correct part of the verb **tener** (*to have*) from the list below.

e.g. Díme, Zeneida – ¿ ... hermanos?   →   Díme, Zeneida – ¿**tienes** hermanos?

El intercambio

PROFESOR Díme, Zeneida – ¿ ... hermanos?

ZENEIDA Sí, ... dos hermanastras, un hermanastro y un hermano gemelo, Iñaki.

PROFESOR ¿Iñaki y tú sois gemelos? ¿Cuántos años ... ?

ZENEIDA Tenemos quince años. Y mi hermanastro Felipe ... once años.

PROFESOR ¿Y tus hermanastras?

ZENEIDA Pepa y Gema son gemelas también – ... seis años.

PROFESOR ¡Vaya! ¿Y tenéis animales en casa también?

ZENEIDA Sí – pues Iñaki y yo ... dos perros, Pepa y Gema tienen tres conejos, y Felipe tiene una serpiente y un loro.

PROFESOR ¡Dios mío! Eso no es una familia – ¡es un zoológico!

tienen   tenéis   tiene   tienes   tengo   tenemos

B Mike is being taken on a guided tour of the town by his exchange host, Pilar. In her description, substitute words for the numbers.

e.g. Aquí en el número 21   →   Aquí en el número **veintiuno**

La calle Sagunto

Aquí en el número 21 vive mi hermano. Un poco más lejos, vive mi tía en el número 55. ¿Ves las cortinas azules? – allí. En el número 100 vive mi cuñado y enfrente en el 102, mis primos. Es una calle muy larga – en el número 515 viven otros primos.

C Ana is explaining the intercom system to her English pen-friend, Helen. Complete her sentences with the floor number.

e.g. Sr. P. Aguirre Roldán 2°   →   El señor Aguirre vive **en el segundo piso**

Los pisos

1 2° Sr. P. Aguirre Roldán   El señor Aguirre vive ...
2 5° Sta. C. Cánovas Carillo   La señorita Cánovas vive ...
3 6° Sres. A. Clemente Lozano   Los señores Clemente viven ...
4 3° Sra. P. Elizalde Gil   La señora Elizalde vive ...
5 1° Dr. F. Guerra Rivas   El doctor Guerra vive ...
6 4° Sres. M. Martínez Poyatos   Los señores Martínez viven ...

The verb **Tener**: *to have*

1 **Tener** is the verb *to have*. The present tense is:

yo	**tengo**	*I have*	nosotros	**tenemos**	*we have*
tú	**tienes**	*you have*	vosotros	**tenéis**	*you have*
él	**tiene**	*he has*	ellos	**tienen**	*they have*
ella	**tiene**	*she has*	ellas	**tienen**	*they have*
usted	**tiene**	*you have*	ustedes	**tienen**	*you have*

2 **Tener** is used:

a to say *has* or *have*, as in English:

Mi padre **tiene** mucha paciencia   *My father **has** lots of patience*
¿**Tienes** hermanos?   ***Have you** got any brothers and sisters?*

b in some common expressions where English uses the verb *to be*:

tener años	*to be ... years old*	**tener hambre**	*to be hungry*
tener calor	*to be hot*	**tener miedo**	*to be afraid*
tener cuidado	*to be careful*	**tener razón**	*to be right*
tener éxito	*to be successful*	**tener sed**	*to be thirsty*
tener frío	*to be cold*	**tener sueño**	*to be sleepy*
tener ganas(de)	*to feel like*	**tener suerte**	*to be lucky*

Examples:

¿Cuántos **años tienes?**   *How **old are you**?*
¡Uf! **Tengo calor**   *Whew! **I'm hot!***
No **tenemos ganas de** salir   *We don't **feel like** going out*
¿**Tenéis sueño**? ¡a la cama!   *Are you **sleepy**? off to bed with you!*

Tener que: *to have to*

3 **Tener que** + INFINITIVE means *to have to*. In English, the infinitive is expressed as *to...*, e.g. *to speak, to eat, to live*. In Spanish, the infinitive ends in -**ar**, -**er**, -**ir**, e.g. **hablar, comer, vivir**.

¿**Tienes que ayudar** en casa?   *Do you **have to** help at home?*
Tengo que hacer mi cama   *I **have to** make my bed*

Number

The following points need particular care:

4 The number **1** has two masculine forms **un** and **uno**. When it is followed by a noun, use **un**. When it is not followed by a noun, use **uno**:

un alumno   ciento **un** alumnos   *one pupil   a hundred and one pupils*
¿**un** boli? no, sólo tengo **uno**   *a biro? No, I've only got one*

5 **100** has two forms, **cien** and **ciento**. Use **cien** if the figure is exactly 100 and **ciento** if **100** is followed by another number:

¡Tiene **cien** años!   *She's a hundred years old!*
¿Cúantas dálmatas? **Ciento** una   *How many dalmations? A hundred and one*

6 Numbers 200 + end in **-os/-as**, depending on the gender of the following noun:

Hay mil doscient**os** alumnos   *There are one thousand two hundred pupils*
Cuesta trescient**as** pesetas   *It costs three hundred pesetas*

For a full list of numbers, see the Appendix, page 154

First, second etc.

7 1st, 2nd etc. are examples of ORDINAL numbers. Those from 1–10 are:

primero 1st	quinto 5th	octavo 8th
segundo 2nd	sexto 6th	noveno 9th
tercero 3rd	séptimo 7th	décimo 10th
cuarto 4th		

a   ordinal numbers change their endings, like adjectives:

El ascensor va hasta la cuart**a** planta   *The lift goes up to the fourth floor*

b   **primero** (*1st*) and **tercero** (*3rd*) lose the **-o** before a masculine singular noun:

El **primer** día en un instituto es horrible   *The first day in school is horrible*
Éste es tu **tercer** cuaderno   *This is your third exercise book*

8 Beyond 10 use ordinary numbers after the noun:

el piso **doce**   *the twelfth floor*

CHAPTER 4   WHAT HAVE YOU LEARNT?

A   Parents always complain about their children! Complete the gaps in Lola and Ana's conversation with the correct part of the verb **tener** or **tener que**.

e.g. ¿Cuántos niños ... usted?   →   ¿Cuántos niños **tiene** usted?

Las Quejas

LOLA   ¿Cuántos niños ... usted?

ANA   Mi marido y yo ... siete hijos en total: tres hijos y cuatro hijas.

LOLA   ¡Uf! Ustedes ... mucho trabajo en casa, con tantos niños.

ANA   ¡Eso sí que es verdad! Como mi marido trabaja fuera hasta las ocho, yo ... hacer todo – la ropa, fregar y, preparar la comida.

LOLA   Pues yo ... dos hijos. Y siempre quieren dinero.

ANA   ¡Los míos también! Mi hijo me dice – ¡Mamá, voy a la discoteca! ¿No ... mil pesetas? –

LOLA   ¿El no ... dinero?

ANA   ¡Qué va! Y yo le digo – Yo, hijo, no ... ni un duro. ¡Si tú quieres dinero, ... trabajar!

LOLA   Son todos iguales. ¡Los niños de hoy no ... nada que hacer!

ANA   Bueno, ... irme – mi hija Alicia está en casa con los pequeños. ¡Adiós!

B   Alicia is helping her younger brother and sisters, who are doing their homework! Write the words in brackets in Spanish.

e.g. Es que sólo tengo ... goma.   →   Es que sólo tengo **una** goma.

Las preguntas

1   Es que sólo tengo [one] goma.

2   ¿Un lápiz? Lo siento, pero no tengo más que [one].

3   ¿Qué página es? Página [a hundred and one].

4   ¡Ésta no es la [first] vez que te dejo mi regla!

5   El problema es que sólo tengo [one] lápiz rojo.

6   ¡Oye, no copies los deberes! ¡Te he dicho [a hundred] veces que no!

7   ¿Otro boli? ¡No! ¡Éste es el [third] boli que has perdido!

8   ¿Una hoja? Bueno, toma – tengo [a hundred and one] hojas.

Help Yourself to Essential Spanish Grammar

UNIT

2

CHAPTER 5   WHAT DO YOU KNOW?

A Santiago is introducing his family. Choose the correct form of the adjective (describing word) from the alternatives given in brackets.

e.g. Todos son (*diferente/diferentes*).   → Todos son **diferentes**.

Mi Familia

1 Tengo cinco hermanos. Todos son (*diferente/diferentes*).
2 ¡Mi hermana (*mayor/mayores*) está (*loco/loca*)!
3 Mi hermana (*menor/menores*), que es (*tímido/tímida*), se llama Clara.
4 Mi hermano Juan tiene 16 años. Es muy (*divertido/divertidos*) y las chicas dicen que es (*guapo/guapa*).
5 Mi hermanito David tiene 8 años. ¡Es (*perezoso/perezosa*) pero es muy (*listo/listos*)!
6 Mi hermana gemela se llama Ana y es más (*hablador/habladora*) que yo.
7 Mis padres son muy (*simpático/simpáticos*).
8 Al otro lado de la ciudad viven mis abuelos: son (*anciano/ancianos*) ya, pero mi abuelo es una persona muy (*animado/animada*) y mi abuela es muy (*trabajador/trabajadora*).

B Zohora's mother is tidying up the clothes on her children's floor. Put the correct endings on the adjectives (describing words) in brackets.

e.g. el bañador …   → el bañador **rojo**

La Ropa

1 el bañador (*rojo*)
2 los guantes (*marrón*)
3 la bufanda (*azul*)
4 el chaleco (*verde*)
5 los pantalones (*gris*)
6 los calzoncillos (*blanco*)
7 el pantalón corto (*naranja*) para el fútbol
8 el jersey (*rosa*) con mangas (*largo*)
9 las zapatillas (*negro*)
10 la chaqueta (*marrón*) de pana
11 las botas (*rojo*) de goma
12 el chandal (*amarillo*) para la gimnasia

Now organise all the clothes into drawers.
e.g. Cajón 1.   Ropa interior y bañadores: **el bañador rojo**

Cajón 1.   Ropa interior y bañadores
Cajón 2.   Ropa exterior
Cajón 3.   Zapatos etc
Cajón 4.   Ropa deportiva
Cajón 5.   El resto

Forming adjectives

1   An ADJECTIVE describes a noun. *Big*, *blue*, *lazy* are all adjectives:

   a **big** meal   **blue** eyes   Mark is **lazy**

2   In Spanish, the endings of adjectives change to match the gender of the noun they describe.

   a   Masculine adjectives ending in **-o**, change to **-a** in the feminine:

MASCULINE	un calcetín blanc**o**	*a white sock*
FEMININE	una blusa blanc**a**	*a white blouse*

   b   Singular masculine adjectives ending in **-e**, **-a**, or in a consonant (e.g. **-l**, **-r**, **-s**) remain the same in the feminine:

MASCULINE	un chaleco **verde**	*a green waistcoat*
	un señor **optimista**	*an optimistic man*
	un jersey **azul**	*a blue jumper*
FEMININE	una camisa **verde**	*a green shirt*
	una señora **optimista**	*an optimistic lady*
	una chaqueta **azul**	*a blue jacket*

   c   Add an **-a**, to form the feminine of adjectives of **nationality**, **region**, or those ending in **-án**, **-ón**, **-ín**, **-or**:

MASCULINE	un niño **español**	*a Spanish boy*
	Pepe es **trabajador**	*Pepe is **hardworking***
FEMININE	una niña **española**	*a Spanish girl*
	Ana es **trabajadora**	*Ana is **hardworking***

   Note that there is no change for **mayor/menor** (*older/younger*) **mejor/peor** (*better/worse*) **interior/exterior** (*inside/outside*), or the colour **marrón** (*brown*):

   un hermano **mayor**   *an older brother*   una hermana **menor**   *a younger sister*
   el **mejor** jugador   *the best player*   la **mejor** jugadora   *the best player*
   un zapato **marrón**   *a brown shoe*   una sandalia **marrón**   *a brown sandal*

3   For PLURAL adjectives, first apply the rules for singular adjectives above, then the following:

   a   For adjectives which end in a vowel in the singular add **-s**; for adjectives which end in a consonant, add **-es**:

SINGULAR	un jersey negro	un pantalón azul
	a black jumper	*a pair of blue trousers*
PLURAL	jerseys negro**s**	pantalones azul**es**
	black jumpers	*blue trousers*

b The final -**z** ending in singular adjectives changes to -**c** in the plural:

una madre feli**z**   *a happy mother*   madres feli**c**es   *happy mothers*

4 ACCENTS on adjectives in the masculine singular are lost in feminine and plural forms:

un estudiante ingl**é**s/una estudiante inglesa   *an English student*
estudiantes ingleses   *English students*

5 The following COLOUR adjectives never change. They are INVARIABLE.

	naranja (*orange*)	**lila** (*lilac*)	**rosa** (*pink*)	**marrón** (*brown*)
colours with	**oscuro** (*dark*)	**claro** (*light*)	**vivo** (*bright*)	**marino** (*navy*)

sombreros naranja   *orange hats*   una chaqueta azul claro   *a light blue jacket*

Position of adjectives (1)

6 In English, adjectives come before the noun. In Spanish, they usually come after:

un alumno **inteligente**   *an intelligent pupil*

Note: if you want to use two adjectives together, link two adjectives with **y** (*and*):

un alumno **inteligente y trabajador**   *an intelligent and hardworking pupil*

7 Some adjectives, however, come BEFORE the noun, such as:

alguno (*some, any*)	**ninguno** (*none, not any*)	**tanto** (*as much*)
mucho (*much, a lot*)	**poco** (*little, few*)	**otro** (*an/other*)
último (*last*)	**próximo** (*next*)	**cada*** (*each, every*)
		todo* (*all, every*)

also ORDINALS (*first, second etc.*)

el **otro** día   *the other day*   la **última** vez   *the last time*
cada semana   *each week*   **todos** los días   *every day*

a **Alguno** and **ninguno** lose the -**o** before a masculine singular noun, and gain an accent on the final -**ú**:

¿Alumno malo? ¡No tengo **ninguno**!   *A bad pupil? I haven't got any!*
No tengo **ningún** cuaderno tuyo   *I have no exercise book of yours*

b **Cada** is INVARIABLE – it does not change in the feminine or in the plural:

cada padre, cada madre   *every father, every mother*

---

*For further usage of **todo** and **cada**, see Chapter 9

CHAPTER 5   WHAT HAVE YOU LEARNT?

A Amalia is writing about her family to her new penfriend. Change the endings on the adjectives in brackets, if necessary, so that they agree with the thing or person they describe.

e.g. Paola quiere ser una diseñadora (*famoso*).   →   Paola es una diseñadora **famosa**.

Los míos

Paola es una diseñadora (*famoso*) – es mi hermana y vive en un piso en París con unas amigas (*divertido*). Su mejor amiga es (*español*) y muy (*trabajador*).

Tiene muchos compañeros (*francés*) – por lo general, son (*guapo*) y (*rico*). Paola es (*pobre*) – tiene que trabajar mucho. ¡Qué lástima!

David es mi hermano – pero es terrible. Es muy (*travieso*) en clase. En su cartera tiene libros (*sucio*) y fruta (*podrido**). ¡Qué asco!

Marisa, mi hermana, es muy (*bonito*), (*delgado*) y (*elegante*). Tiene los ojos (*verde*). ¡Qué suerte!

Quiero mucho a mis padres – son (*generoso*). Cada año vamos de vacaciones a un país (*diferente*). Este año nos vamos a Argentina.

B Not everything is going well in Paris for Paola! Complete her complaints by deciding whether the adjective goes in front of the noun or after it.

e.g. 1 Tengo que trabajar <u>los días.</u>   →   Tengo que trabajar **todos los días**.

¡No es justo!

1 Tengo que trabajar <u>los días</u> – ¡no es justo!   (*todos*)
2 <u>Sábado</u> por la mañana tengo que trabajar también. (*cada*)
3 En mi oficina tengo dos <u>compañeros</u> que nunca (*perezosos*)
   trabajan los sábados.
4 Estas <u>semanas</u>, tenemos <u>clientes</u>, y hay (*últimas, muchos*)
   mucho que preparar.
5 Soy una <u>empleada</u> – no puedo dejar todo sin hacer. (*consciente*)
6 Preparo <u>los dibujos</u> primero.   (*difíciles*)
7 Voy a trabajar hasta medianoche – ¡no es la <u>vez</u>, (*primera*)
   pero va a ser la última!

---

* *podrido*: rotten

UNIT

2

A The twins, Quique and Rosa, won't leave their brother, Toni, in peace. Complete
their interruptions with the correct possessive adjective (e.g. *my/your/his/her/our*)
from the selection below.

e.g. ¡Toni! ¡Quiero ver … revista!   →   ¡Toni! ¡Quiero ver **tu** revista!

Quique y Rosa

QUIQUE ¡Toni! ¡Quiero ver [YOUR] revista!

TONI   No puedes. No es [MY] revista. Es de Tomás.

ROSA   ¿Por qué tienes [HIS] revista?

TONI   Porque él tiene [MY] tebeos.

QUIQUE No son [YOUR] tebeos, Toni. ¡Son [OUR] tebeos!

TONI   Quique y Rosa, ¡éstos son [YOUR] juguetes! Dejadme en paz.

ROSA   ¡Mamá! ¡Toni no nos deja [HIS] tebeos!

TONI   ¡Sois imposibles!

sus   vuestros   su   mi   tu   mis   tus   nuestros

B Merche, a friend of Toni's, arrives with some bad news about a classmate. Decide
whether the adjectives go before the noun they describe, or after.

e.g. ¡Qué <u>noticias</u>!   →   ¡Qué **malas** noticias!

¡Ay, qué pena!

TONI   ¡Qué <u>noticias</u>!   (*malas*)

MERCHE ¿Qué pasa?

TONI   ¿Conoces a la <u>chica</u> en tu clase?   (*nueva*)

MERCHE ¿Belén? ¿La que vive en la <u>torre</u> donde hubo* un   (*grande*)
        incendio la <u>semana</u>?   (*pasada*)

TONI   Sí – ¡pues hubo otro incendio en la <u>torre</u> anoche!   (*misma*)
        El piso de Belén está completamente destrozado.

MERCHE ¡Ay, qué pena! ¡La <u>familia</u> ! ¿Dónde van a vivir?   (*pobre*)

TONI   Hay <u>posibilidades</u>.   (*varias*)

MERCHE A lo mejor, pueden alquilar un <u>piso</u> aquí.   (*moderno*)

TONI   O tal vez volver a su <u>pueblo</u> y vivir con los abuelos.   (*antiguo*)

---

* hubo: *there was*

Position of adjectives (2)

1 These are common adjectives which can go either **before** or **after** the noun: **bueno** (*good*), **malo** (*bad*), **mejor** (*best*), **peor** (*worst*):

¡buena idea!	*good idea!*	**malas** noticias	*bad news*
ideas **buenas**	*good ideas*	costumbres **malas**	*bad habits*

Before a masculine singular noun, **bueno** and **malo** lose the final -**o**:

Hace **buen** tiempo	*The weather's good*
Hace **mal** tiempo	*The weather's bad*

2 Some adjectives change in meaning, depending on whether they go **before** or **after** the noun:

	BEFORE	AFTER
gran/grande	un **gran** hombre *a great man*	un hombre **grande** *a big man*
pobre	¡los **pobres** padres! *the poor parents!*	los padres **pobres** *poor parents (have little money)*
nuevo	un **nuevo** día *a new/another day*	un compact-disc **nuevo** *a (brand) new compact disc*
mismo	es la **misma** cosa *it's the same thing*	lo hago yo **mismo** *I do it myself*
antiguo	mi **antiguo** novio *my old/former boyfriend*	vivo en una casa **antigua** *I live in an old house*
varios	**varios** discos *several records*	discos **varios** *different records*

Indicating Possession ('s in English)

3 English uses **'s** to show when something/someone belongs to someone, e.g. Juan**'s** biro. Spanish uses **de** (*of*) to indicate possession:

la hermana **de** mi padre	el boli **de** Juan
my Dad's sister (the sister of my Dad)	*Juan's biro (the biro of Juan)*

Help Yourself to Essential Spanish Grammar

Possessive Adjectives

4 POSSESSIVE ADJECTIVES (*my*, *your* etc.) indicate who owns something. They always go before the noun.

	SINGULAR		PLURAL	
	masc.	fem.	masc.	fem.
my	**mi** primo	**mi** prima	**mis** primos	**mis** primas
your	**tu** hermano	**tu** hermana	**tus** hermanos	**tus** hermanas
his/her/your	**su** abuelo	**su** abuela	**sus** abuelos	**sus** abuelas
our	**nuestro** conejo	**nuestra** gata	**nuestros** tíos	**nuestras** tías
your	**vuestro** piso	**vuestra** casa	**vuestros** hijos	**vuestras** hijas
their/your	**su** niño	**su** niña	**sus** niños	**sus** niñas

Where it is not clear whether **su** means *his*, *her*, *your*, *their*, one of the following is added: **de él, de ella, de ellos, de ellas, de usted, de ustedes**:

¿Ésta es tu bolsa? No, es su bolsa   ¿La bolsa **de él**?   No, **de ella**
Is this your bag?   *Is it his?*   *No, it's hers*

Possessive pronouns

5 POSSESSIVE PRONOUNS (mine, yours, etc.) replace possessive adjectives + nouns to show when someone owns something. For example, 'it's *mine*' can replace 'it's *my* coat':

	SINGULAR		PLURAL	
	masc.	fem.	masc.	fem.
mine	**el mío**	**la mía**	**los míos**	**las mías**
yours	**el tuyo**	**la tuya**	**los tuyos**	**las tuyas**
his/hers	**el suyo**	**la suya**	**los suyos**	**las suyas**
ours	**el nuestro**	**la nuestra**	**los nuestros**	**las nuestras**
yours	**el vuestro**	**la vuestra**	**los vuestros**	**las vuestras**
theirs/your	**el suyo**	**la suya**	**los suyos**	**las suyas**

a Possessive pronouns agree with the nouns they replace in terms of number and gender:

El cuaderno es más viejo que **el mío**   La cartera estaba al lado de **la mía**
The exercise-book is older than mine   *The school-bag was beside mine*

b The **el, la, los, las** part of the possessive pronoun is frequently omitted after the verb **ser**:

Este libro es **mío**   ¿Estas tijeras son **tuyas**?
This book is mine   *Are these scissors yours?*

CHAPTER 6   WHAT HAVE YOU LEARNT?

A Miguel meets his ageing neighbour who praises the former Spanish dictator Franco.
Write the words in brackets in Spanish either before or after the underlined noun,
with the correct endings.

e.g. Era un hombre [GREAT]   →   Era un **gran** hombre

Franco

RAUL	Era un <u>hombre</u>, Franco.	[GREAT]
MIGUEL	¿De verdad?	
RAUL	Siempre lleno de <u>ideas</u>.	[GOOD]
MIGUEL	¿Sí?	
RAUL	Siempre tenía tiempo para la <u>gente</u>.	[POOR]
MIGUEL	No me digas.	
RAUL	Este <u>gobierno</u>, es imposible.	[NEW]
MIGUEL	¿Por qué?	
RAUL	Porque no aprecian las <u>maneras</u> de hacer las cosas.	[OLD]
MIGUEL	¿Sí?	
RAUL	Es la <u>cosa</u> todos los días – corrupción, escándalos …	[SAME]
MIGUEL	¿Y no había <u>escándalos</u> en la época de Franco?	[BIG]
RAUL	¡Qué va!	
MIGUEL	Pues yo tengo <u>periódicos</u> de los años de Franco, y no todo era tan bonito como lo dice usted.	[SEVERAL]

B Ana is infuriated by her untidy sisters, and writes to a magazine for advice. Choose
the correct word in brackets.

Querida Corazón …

¿Me puede ayudar? ¡Me llamo Ana, y estoy harta! Tengo que compartir (*mi/mío*)
dormitorio con (*míos/mis*) dos hermanas. (*Mi/mía*) hermana menor, Alicia, no hace
(*su/suya*) cama y Rafaela, la mayor, no hace la (*su/suya*) tampoco. Alicia no recoge
nunca (*sus/suyas*) cosas. Es que el cuarto es muy pequeño. Mi hermano tiene suerte:
(*suyo/su*) dormitorio es grande y para él sólo; está muy ordenado, pero Mamá dice
que (*nuestro/el nuestro*) es una pocilga. ¿Qué puedo hacer?

Querida Ana,
¿Por qué no habláis con (*los vuestros/vuestros*) padres? Tal vez podéis cambiar de
habitación. Y muchos jóvenes tienen problemas con (*suyas/sus*) hermanos: ¡me
acuerdo de discusiones interminables con los (*mis/míos*)! ¡Buena suerte! Corazón.

Revision test 4–6

A Pili and Gabi are besieged with questions from their anxious grandmother. Answer for them in Spanish, by making sentences from the expressions in brackets.
e.g. 1 ¿Por qué abres la ventana, Pili?   →   Porque **tengo calor**.

¿Por qué ...?
1 ¿Por qué abres la ventana, Pili?   *tener calor*
2 ¿No quieres un refresco, Gabi? ¿Por qué?   *no tener sed*
3 Pili y Gabi – ¿por qué no vais a cenar?   *no tener hambre*
4 Pili, ¿por qué no quieres ver la película de horror?   *tener miedo*
5 ¿Te pones la chaqueta, Gabi? ¿Por qué?   *tener frío*
6 Gabi y Pili, ¿por qué os vais a la cama ya?   *tener sueño*

B How good is your general knowledge? Write the numbers below in Spanish, in the appropriate sentence.
e.g. 1 Hay ... días en febrero   →   Hay **veintiocho** días en febrero

Números
1 Hay ... días en febrero.
2 Las historias de 'Las ... noches'.
3 Hay ... milímetros en medio metro.
4 El año bisiesto tiene ... días.
5 El tablero de ajedrez tiene ... casillas.
6 Hay ... segundos en una hora.

        1001   64   3600   500   28   366

C Try this puzzle on the days of the week, months and seasons. Fill in the gaps with the appropriate Spanish ordinal number e.g. '*first*', '*second*' etc.
e.g. Lunes es el ... día de la semana.   →   Lunes es el **primer** día de la semana.

El puzzle
1 Lunes es el ... día de la semana.
2 El ... día de la semana es miércoles.
3 La ... estación del año es la primavera.
4 Mayo es el ... mes del año.
5 El ... mes es junio.
6 Abril es el ... mes.
7 El verano es la ... estación del año.
8 El ... día de la semana es domingo.
9 ¿Octubre? Es el ... mes.
10 La ... estación, otoño, es la que más me gusta.

D The Scottish Tourist Board has produced a brochure for Spanish tourists. Make the adjectives in brackets agree with the nouns they describe.

e.g. Las (*largo*) playas de arena …   →   Las **largas** playas de arena …

East Lothian

Las (*largo*) playas de arena y los (*dorado*) campos de cereales son las (*primero*) impresiones que tendrá de East Lothian, una región (*renombrado*) por sus (*soleado*) veranos. Las (*histórico*) comunidades de Gifford o Haddington, (*situado*) en la (*bonito*) campiña al pie de las (*impresionante*) colinas de Lammermuir, merecen ser exploradas. Entre las (*mucho*) atracciones de la costa se encuentra Bass Rock, con su (*famoso*) colonia de alcatraces. Se puede visitar también el (*hermoso*) pueblo de Dunbar, cerca del John Muir Country Park, un bosque (*precioso*) con senderos que llegan a una costa que se conserva en su estado (*natural*): todo a (*poco*) distancia de la capital de Escocia.

E Anita and Trini are studying with interest the list of new members of their class in their international school. Read the class-list and complete the gaps in their conversation with the correct nationality.

e.g. Raoul es …   →   Raoul es **francés**.

La lista

	Chicos		Chicas
	Raoul Sabatier (Francia)		Ana Couthinho (Portugal)
	Nikos Kokinopoulos (Grecia)		Martine Arlette (Canadá)
	Jas Izbeki (EE.UU)		Tanja Hirshfelder (Alemania)

ANITA ¡Mira! ¡Tenemos compañeros nuevos! Raoul es …

TRINI Y Nikos es … Hay un chico que se llama Jas – ¡qué nombre más raro!

ANITA No sé como se pronuncia. Jas es …

TRINI Y Ana es … A lo mejor habla español, o lo entiende.

ANITA Luego, está Martine – es … Me gustaría visitar el Canadá un día.

TRINI La última es Tanja, que es …

ANITA Pues yo no sé nada de Alemania. ¡Va a ser un año muy interesante!

F Miguel has had enough of his untidy children and has posted a cross letter in the kitchen on his way to work. Put the words in brackets into Spanish.

¡Atención!

1 Felipe, [MY] zapatillas nuevas – ¿dónde están? ¡No los encuentro!

2 Merche, [YOUR] cartera está en [OUR] dormitorio. ¿Por qué? ¡Y la raqueta encima de la cama no es [MINE] tampoco!

3 Gabi y Unai – [YOUR] zapatillas nuevas están delante de la tele. ¡No es su sitio!

4 Marta – Antonia ha llamado por teléfono: ¿puedes ir a verla a [HER] casa? ¡Y estoy disgustado con Unai y Gari – [THEIR] chaquetas están en las escaleras y el montón de libros en la cocina es [THEIRS] también! ¡Hasta luego!

Tiempo Libre

A   In his free time, Ramón, a Spanish journalist, is researching claims that where people go on holiday is linked to which country they come from.
Read his article and select the correct part of the verb **ir** (*to go*) in brackets.

¿Adónde van?

¿Adónde (*vas/va*) usted de vacaciones? Según un estudio, depende de la nacionalidad de la persona. Los británicos (*voy/van*) a la costa mediterránea, pero si nosotros los españoles (*va/vamos*) al extranjero, preferimos explorar las grandes ciudades de Europa. La familia francesa típica no (*va/vais*) al extranjero – prefiere quedarse en Francia. Los escandinavos (*va/van*) a Suiza o a Europa Occidental.

B   A coach-load of young teenagers on a youth club trip stop at a garage on the motorway, and are full of questions. Match the beginnings and ends of their questions.

Preguntas y más preguntas

1 ¿Cuándo hay que …	a	una Coca-cola?
2 ¿Qué se puede …	b	pasamos aquí? ¿Una hora?
3 ¿Cuánto cuesta …	c	volver al autocar?
4 ¿Dónde están …	d	a la tienda conmigo?
5 ¿Quién quiere ir …	e	comprar – hay churros con chocolate?
6 ¿Cuánto tiempo …	f	los servicios?

C   Celia wants her friend Ana to go with her to the shop in the service-station. Read their conversation, and select the most appropriate expressions from the list below to fill in the gaps.

En la estación de servicio

CELIA   Oye, Ana – ¿no vienes a la tienda …?

ANA   ¿Contigo? No sé. ¿No sabes dónde está Marta? No quiero ir ….

CELIA   Mira, está allí con Paco. A lo mejor Marta va … a la cafetería.

ANA   Entonces voy … también. ¿Te traigo algo de comer?

CELIA   No, gracias – nada …. Me compro un poco de chocolate en la tienda.

ANA   Pero ¿de quién es esta chaqueta en el asiento? ¿Es de Paco?

CELIA   Vamos a mirar la etiqueta dentro – sí, es ….

ANA   ¡Qué despistado es! Se la llevo. Hasta pronto, Celia.

sin ella   de él   con ellos   conmigo   con él   para mí

The verb **ir**: *to go*

1 **Ir** is the verb *to go*. The present tense is as follows:

yo	**voy**	*I go*	nosotros	**vamos**	*we go*
tú	**vas**	*you go*	vosotros	**vais**	*you go*
él	**va**	*he goes*	ellos	**van**	*they go*
ella	**va**	*she goes*	ellas	**van**	*they go*
usted	**va**	*you go*	ustedes	**van**	*you go*

Examples:

¿**Vas** pronto?   *Are you going soon?*   **Van** mañana   *They go tomorrow*

2 The verb ir is followed by **a** meaning *to*:

Voy **a** Francia   *I'm going to France*
¿Vas **a** la pista de hielo?   *Are you going to the ice-rink?*
Vamos **a** las tiendas   *We're going to the shops*

Remember that with masculine nouns, **a** and **el** combine to make **al**:

¿Vais **al** parque?   *Are you going to the park?*

3 The verb **ir** + **a** + *infinitive* indicates the future:

¿**Vas a viajar** en avión?   *Are you going to travel by plane?*
Voy a pasar dos días en París   *I'm going to spend two days in Paris*

'A' meaning 'away'

4 '**A**' can be used when referring to distance in Spanish, where in English we use the word *away*.

El banco está **a** cien metros   *The bank is a hundred metres away*
¿Toledo? – está **a** dos kilómetros   *Toledo? – it's two kilometres away*

Questions

5 To ask a question, you can simply raise your voice at the end of a sentence.

¿**Te gusta?**   *Do you like it?*   ¿**Vas** a la tienda?   *Are you going to the shop?*

Help Yourself to Essential Spanish Grammar

6   You can also use a question word:

¿cómo ...?	**¿Cómo** vas a viajar?
how ...?	*How are you going to travel?*
¿cuándo ...?	**¿Cuándo** vas de vacaciones?
when ...?	*When are you going on holiday?*
¿cuánto ...?	**¿Cuánto** cuesta el vuelo?
how much ...?	*How much does the flight cost?*
¿dónde ...?	**¿Dónde** vas a alojarte?
where ...?	*Where are you going to stay?*
¿adónde ...?	**¿Adónde** vas?
where to ...?	*Where are you going?*
¿qué ...?	**¿Qué** vas a hacer?
what ...?	*What are you going to do?*
¿quién ...?	**¿Quién** va contigo?
who ...?	*Who is going with you?*
¿de quién ...?	**¿De quién** es este asiento?
whose ...?	*Whose seat is this?*
¿por qué ...?	**¿Por qué** quieres ir a Ibiza?
why ...?	*Why do you want to go to Ibiza?*

Note that the question word ¿**Cuánto**? is like an adjective. It agrees with the noun it describes:

¡**Cuánta** gente hay!	*What a lot of people there are!*
¿**Cuántos** alumnos hay?	*How many pupils are there?*

Pronouns after *for, from* etc.

7   After **para** (*for*), **de** (*from, of*), **en** (*in*), **sin** (*without*) and **con** (*with*) use the following pronouns:

mí	*me*	**nosotros/as**	*us*
ti	*you*	**vosotros/as**	*you*
él/ella	*him/her*	**ellos/ellas**	*them*
usted	*you*	**ustedes**	*you*

¿Es para **mí**?   *Is it for **me**?*   Voy sin **ella**   *I'm going **without her***

Nosotras and **vosotras** are used when those referred to are female:

!Ana y María, voy con **vosotras**!   *Ana and María, I'm going with **you**!*

After **con**, don't use **mí** or **ti**; use **conmigo** (*with me*) and **contigo** (*with you*):

¿Vienes **conmigo**? Voy **contigo**   *Are you coming **with me**? I'll go **with you***

CHAPTER 7   WHAT HAVE YOU LEARNT?

A Ana and Paco are discussing their plans for the summer holidays. Fill in the gaps
with the correct part of the verb **ir** (*to go*).
e.g. Paco, ¿adónde … de vacaciones? → Paco, ¿adónde **vas** de vacaciones?

Las vacaciones de verano

ANA   Paco, ¿adónde … de vacaciones?

PACO   No lo sé. Mi familia … a Francia, pero yo no.

ANA   ¿Por qué no … tú?

PACO   Mis dos primos… también – ¡pero son niños horrorosos! ¿Y tú?

ANA   Mi hermano mayor, Enrique, y yo … a Inglaterra.

PACO   ¿… vosotros a Londres?

ANA   Sí, y luego a Edimburgo. Normalmente, yo … a casa de mis tíos en Oxford,
pero este año, no.

PACO   ¿Por qué no?

ANA   Porque mis tíos … a los Estados Unidos por tres semanas.

PACO   ¡Pues tienes suerte, Ana! Me encantaría visitar Gran Bretaña.

B Ana discovers that suspicious Security guards can ask plenty of probing questions.
Choose the correct question word(s) from the list below to complete their queries.
e.g. ¿De … es esta maleta? → ¿De **quién** es esta maleta?

En el aeropuerto

1 ¿De … es esta maleta?   5 ¿… vas a volver a España? ¿En avión?

2 ¿… vas de vacaciones?   6 ¿… tiempo vas a quedarte en Gran Bretaña?

3 ¿… años tienes?   7 ¿… vas a Inglaterra? ¿Tienes familia allí?

4 ¿… es tu cumpleaños?   8 ¿… tienes en esa bolsa?

qué   cuándo   quién   adónde   cómo   por qué   cuántos

C Ana and Enrique are met at the airport by a Spanish friend, who barely stops talking
as they make their way out. Put the words in brackets into Spanish.

¡Qué habladora!

¿Es para [ME], el regalo? ¡Qué amable! Mi marido está allí en el quiosco – ¿ves? Sí,
tu amigo está con [HIM] también. ¿Qué tal tu madre? Hablé con [HER] ayer. Va a
pasar dos semanas tranquilas sin [YOU] dos. ¡Rápido, o el autobús va a salir sin [US]!

UNIT

3

CHAPTER 8   WHAT DO YOU KNOW?

A Does your star-sign have any influence on the kind of holiday activities you enjoy?
Choose the appropriate verb from the list below and fill in each gap with the **yo** (*I*)
form of the verb.

e.g. ¡… toda la mañana en la playa!   →   **¡Paso** toda la mañana en la playa!

Un día ideal

– *Juan, eres un jóven Pisces. ¿A los Pisces les gustan las vacaciones acuáticas?*
– A mí, sí. ¿Mi día ideal? ¡… toda la mañana en la playa! Si hace buen tiempo, …
  en el mar y … el sol. Luego, por la tarde, depende. Si tengo mucha energía, …
  algún deporte acuático con mis amigos: esquí o vela.

tomar   hacer   nadar   pasar

– *Señora Carilla, usted es Escorpión. ¿Su día ideal consiste en algo más tranquilo?*
– Sí. Por la mañana, … la última novela de los 'best-sellers' en mi jardín. Luego,
  sobre las dos, … en la terraza de un restaurante tranquilo cerca de mi casa. Por la
  tarde, muchas veces … un museo o una exposición interesante en el centro. Y por
  la noche … al teatro o al cine si ponen algo bueno que me interesa.

salir   visitar   comer   leer

B Juan is packing for his windsurfing competition in the USA, when his friend Santi
arrives with some interesting news. Choose the correct word in brackets.

¡Qué rabia!

JUAN   ¿Cuándo vas a los Estados Unidos, Santi?
SANTI   Bueno, me voy (*el/los*) seis de agosto y vuelvo en quince días.
JUAN   ¿Así que no vas a estar aquí (*el/en*) fin de semana?
SANTI   No. ¿Por qué?
JUAN   Bueno, ¿sabes que (*el/los*) sábados de agosto invitamos a varios expertos al
           club náutico? ¡Viene Marcos Martín!
JUAN   ¿El famoso surfista? ¿Viene (*en/el*) sábado?
SANTI   Sí, para mostrarnos sus técnicas del windsurf.
JUAN   ¡Qué rabia! Estoy fuera a mediados (*de/en*) agosto – ¡y viene mi héroe aquí!
SANTI   ¿Por qué note vas (*de/en*) septiembre?
JUAN   No sé …

Present tense

1 The PRESENT tense is used to say:

what we are doing at the moment	*I'm reading* a new book
what we usually do	*I read* a lot of science-fiction
to emphasise what we do	*I do read* other things as well!

Regular verbs

2 In Spanish there are what are known as regular and irregular verbs. Regular verbs end in **-ar**, **-er**, **-ir**. To form the present tense, remove these endings from the verb STEM, e.g. **habl-ar**, **com-er**, **viv-ir**, and add the following endings:

a   Verbs ending in **-ar** e.g. **hablar** (*to speak*)   →   **habl-**.

yo	habl**o**	*I speak*	nosotros	habl**amos**	*we speak*
tú	habl**as**	*you speak*	vosotros	habl**áis**	*you speak*
él	habl**a**	*he speaks*	ellos	habl**an**	*they speak*
ella	habl**a**	*she speaks*	ellas	habl**an**	*they speak*
usted	habl**a**	*you speak*	ustedes	habl**an**	*you speak*

b   Verbs ending in **-er** e.g. **comer** (*to eat*)   →   **com-**.

yo	com**o**	*I eat*	nosotros	com**emos**	*we eat*
tú	com**es**	*you eat*	vosotros	com**éis**	*you eat*
él	com**e**	*he eats*	ellos	com**en**	*they eat*
ella	com**e**	*she eats*	ellas	com**en**	*they eat*
usted	com**e**	*you eat*	ustedes	com**en**	*you eat*

c   Verbs ending in **-ir** e.g. **vivir** (*to live*)   →   **viv-**.

yo	viv**o**	*I live*	nosotros	viv**imos**	*we live*
tú	viv**es**	*you live*	vosotros	viv**ís**	*you live*
él	viv**e**	*he lives*	ellos	viv**en**	*they live*
ella	viv**e**	*she lives*	ellas	viv**en**	*they live*
usted	viv**e**	*you live*	ustedes	viv**en**	*you live*

3 Remember the SUBJECT PRONOUNS (*yo, tú, él, ella* etc.) are normally left out.

¿Dónde vives?   *Where do you live?*   Vivo en York   *I live in York*

but can be used to make the meaning clear or for emphasis:

Él vive en el centro, pero **ella** no   *He lives in the centre, but she doesn't*

Help Yourself to Essential Spanish Grammar

Irregular verbs

4 There are some verbs which do not follow the pattern in the yo form. For example, the verb **hacer** (*to make/do*):

dar	*to give*	Yo **doy** a los pobres	*I give to the poor*
hacer	*to do, to make*	Yo **hago** mi cama	*I make my bed*
poner	*to put (on)*	Yo **pongo** la fecha arriba	*I put the date at the top*
salir	*to go out*	Yo **salgo** con Juan	*I'm going out with Juan*
traer	*to bring*	Yo **traigo** regalos	*I'm bringing presents*
ver	*to see, watch*	Yo **veo** la tele	*I watch TV*
conducir	*to drive*	Yo **conduzco** un Seat	*I drive a Seat*
conocer	*to know (people)*	Yo **conozco** a Arantxa	*I know Arantxa*
saber	*to know (facts)*	Yo **sé** que no viene	*I know he's not coming*

5 Some very common verbs do not follow any pattern and are treated separately:

tener   *to give* (p 16)   **estar/ser**   *to be* (p 6, 10)   **ir**   *to go* (p 30)
decir   *to say* (p 115)

Common irregular verbs are listed in full in the Appendix, page 130

Days and months: on, in

6 To say *on* or *at* with dates and days of the week, e.g. *on Monday/at the weekend*, use **el** and **los**.

Llego **el** dos de agosto   *I'm arriving **on** the second of August*
El lunes voy al dentista   ***On** Monday, I'm going to the dentist*
Los sábados voy a las tiendas   ***On** Saturdays I go to the shops*
El fin de semana, salgo con mis amigos   ***At** the weekend, I go out with my friends*

7 When talking about months of the year on their own, use **en** to mean *in*:

en febrero   *in February*

8 Beginnings, middles and ends of months are expressed in the following way:

a primeros de julio   *at the beginning of July*
a mediados de agosto   *in the middle of August*
a finales de septiembre *at the end of September*

CHAPTER 8   WHAT HAVE YOU LEARNT?

A The Soriano family are on holiday at the University of Santander, where they hope to learn new hobbies and skills. Read their interview with the local journalist, Iñigo, and write the verbs in brackets in the present tense.

e.g. ¿por qué (pasar) ustedes …?   →   ¿por qué **pasan** ustedes …?

La Universidad de Santander

IÑIGO   Señores Soriano, ¿por qué (*pasar*) ustedes las vacaciones aquí?

SR.   Nosotros – mi mujer y mi niña Mar – (*vivir*) cerca de Madrid …

SRA.   … y una semana aquí en la costa del norte (*parecer*) ideal.

IÑIGO   Y tú, Mar, ¿qué (*hacer*) en tu cursillo?

MAR   (*Aprender*) a hacer vela. A veces (*salir*) en un barco yo sola – ¡es muy emocionante! – pero normalmente (*practicar*) con mi pareja.

IÑIGO   Y ustedes, ¿qué (*hacer*)?

SR.   ¡Yo (*cocinar*)! En casa, (*hacer*) el desayuno, pero es todo.

IÑIGO   Señora, ¿le parece que su marido (*necesitar*) aprender a cocinar?

SRA.   ¡Sí, por supuesto! Por la tarde, mi marido (*traer*) a la residencia los platos que ha preparado. Son deliciosos… Mi hija y yo (*comer*) todo lo que él (*preparar*).

IÑIGO   ¿Y su mujer (*aprender*) algo útil y práctico también, Señor Soriano?

SR.   ¡No! ¡Mi mujer (*pintar*) a la acuarela y (*visitar*) exposiciones!

IÑIGO   ¿Y el año que viene?

SR.   No lo (*saber*) todavía. Lo bueno es que ahora yo (*conocer*) a mucha gente y tengo amigos nuevos. ¡A ver lo que (*decir*) mi mujer!

B The noticeboard at the Soriano's Halls of Residence advertises lots of activities for the holiday months. Fill in the gaps correctly with **a**, **el**, **los**, **en** or **de**.

Los anuncios

1 ¿Le interesa aprender el piragüismo? Clases con Toni empiezan … lunes 12 … julio.

2 … domingos por la tarde … agosto – recitales de piano, aula 5, 20.00h.

3 … primeros … agosto – posibilidad de visitas a las cuevas de Altamira. Infórmese en la recepción.

4 Llegada del grupo musical Los Garay del Perú … treinta de julio. Recepción para todos a las 21.00, sala 3.

5 ¡Atención! … fin de semana 17–18 julio se sirve la cena a las 21.30.

6 … septiembre, no habrá clases de yoga con la Señora Puig.

7 Todos los cursillos terminan … finales … septiembre este año.

UNIT

3

.

CHAPTER 9   WHAT DO YOU KNOW?

A A group of students are choosing a team to represent their college in a tennis match.
Fill in the gaps with the correct form of the verb **jugar** from the list below.
e.g. pero yo no … al tenis.   →   pero yo no **juego** al tenis.

Jugamos al tenis

PACO   Pues lo siento amigos, pero yo no … bien al tenis.
FERNANDA Sylvia sí que … ¡Es buenísima!
PACO   Sí, es verdad. Y Xavier es fenomenal. ¿Por qué no … tú, Xavier?
XAVIER   Lo siento – no estoy libre el sábado.
FERNANDA ¿Elena y Gabi? ¿… al tenis vosotros dos?
ELENA   Bueno, sí – pero no … muy bien.
FERNANDA Faltan cinco días – ¡hay que practicar cada tarde! ¿De acuerdo?

jugáis   juegas   juego   juega   juegamos

B Enrique's sports' coach has a recipe for success written on the wall of the changing
room: put the words in brackets into Spanish.

Receta para ganar la Copa
1 Treinta minutos de ejercicos cada [day] …
2 más dos horas en la piscina cada [week] …
3 más un fin de semana de entrenamiento intensivo cada [month] …
4 ¡y ganamos la Copa cada [year]!

C The coach is not looking forward to spending Saturday with his pupils. Read his
disgruntled thoughts. Fill in the gaps with the appropriate phrases from the list below.

El profe de deportes
Enseño … día – ¡y luego preparo clases … tarde! Normalmente, paso … sábados en
el campo de deporte viendo los partidos, y paso … vacaciones preparando materiales
para el nuevo trimestre. Antes de volver en septiembre, tengo pesadillas … noche.
Durante el trimestre, paso … fines de semana pensando en el lunes. No sé por qué
soy profesor – ¡qué vida!

todos los   todo el   toda la   todas las   toda la   todos los

Stem-changing verbs

1 Some verbs have a change in their STEM, except in the **nosotros** and **vosotros** form. Their endings follow the patterns for regular verbs.

ending in …	-ar, -er, -ir			-ir
stem change	-u → ue	-o → ue	-e → ie	-e → i
	jugar *to play*	volver *to return*	preferir *to prefer*	servir *to serve*
yo	j**ue**go	v**ue**lvo	pref**ie**ro	s**i**rvo
tú	j**ue**gas	v**ue**lves	pref**ie**res	s**i**rves
él, ella	j**ue**ga	v**ue**lve	pref**ie**re	s**i**rve
usted	j**ue**ga	v**ue**lve	pref**ie**re	s**i**rve
nosotros	jugamos	volvemos	preferimos	servimos
vosotros	jugáis	volvéis	preferís	servís
ellos, ellas	j**ue**gan	v**ue**lven	pref**ie**ren	s**i**rven
ustedes	j**ue**gan	v**ue**lven	pref**ie**ren	s**i**rven

Examples:

¿**Juegas** mucho al fúbol?   *Do you play a lot of football?*
Vuelvo hoy y Paco **vuelve** mañana   *I return today and Paco returns tomorrow*
Preferimos beber el té en Inglaterra   *We prefer to drink tea in England*
Los españoles **prefieren** el café   *The Spanish prefer coffee*
La cena se **sirve** desde las nueve   *The evening meal is served from nine*

2 Also note that the stem-changing verb **venir** (*to come*) is irregular in the **yo** form:

Yo **vengo** al instituto a pie   *I come to school on foot*
¿Cómo **vienes** tú?   *How do you come?*

Common stem-changing verbs are given in full in the Appendix, p 130

Each, every, all

3 **Cada** means *each* or *every*. Note that it remains unchanged, even when linked to a feminine/plural noun.

cada día	*each day*	**cada** semana	*each week*
cada mes	*each month*	**cada** año	*each year*
cada dos días	*every two days*	**cada** quince días	*every two weeks*

Examples:

> **Cada** año, voy a las Islas Canarias   *Each year, I go to the Canary Islands*
> **Cada** noche, hay un montón de deberes   *Every night, there's a load of homework*

4 **Todo** means *every* and *all*. It changes form according to the gender and number of the noun it is linked to and is followed by **el, la, los** or **las**:

todo el día	*all day*	**todos los** días	*every day*
todo el mundo	*everyone*	**todas las** chicas	*all the girls*

It can also mean *whole*:

toda la clase	*the **whole** class*	**todo el** año *the **whole** year*

Examples:

> **Todos** los chicos en mi clase son majos   *All the boys in my class are nice*
> No saqué "sobresaliente" en **todo** el año   *I didn't get "excellent" in the whole year*

Saying how often

5 **Vez** or **veces**, meaning *time* or *times* is used is used to say how often e.g. *once, twice* etc:

una vez *once*	**dos veces** *twice*	**tres veces** *three times*

and also to say *often*, *not very often*, and *how often*?

muchas veces	*often*	**¿cuántas veces?**	*how often?*
pocas veces	*not very often*	**raras veces**	*rarely*

6 To say how often something happens (*a* or *per* month etc) use **al, a la**:

al día *per day*	**a la** semana *per week*	**al** mes *a month*	**al** año *per year*

Examples:

> Juego al squash dos veces **a la** semana   *I play squash twice **a** week*
> Voy a la piscina una vez **al** mes   *I go to the pool once **a** month*
> Duermo sólo cinco horas **al** día   *I sleep only five hours **per** day*

CHAPTER 9   WHAT HAVE YOU LEARNT?

A Inma is a fan of the Internet. Read the interview between her and Pablo, and put the verbs in brackets into the correct form of the present tense.

e.g. ¿*(tener)* tu proprio ordenador? → **¿tienes** tu propio ordenador?

Inma y Internet

PABLO Inma, ¿*(tener)* tu proprio ordenador?

INMA ¡Ojalá! No, *(soler)* usar el ordenador de mi madre.

PABLO ¿Tú *(poder)* conectarte cuando quieras?

INMA No, siempre *(pedir)* permiso a mi madre antes. Si ella lo necesita para trabajar, entonces *(volver)* a pedirle más tarde.

PABLO ¿Qué tipo de cosas *(preferir)* tú hacer con tus amigas en la red?

INMA Normalmente mi amiga Carla y yo *(empezar)* con los canales de chat. Me gusta conectarme con chicas ingleses. A veces yo no *(entender)* lo que *(decir)*, ¡y *(perder)* mucho tiempo buscando en el diccionario!

B Are you lazy? Help prepare this questionnaire on lifestyles by replacing the English in brackets with the correct Spanish word.

e.g. 1a [EVERY DAY] → **todos los días**

¿Eres perezoso o no?

1 Haces los deberes
a [EVERY DAY]
b de vez en cuando
c muy pocas veces

2 Recoges tu cuarto
a cada día
b [ONCE A WEEK]
c una vez al mes

3 Practicas el deporte
a dos veces a la semana
b cada quince días
c [ONCE OR TWICE A YEAR]

4 Vas a la piscina
a [EACH WEEK]
b una vez a la semana
c una o dos veces al mes

5 Juegas en un equipo
a cada sábado
b cada seis meses
c [NOT VERY OFTEN]

6 Haces aerobic
a cada noche
b [TWICE A MONTH]
c raras veces

Now do the test to find out whether you are lazy or not!

Mayoría de a: ¡qué bien! – eres muy activo/a. Mayoría de b: debes esforzarte un poco más. Mayoría de c: ¡qué perezoso/a eres!

Revision test 7–9

A Ana feels exhausted just looking at the family noticeboard for next week! Use her notes below to work out what she says to her friend about her busy family's schedule. Fill in the gaps with the correct part of the verb **ir** (*to go*).
e.g. Carmen – al conversatorio.   →   Carmen **va** al conservatorio.

La agenda

lunes 22	Carmen … al conservatorio (exámen de música).
martes 23	Yo … al médico a las 11.00.
miércoles 24	Martín y José … al partido de fútbol (16.30).
jueves 25	Enrique y yo … al teatro (21.00).
viernes 26	¡Atención, Felipe! Tú y Rosario … al dentista a las 11.00.
sábado 27	José … al campamento (10.00 en el colegio).

B You read an article about the pilgrim route to Santiago. It finishes with a list of points to think about. Insert the correct question word in the gaps provided.
e.g. ¿Con … vas?   →   ¿Con **quién** vas?

El Camino de Santiago

1 ¿Con … vas? ¡Si vas con un amigo o una amiga, hay que ser compatible!
2 ¿… vas a viajar? ¿A pie? ¿En bicicleta?
3 ¿… vas a quedarte de noche? El camping es más barato, pero hay que llevar más cosas.
4 ¿… dinero vas a necesitar? Es importante llevar algo para emergencias.
5 ¿… tipo de zapatos vas a llevar? Necesitas algo cómodo y fuerte – y dos pares.
6 ¿… piensas llegar a Santiago? Mejor evitar el 25 de julio – Día del Apóstol – porque habrá mucha gente en la capital.

C Some students on an orienteering course have forgotten various items they need for camping. Luckily the leader has extras and hands them out. Fill in the gaps by putting the English word in brackets into Spanish as required.
e.g. Esta tienda es … [FOR ME].   →   Esta tienda es **para mí**.

En el camping

1 Vamos a ver. Esta tienda es …	[FOR ME]
2 ¡Oye – tú, Charo! La lámpara de bolsillo es …	[FOR YOU]
3 ¿Dónde está Nacho? Bueno, las cerillas son …	[FOR HIM]
4 ¿Y María? El plato, el cuchillo y el tenedor son …	[FOR HER]
5 Ximena y Nuria, los dos sacos de dormir son …	[FOR YOU]
6 ¡Quiero comprar una barra grande de chocolate! ¡Es …!	[FOR US!]
7 ¿Quién viene al supermercado …?	[WITH ME]

D Ronaldo, a famous footballer, talks to a magazine about his hobbies and what he likes best in life. Put the verb in brackets into the correct form of the present tense.
e.g. Ronaldo (*disfrutar*) con un buen CD.   →   Ronaldo **disfruta** con un buen CD.

El futbolista
Música y cine

Ronaldo (*disfrutar*) con un buen CD o una buena película. En música (*preferir*) la samba y en el cine lo tiene bien claro: las películas de acción. Él siempre (*ver*) las películas en el vídeo de su casa:
– 'Si (ir) al cine, (*llegar*) tarde, porque la gente me (*pedir*) autógrafos. Es el precio de la fama' – dice Ronaldo.

Comidas

¿Qué tipo de comida le gusta más? Depende.
– Me encanta la comida brasileña, y ¡más todavía si es mi madre quien (*cocinar*)! Si yo (*salir*) a cenar fuera de casa, siempre (*comer*) hamburguesas, o pizzas.

Amor

Ronaldo está enamorado de la futbolista y modelo Susana Werner. Lo difícil es que él (*jugar*) en Barcelona y ella (*vivir*) en Brasil. Muchos kilómetros les (*separar*) pero los dos (*pasar*) las vacaciones juntos en América o en Europa.
– Estoy enamoradísimo y (*querer*) formar una familia – (*afirmar*) Ronaldo.

E Trinidad receives a telegram about her aunt Rosa, who is ill and coming to stay. She reads it aloud to the family. Write her sentences in full by using the information underlined.
e.g. Rosa: tratamiento agosto.   →   Rosa necesita tratamiento **en** agosto.

El Telegrama

1	Rosa: tratamiento <u>agosto</u>.	Rosa necesita tratamiento …
2	Llegada 5 <u>agosto</u>.	Llega aquí …
3	Cita con médico: <u>lunes</u>.	Tiene cita con el médico …
4	Descanso total <u>fines de semana</u>.	Necesita descanso total …
5	Vuelta Oreña <u>finales agosto</u>.	Vuelve a Oreña …

F Carlos has met Begoña on an Internet chat-line, and sends her an e-mail about himself and his hobbies. Write the words in brackets in Spanish.

El correo electrónico

Querida Begoña,
Quieres saber algo de lo que hago en mi tiempo libre. Bueno, juego al squash [THREE TIMES A WEEK] y practico la natación [EVERY DAY]. Voy al gimnasio [EVERY TWO DAYS] para entrenarme. Me encanta el ciclismo y [ONCE A MONTH] voy a la montaña con un grupo de amigos. Soy una persona muy activa: ¡sólo duermo cinco horas [PER DAY]! Como sabes, me encanta la informática. ¿Y tú? ¿[HOW MANY TIMES] navegas por Internet [PER WEEK]? Leo mi correo electrónico [EVERY NIGHT] antes de irme a la cama, así que ¡escríbeme pronto!

La Rutina

A Alicia does not enjoy school! Replace the underlined expressions with the **yo** form of the appropriate verb from the list below.

e.g. 1 <u>Abro mis ojos</u> a las siete   →   **me despierto**

La rutina

1 <u>Abro mis ojos</u> a las siete. ¡Qué disgusto!
2 <u>Tomo una ducha</u>. ¡Qué frío!
3 <u>Me pongo</u> mi uniforme escolar. ¡Qué asco!
4 <u>Salgo</u> a las ocho menos cuarto. ¡Qué temprano!
5 En clase <u>estoy aburrida</u>. ¡Qué rollo!
6 <u>Voy a la cama</u> muy tarde. ¡Qué bien!

me voy   me acuesto   me aburro   me despierto   me ducho   me visto en

B Alicia's older brother Ricardo has a very relaxed weekend. Match up the two halves of the sentences correctly.

El fin de semana

1 El sábado no hago mucho	a medianoche.
2 No desayuno, pero tomo algo ligero a la	b de la tarde.
3 Me acuesto muy tarde, a	c por la mañana.
4 El domingo no me levanto hasta las once	d una.
5 Salgo con mis amigos a	e de la mañana.
6 No vuelvo a casa hasta las seis o siete	f mediodía.

C Alicia's bossy mother calls up a series of instructions to her as she's getting dressed. Fill the gaps with **antes de** (*before*) or **después de** (*after*) as the meaning requires.

La pobre Alicia

1 ¡Alicia! ¡Haz tu cama … bajar para desayunar!
2 ¡No te olvides de lavarte los dientes … desayunar!
3 Y … irte al insti, prepárate un bocadillo para el recreo.
4 … volver a casa, ¡haz tus deberes en tu cuarto y no delante de la tele!
5 Y … las seis ve a la casa de tu tía para recoger a tu hermano. Tu tía sale a las seis en punto, ¡así que no llegues tarde!
6 … recoger a tu hermano, dale algo de comer aquí en casa: fruta o yogur.

The present tense: reflexive verbs

1 REFLEXIVE VERBS describe actions which you do to yourself, such as washing and dressing oneself. When forming a reflexive verb, a REFLEXIVE PRONOUN (**me**, **te**, **se**, **nos**, **os**, **se**) goes before the verb:

		levantar**se**	*to get (oneself) up*
yo	**me**	levanto	*I get up*
tú	**te**	levantas	*you get up*
él, ella	**se**	levanta	*he/she gets up*
usted	**se**	levanta	*you get up*
nosotros	**nos**	levantamos	*we get up*
vosotros	**os**	levantáis	*you get up*
ellos, ellas	**se**	levantan	*they get up*
ustedes	**se**	levantan	*you get up*

¿A qué hora **te levantas**?　　*What time do you get up?*
Me levanto temprano　　*I get up early*
Nos levantamos tarde los sábados　　*We get up late on Saturdays*

2 Some common verbs (e.g. *despertarse, acostarse, vestirse*) are also STEM-CHANGING verbs:

Me desp**ie**rto a las ocho　　*I get up at eight*
Me v**i**sto en seguida　　*I get dressed straightaway*
Me ac**ue**sto a las once　　*I go to bed at eleven*

See stem-changing verbs in Chapter 9, p 38 and the Appendix, page 130

3 When using the infinitive form (e.g. **levantar**) of a reflexive verb, the reflexive pronoun is added to the end of the verb, e.g. **levantarse**. Note that the reflexive pronoun must agree with the person doing the action.

¡(Yo) No quiero levantar**me**!　　*I don't want to get up!*
Ana no tiene ganas de levantar**se**　　*Ana doesn't feel like getting up*

See stem-changing verbs in Chapter 9, p 38

The time of day: *at, in*

4 To say *in the morning/afternoon/evening/night* without wanting to specify a particular time, use **por**:

Examples:

por la manana	*in the morning*
por la tarde	*in the afternoon*
el martes **por** la mañana	*on Tuesday morning*
los jueves **por** la tarde	*on Thursday afternoons*

5 When wanting to specify a particular time of day, use **de**:

a las once **de** la mañana	*at eleven **in** the morning*
a las diez **de** la noche	*at ten **at** night*

6 To say *at one o'clock*, *at two o'clock* etc, *at midday*, use **a**:

a la una	*at one o'clock*
a las dos y media	*at half past two*
a las tres y cuarto	*at a quarter past three*
a las cuatro menos cuarto	*at a quarter to four*
a mediodía/medianoche	*at midday/midnight*

Ordering events

7 The simplest ways of expressing the order in which things happen is to use words like *then*, *next*, *later*:

primero	*first*	**después**	*after(wards)*
luego	*then*	**más tarde**	*later*
antes	*before(hand)*	**un poco más tarde**	*a little later*

me visto y **luego** desayuno	*I get dressed and **then** I have breakfast*
un poco más tarde voy al instituto	*a little later I go to school*

8 The following expressions also indicate the order of events, e.g. *before*, *after*. They are always followed by the infinitive:

después de *after (...ing)*	**antes de** *before (...ing)*	**al** *on (...ing)*

Después de desayunar, salgo de casa	***After** having breakfast, I leave the house*
Antes de salir, hago mi cama	***Before** leaving, I make my bed*
Al llegar al instituto, voy a mi aula	***On** arriving at school, I go to my classroom*

CHAPTER 10   WHAT HAVE YOU LEARNT?

A It is Sunday and Iñigo has left his timetable at college. He rings his friend Antón to find out what they have on Monday. Fill the gaps with **a**, **por**, or **de**, as appropriate.

El horario

IÑIGO   ¿Qué asignaturas tenemos mañana ... la mañana?

ANTÓN   ... las nueve tenemos música.

IÑIGO   ¿No tenemos música ... la una ... la tarde?

ANTÓN   No – el lunes no. Y luego ... las diez hay dos horas de ciencias.

IÑIGO   ¿Hay asamblea ... mediodía o ... la tarde?

ANTÓN   No hay mañana. Hay geografía ... la una. ¿Has hecho tus deberes?

IÑIGO   ¡Se me olvidó! Tendré que hacerlos. Y son las diez ... la noche ya.

         ¡A qué me acuesto ... medianoche!

B On his way to bed, Iñigo reads an article in a teenage magazine about optimists and pessimists. Write the verbs in brackets in the present tense.

e.g. (*levantarse*) temprano   →   **te levantas** temprano

¿Optimista o pesimista?

Si tú eres optimista ...   1 (*levantarse*) temprano casi todos los días.

                           2 (*ducharse*) o (*bañarse*) cantando.

                           3 (*vestirse*) bien y estás contento/a con tu cuerpo.

                           4 (*divertirse*) mucho – todo le parece interesante.

La persona pesimista ...   5 (*preocuparse*) mucho de su aparencia física.

                           6 no (*organizarse*) bien – es despistado/a.

                           7 (*aburrirse*) fácilmente.

                           8 (*acostarse*) muy tarde.

C Iñigo spots an item about a Polar explorer. Rewrite the description, beginning each sentence with the phrases in brackets and altering the verb and sentence as necessary.

e.g. Cuando se despierta   →   **Al despertarse**

Al Polo Sur

1 Cuando se despierta, se pone en contacto con Madrid.   (*al*)

2 Se levanta y luego prepara una comida.   (*después de*)

3 Se viste en un mono de nieve, se pone una crema.   (*antes de*)

4 Se marcha temprano, pero primero escucha el pronóstico.   (*antes de*)

5 Cuando llega al próximo campamento, primero monta la tienda.   (*después de*)

UNIT

4

CHAPTER 11   WHAT DO YOU KNOW?

A A survey of Spanish teenagers' attitudes to foreign foods was carried out in school canteens over a period of six months and showed up some interesting results. Fill in the gaps with the correct present tense form of the verb **gustar** (*to like*), i.e. **gusta** or **gustan**.

La encuesta

1 A 95% les ... la coca-cola.
2 A 92% les ... los helados italianos.
3 A 87% les ... las hamburguesas.
4 A 85% les ... la lasaña.
5 A 80% les ... el queso holandés.
6 A 76% les ... las perritos calientes.
7 A 70% les ... los espaguetis.
8 A 15% les ... el rosbif.

B Jon is playing host to Conchita, an exchange partner from Scotland, and, during a free period at school, wants to find out more about her hobbies. Choose the correct word from the alternatives in brackets.

¿Qué les gusta hacer?

JON   Oye, Conchita, ¿qué tipo de música (*me/te*) interesa?
CONCHITA Pues, a mí (*me/le*) encanta la música 'hip-hop'. ¡Pero a mis padres, no (*le/les*) gusta nada!
JON   ¿Y tu hermano? ¿(*Le/Te*) parecen buenos los grupos británicos?
CONCHITA Sí. A nosotros (*nos/os*) interesa la música inglesa y americana.
JON   ¿Qué hacéis el fin de semana? ¿(*Os/nos*) gusta salir?
CONCHITA Mucho. ¿(*Te/le*) gustaría venir con nosotros al club juvenil el viernes?
JON   ¡Cómo no!

C Conchita's mother tells a neighbour how Jon is managing during his stay. Choose the expression from the list below which best fits each gap.

Lo mejor y lo peor

... es que le encanta España, y Conchita es muy amable con él. ¡Pero ... es que hablamos muy rápido, y le resulta difícil entender! Para él, ... es que va al instituto con Concha. ¡Dice que no entiende nada de nada! Pero ... es que sale con Concha y sus amigos por la tarde y lo pasa bomba.

lo malo   lo divertido   lo aburrido   lo bueno

Gustar and similar verbs

1 **Gustar** usually means *to like*. Its exact meaning is *to please*:

me	gusta	jugar al fútbol
(to me)	*(is pleasing)*	*(to play football)*
me	gusta	el chocolate
(to me)	*(is pleasing)*	*(chocolate)*
me	gustan	las aceitunas
(to me)	*(are pleasing)*	*(olives)*

2 The endings of **gustar** are always in the *s/he* or *they* form, which is **-a** or **-an** in the present tense.

Me gust**a el** café	*I like coffee*
Me gust**a la** coca-cola	*I like coca-cola*
Me gust**an los** bocadillos de jamón	*I like ham sandwiches*
Me gust**an las** hamburguesas	*I like hamburgers*

3 When followed by a verb, use the singular form (*s/he*) of the verb **gustar**, which is **-a** in the present tense.

¿Qué te gust**a** hacer?	*What do you like doing?*
Me gust**a** salir con mis amigos	*I like to go out with my friends*

4 Where English uses *I like*, *you like*, Spanish uses *it/they are pleasing to me*, *to you*, etc. These are called INDIRECT OBJECT PRONOUNS. They are as follows:

me	gusta	*I like*	**nos**	gusta	*we like*
te	gusta	*you like*	**os**	gusta	*you like*
le	gusta	*he, she likes* *you like*	**les**	gusta	*they like* *you like*

Examples:

No **me** gusta nada el hockey	*I don't like hockey at all*
¿Por qué no **te** gusta?	*Why don't you like it?*
¿**Le** gustan las corridas de toros?	*Does he like bull-fights?*
No **nos** gusta mucho el calor	*We don't like the heat very much*
¿**Os** gustan las películas de horror?	*Do you like horror films?*
Señor y Señora Ruiz ¿**les** gusta Gales?	*Mr. and Mrs. Ruiz, do you like Wales?*

Help Yourself to Essential Spanish Grammar

5 Where there is possible confusion over the meaning of **le** or **les**, add **a** and the name of the person or the **pronoun**, to make it clear:

WITH NAMES	
No **le** gusta **a Isabel** el pescado	*Isabel doesn't like fish*
No **les** gusta **a Juan** y **Paco** tampoco	*Juan and Paco don't like it either*

WITH PRONOUNS	
Le gusta **a él** la carne	*He likes meat*
Le gusta **a ella** también	*She likes it as well*
Le gusta **a usted** el pescado frito ¿verdad?	*You like fried fish, don't you?*
Les gusta **a ellos** la sangría	*They (male) like sangría*
Les gusta **a ellas** más el jerez	*They (female) like sherry more*
Les gusta a **ustedes** el vino de Málaga, ¿no?	*You like Málaga wine, don't you?*

6 There are other verbs which behave in the same way as **gustar**. They are:

encantar	*to really like, love*	**interesar**	*to interest*
apetecer	*to feel like*	**doler**	*to hurt*

Examples:

Me encanta la música rock	*I love rock music*
¿**Te interesa** ir al concierto?	*Are you interested in going to the concert?*
Me duelen los pies/tengo dolor de cabeza	*My feet hurt/I've got a headache*
No me apetece salir esta tarde	*I don't feel like going out this evening*

Using **lo** and **lo que**

7 To express *the … thing* (e.g. *the good thing*) in Spanish, use **lo** with an adjective in the masculine singular:

Lo bueno es que no tengo exámenes	*The good thing is that I don't have exams*
Lo malo es que hay muchas pruebas	*The bad thing is that there are lots of tests*
Lo bonito es que son amigos	*The nice thing is that they are friends*

8 When talking about a general idea or action, use **lo que** to mean *what* or *which*:

Lo que no me gusta, es que hay mucho tráfico	*What I don't like is that there is a lot of traffic*
Siempre tiene razón – **lo que** me fastidia mucho	*He's always right, which really gets on my nerves*

CHAPTER 11　WHAT HAVE YOU LEARNT?

A The mothers of host families on an exchange find it hard to please their fussy guests!
Complete their sentences with **me, te, le, nos, os, les** as appropriate.

e.g. A los jóvenes no ... interesa → A los jóvenes no **les** interesa

Los jóvenes tiquismiquis

INMA A los jóvenes de cualquier nacionalidad, no ... interesa la cultura.

ROSA ¡Es verdad! A la inglesa que tengo yo, sólo ... gusta salir con amigos.

TERE Pero cuando tú tenías catorce años, ... gustaba salir también, ¿no?

INMA ¡Y además son muy tiquismiquis! A la niña japonesa no ... apetece nada. ¡No quiere comer nada!

TERE ¡Pues yo tengo dos chicos escoceses en casa, y ... gusta todo!

ROSA Tienes suerte, hija. A mí, ... encanta cuando los niños comen bien.

TERE Pero cuando estáis en el extranjero vosotras, ¿... gusta siempre la comida?

INMA Sí, tienes razón. Muchas veces sólo probamos lo que ... gusta en casa.

ROSA Bueno, vamos al castillo: ¡a ver si ... interesa a mis dos chicas!

B Cathy is a student staying with a Spanish family. They have asked her to jot down foods she likes and doesn't like. Use the table below to work out what she says: use **(no) me gusta mucho, (no) me gustan mucho.**

e.g. la coca-cola → **Me gusta mucho** la coca-cola.

　　 el zumo de piña → **No me gusta mucho** el zumo de piña.

Mis gustos

	+			–
1	la coca-cola	6		el zumo de piña
2	las hamburguesas	7		el pescado
3	la fruta	8		las aceitunas
4	el chocolate	9		la leche
5	los mariscos	10		los bocadillos de jamón

C One of the students on the exchange is asked for his impressions of Spain. Insert **lo** or **lo que** in the gaps as appropriate.

En mi opinión

Me gusta mucho España en general. ... bueno es que la gente es muy simpática, pero ... me fastidia es que los españoles hablan tan rápidamente. El paisaje es muy bonito y ... mejor es que todavía hay ciudades y regiones enteras sin turistas. Pero ... no me gusta nada, es la contaminación del paisaje por todas partes – la conciencia ecológica no existe en muchos sitios. Esto es ... peor para mí.

Help Yourself to Essential Spanish Grammar

UNIT

4

CHAPTER 12   WHAT DO YOU KNOW?

A   Carmen is unhappy about her family's move to the outskirts of Madrid. Choose the correct word in brackets to complete her letter to an agony aunt.

¡No me gusta mi nueva casa!
Querida Corazón,
No me gusta mi nueva casa, (*ni/no*) el cambio de mi rutina. Vivo ahora en las afueras de Madrid, pero no me gusta (*nada/nunca*). Mis antiguos amigos viven en el centro, y no quieren venir aquí (*nunca/ni*), donde es aburrido y (*no/ni*) hay mucha movida. El fin de semana, no veo a (*nada/nadie*). No hay (*ni/nada*) cine (*ni/no*) discoteca.
¡Ayúdame!
Carmen.

B   The agony aunt replies to Carmen's letter. Decide whether **a** is needed before the underlined words or not.
e.g. para conocer <u>(?) otras personas</u>   →   para conocer **a** otras personas

Mis recomendaciones
1   Hay que hacer un esfuerzo para conocer <u>(?) otras personas</u> – ¡anímate!
2   Haz un cursillo de noche: pide <u>(?) información</u> en el ayuntamiento.
3   Invita <u>(?) una compañera</u> de clase a tu casa; así vas a hacerte amigas.
4   Visita <u>(?) el hospital</u> o la clínica cerca, para ver si necesitan voluntarios.
5   Pregunta <u>(?) tu tutor</u>, para ver si hay clubs después del día escolar.
6   Si te sientes muy sola y muy triste, llama <u>(?) la organización</u> Juventud.

C   Carmen gets a Saturday job in a Chemist's. She is left alone to cope one day, and discovers to her horror that they seem to have run out of almost everything! Complete the gaps with one of the words from the list below.

Lo siento ...
1   – Quiero un bote de crema Parasol.   – Lo siento, no queda ...
2   – ¿Tiene una caja de tiritas?   – Es que no hay ... en el almacén.
3   – Por favor, ¿tiene pastillas Sanatos?   – No quedan .... Lo siento mucho.
4   – Quisiera un paquete de tisús Mari.   – Lo siento, no queda ... paquete.
5   – ¿No hay tubos de pasta de dientes?   – Vendí los últimos ayer. No tenemos ...

ningunas   ningún   ninguna   ningunos   ninguno

The personal **a**

1 The personal **a** is used before a person or a person's name when something is done to them, or something happens to them.

> Pegó **a** Juan   He hit Juan
> Pegó **a** su padre   He hit his father

2 **A** is also used with verbs which, in English, we do not think of as being action verbs: **ver** (*to see*), **conocer** (*to get to know*), **preguntar** (*to ask*):

> No veo **a** María   *I don't see María*
> Conocí **a** muchos jóvenes   *I got to know lots of young people*
> ¡Pregunta **a** tu profe!   *Ask your teacher!*

3 The personal **a** is <u>not</u> used after the verb **tener** (*to have*):

> Tengo dos hermanos   *I have two brothers*

4 The verb **querer** on its own means *to want* (*to*). When the personal **a** is placed after it, it means *to love*:

> Quiero un hermano   *I want a brother*
> Quiero **a** mi hermano Paco   *I love my brother Paco*

Negatives

5 NEGATIVE words indicate that something does <u>not</u> happen or that you are <u>not</u> doing something. The following are negative sentences:

> I do **not** like him, and she does**n't** either   He has **not** a clue. I have**n't** either!

6 In Spanish, *not* is expressed by the word **no**. It always comes before the verb, and before the reflexive pronoun if there is one:

> **No** tengo un boli   *I haven't got a biro*
> Merche **no** vive con sus padres   *Merche doesn't live with her parents*
> **No** me levanto muy temprano   *I do **not** get up very early*

Help Yourself to Essential Spanish Grammar

7 The other most common negative words are:

nada   *nothing*   **nadie**   *no-one*
nunca/jamás *never*   **ni … ni** *neither … nor*

¿Qué tienes en la mano? **Nada**   *What have you got in your hand? **Nothing***
¿Quién quiere un té? **Nadie**   *Who wants tea? **No-one***
¿Vas mucho al teatro? **Nunca**   *Do you often go to the theatre? **Never***
No tengo **ni** tiempo **ni** dinero   *I've **neither** time **nor** money*

8 a The negatives **nada**, **nadie**, **nunca/jamás** have two possible positions: either before the verb on their own, or after the verb which then takes **no** in front:

No viene **nunca** *He never comes*   **No** vive **nadie** allí *No-one lives there*
Nunca viene *He never comes*   **Nadie** vive allí *No-one lives there*

None, not … any

9 The following negative phrases, **no** + noun (e.g. *no book*), ***not … any*** and ***none*** are expressed in Spanish by the adjective **ninguno**. The word **ninguno** agrees with the noun it describes:

MASC. SING.	**ninguno**	¿**Un** cuaderno? No tengo **ninguno** *An exercise book? I haven't got **any***
FEM. SING.	**ninguna**	¿**Una** manzana? Lo siento – no queda **ninguna** *An apple? I'm sorry, there's **none** left*
MASC. PL.	**ningunos**	¿**Unos** discos compactos baratos? ¡No hay **ningunos**! *Some cheap CDs? There aren't **any**!*
FEM. PL.	**ningunas**	¿**Unas** naranjas? No quedan **ningunas** *Some oranges? There are **none** left*

When **ninguno** comes before a masculine singular noun, it becomes **ningún**:

No hay **ningún** plátano en la cesta *There's **no** money in my purse*

Neither, not … either

10 **Tampoco**, meaning *either*, *neither*, is the negative word which replaces **también** (*also, as well*), and often goes after the verb which takes **no** in front:

María viene **también**   *María is coming **as well***
Pablo **no** viene **tampoco**   *Pablo is **not** coming **either***
Yo **tampoco**   *Me **neither***

CHAPTER 12   WHAT HAVE YOU LEARNT?

A Ramón is chatting to his friend Leo about his helpful family. Leo's family is the opposite. Change Ramón's descriptions, using the expressions in brackets to explain what Leo's family is like.

e.g. Mi mujer hace mucho.   →   Mi mujer **no** hace mucho.

¡Qué desastre de familia!

1 Mi mujer hace mucho.   *(no)*
2 Nuestro hijo mayor prepara la comida.   *(jamás)*
3 Mi hija mayor hace su cama.   *(no ... nunca)*
4 Mi padrastro lava los platos.   *(nadie)*
5 La madre de mi mujer pone y quita la mesa.   *(ni ... ni...)*
6 Mi hija menor ayuda en casa.   *(no ... a nadie)*

B Leo is having trouble getting his daughter Belén organised for school. Put Belén's replies into Spanish.

e.g. No, I haven't got one.   →   **No, no tengo ninguno.**

La chica despistada

PAPÁ   ¿Estás preparada? ¿Tienes un boli?
BELÉN   [NO, I HAVEN'T GOT ONE.]
PAPÁ   Toma. ¿Y tus zapatillas?
BELÉN   [I HAVEN'T GOT ANY.]
PAPÁ   ¡Cómo qué no! ¡Están en tu cuarto! ¿Y la llave de la casa?
BELÉN   [I HAVEN'T GOT ONE.]
PAPÁ   Te presto la mía – toma. ¿Has hecho los deberes?
BELÉN   [I HAVEN'T GOT ANY.]
PAPÁ   ¡Qué raro! Pero, ¿no tienes una bolsa para tus cosas?
BELÉN   [NO, I HAVEN'T GOT ONE.]
PAPÁ   ¡Dios mío! Toma esta bolsa de plástico. Corre – ¡allí viene el autobús!
BELÉN   [I HAVEN'T GOT ANY MONEY!]

C Zeneida, Ramon's wife, is very keen to make friends with Marifé and agrees with her all the time. Complete Zeneida's replies with either **también** or **tampoco** as the meaning requires.

e.g. 1 – No me gusta levantarme temprano el sábado.   →   A mí **tampoco**.

Marifé	Zeneida
1 – No me gusta levantarme temprano el sábado.	– A mí ...
2 – Y desayuno en la terraza – es mi lugar favorito.	– Yo ...
3 – A veces mi marido prepara churros que no me gustan nada.	– A mí ...
4 – Lo que me encanta, es un buen café con leche.	– A mí ...
5 – Después, doy un paseo por el parque o al lado del río.	– Yo ...
6 – No me gusta el parque, porque hay muchos gamberros allí.	– A mí ...

Revision test 10–12

A Things are not always perfect in Ahmed's house in the morning. Read his letter to his friend, and put the verb in brackets into the correct form for the person.

e.g. Pues nosotros no (*llevarse*) bien → Pues nosotros no **nos llevamos** bien

La carta de Ahmed

Quieres saber algo de mi familia, ¿verdad? ¡Pues nosotros no (*llevarse*) bien por la mañana! Yo (*levantarse*) a las siete en punto, y mis padres (*despertarse*) también – pero como sólo tenemos un cuarto de baño, mi madre (*meterse*) primero mientras que yo (*lavarse*) los dientes en el lavabo del aseo y papá prepara el desayuno. A veces, papá (*afeitarse*) en la cocina, ¡pero mi madre (*ponerse*) furiosa si lo hace! Yo (*reírse*) mucho cuando mis padres (*enfadarse*) porque nunca dura mucho tiempo, y luego hacen las paces. ¿Y tú? ¿(*Llevarse*) bien por la mañana con tu familia o (*pelearse*) también? ¡Escríbeme pronto!

B "It's a dog's life" says Sofía, as she tells us about her day. Put the words in brackets into Spanish.

¡Qué vida de perro!

1 Me levanto a las seis y media [IN THE MORNING].
2 [THEN], me ducho y me visto. ¡Siempre tengo prisa!
3 [A LITTLE LATER] me tomo un café con leche y una tostada.
4 [AFTERWARDS] me preparo un bocadillo para el almuerzo.
5 Preparo la cena y despierto a mi marido [AT EIGHT] – él cuida a los niños.
6 Diez minutos [LATER] cojo el autobús a la oficina.
7 Vuelvo a casa, muy cansada [AT SEVEN IN THE EVENING].
8 Traigo tanto trabajo a casa, que me acuesto [AT MIDNIGHT]. ¡Qué vida de perro!

C The life of an air-hostess after take-off is a busy one! Change the sentences below, so that they each start with the phrase from the brackets.

e.g. *Me levanto* de mi asiento … (*Después de …*) → Después de **levantarme** de mi asiento, voy a ver a los pasajeros.

La azafata

1 *Me levanto* de mi asiento y voy a ver a los pasajeros.   (*Después de …*)
2 El capitán verifica su posición *y luego se relaja un poco*.   (*Antes de …*)
3 *Cuando ven* los carritos, los viajeros se preparan para comer.   (*Al …*)
4 *Recogemos* todo *y luego* nos descansamos un poco.   (*Después de … *)
5 *Cuando aterrizamos*, nos despedimos de nuestros clientes.   (*Al …*)
6 *Vuelvo* al terminal, pongo la cabina en orden.   (*Antes de …*)

D Jaime is a researcher for a health magazine, and is trying to find out what people like to eat for their main meal. Fill in the gaps with the correct indirect pronoun (**me, te, le, nos, os, les**) and the correct form of the verb **gustar**.

e.g. ¿Qué ... ... comer al mediodía? → ¿Qué **le gusta** comer al mediodía?

Una encuesta

JAIME   ¿Qué ... ... comer al mediodía, Señorita?

SEÑORITA   ... ... los perritos calientes, sobre todo.

JAIME   Señor y Señora, ¿qué ... ... tomar para la comida principal?

SR. Y SRA. ... ... mucho el pescado. Más que la carne.

JAIME   Y tú, chiquitito – ¿qué te gusta comer?

CHICO   ¡... ... los helados de chocolate!

SRA.   A mi hijo ... ... mucho los dulces – churros, donuts, y pasteles.

JAIME   ¡Es normal!

JAIME   ¡Hola, jóvenes! ¡Un momento! ¿Qué ... ... comer al mediodía?

JÓVENES   Somos de padres italianos, así que ... ... las pastas y las pizzas.

JAIME   ¿Y tus amigos españoles? ¿Qué prefieren?

JÓVENES   ... ... más algo típico español – una tortilla, o una paella.

JAIME   Gracias – ¡que aproveche!

E Silvia has written to the penfriends' section of her favourite music magazine. Write the personal **a** before the underlined words if necessary.

e.g. conocer gente   →   conocer **a** gente

Punto de encuentro

¡Hola! Soy Silvia y me gustaría conocer <u>gente</u> de todo el mundo. Me encanta también el cine: me gusta ir a ver <u>las películas</u> de acción, y los dibujos animados de Disney. También quiero mucho <u>mi serpiente</u> – tengo <u>una cobra</u>, que se llama Coki. Si queréis <u>una amiga</u> divertida, escribid a Silvia, c/ San Clemente 132, Alhucemas o por correo electrónico a Fer0634@.ols.com.es. (¡Pregunta a <u>tus padres</u> primero!)

En la calle y la ciudad

A Marisa sets off from the station for the park with her unruly younger brothers.
  Choose the most appropriate expression in brackets to complete her sentences.
  e.g. Juanito, quédate aquí a mi lado. Camina (*rápidamente/lentamente*).
  ‣ Juanito, quédate aquí a mi lado. Camina **lentamente**.

Vamos al parque
1 Juanito, quédate aquí a mi lado. Camina (*rápidamente/lentamente*).
2 ¡Anda por la acera y no por la carretera! Te comportas
  (*estúpidamente/prudentemente*).
3 Vale, Paquito. Puedes ir hasta la entrada. Pero espera allí
  (*tranquilamente/ruidosamente*).
4 Juanito, ¡sal de allí! Pon la silla de la cafetería (*bien/mal*).
5 ¡A qué sí, entiendes! ¡Me entiendes (*mal/perfectamente*)!
6 ¡Cuidado con esa taza! Se rompe (*difícilmente/fácilmente*).
7 No, no vamos a tomar algo en la cafetería.Vamos al parque para merendar. Se
  abre (*normalmente/raramente*) a las diez.

B At the train station, some tourists and their children are not sure how to find their
  way, and ask for directions at the information desk. For each underlined command,
  write down whether it is **tú**, **vosotros**, **usted** or **ustedes**.
  e.g. ¿Para ir a la farmacia? Suban la calle.   → **ustedes**

¿Por dónde?
1 – ¿Para ir a la farmacia? <u>Suban</u> la calle.
2 – ¿El museo? Está en la Plaza Mayor. <u>Siga</u> todo recto, y está al final.
3 – ¿La juguetería más cercana? <u>Cruzad</u> la calle, y hay una enfrente.
4 – ¿Dónde está el restaurante 'El Capricho'? <u>Coja</u> la calle de enfrente.
5 – ¿Los servicios? <u>Tuerce</u> a la derecha, chico. Está cerca del quiosco.
6 – ¿Para ir a la piscina? <u>Baje</u> la avenida Bolivar, y está a la izquierda.
7 – ¿Dónde está el Hotel Alfonso? <u>Tomen</u> la primera a la derecha.
8 – ¿El cine? <u>Doblad</u> la esquina y está a la derecha, al final de la calle.

Adverbs

1 ADVERBS describe how something is done, and often end in -*ly* in English:

*He works **slowly** and **carefully***   *Can you do it **quickly?** – **possibly***

2 To form adverbs, choose the appropriate adjective, make it feminine and add -**mente**:

ADJECTIVE			ADVERB	
	MASC.	FEM.		
quiet	tranquilo	→ tranquila	tranquil**amente**	*quietly*
easy	fácil	→ fácil	fácil**mente**	*easily*

Examples:

Juan habla clara**mente**   *Juan speaks clearly*
Ellos caminaban lenta**mente**   *They were walking slowly*

3 When two or more adverbs come together, the first one loses the -**mente**:

Habló **sincera** y tranquilamente   *She spoke sincerely and quietly*

4 The following common adverbs do not end in -**mente**:

bien	*well*	Alicia hace todo **bien**	*Alicia does everything **well***
mal	*badly*	Juan lee **mal**	*Juan reads **badly***
despacio	*slowly*	Habla más **despacio**	*Speak more **slowly***

5 The adverb *quickly* or *fast* has two forms, **rápido** and **rápidamente**:

Escribe muy **rápidamente**   *He writes very **fast***
¡Juan, corre! ¡**Rápido**!   *Juan, run! **Quickly!***

Positive Commands

6 A positive command is an order or instruction to do something:

***Put away** your books!*   *Please **speak** more slowly*

7 When speaking to someone to whom you would normally use the familiar **tú** or **vosotros**, form commands as follows:

	tú *(one person)*		vosotros *(more than one)*	
	remove the -s from the 'tú' form of the present tense		*change the last -r of the infinitive to a -d*	
-ar	hablas → **¡habla!**	*speak!*	hablar → **¡hablad!**	*speak!*
-er	comes → **¡come!**	*eat!*	comer → **¡comed!**	*eat!*
-ir	escribes → **¡escribe!**	*write*	escribir → **¡escribid!**	*write!*

¿Tú no tienes un boli? **toma** el mío   *You haven't a biro? take mine*
¡Vosotros – **sacad** los libros!   *You lot – take out your books!*

8 When speaking to those to whom you would normally use the formal **usted** or **ustedes**, use the PRESENT TENSE to form commands as follows:

	usted (one person)		ustedes (more than one)	
	change last letter of the 'usted' form as follows:		*change last letters of the 'ustedes' form as follows:*	
-ar	habla → ¡hable!	*speak!*	hablan → ¡hablen!	*speak!*
-er	come → ¡coma!	*eat!*	comen → ¡coman!	*eat!*
-ir	escribe → ¡escriba!	*write!*	escriben → ¡escriban!	*write!*

Gracias a usted por todo – **¡Escriba** pronto!   *Thank you for everything – write soon!*
¿Ustedes son ingleses? **¡Prueben** la sidra!   *You're English? Try the cider!*

9 There may be spelling changes as well, in order to keep the same sound:

g → j	coger	*to catch*	→ **¡coja**
c → qu	buscar	*to look for*	→ bus**qu**e

10 Some common verbs are irregular in parts of their command forms:

		tú	vosotros	usted	ustedes
decir	*to say, tell*	**di**	decid	**diga**	**digan**
estar	*to be (stay)*	**está**	estad	**esté**	**estén**
hacer	*to do, make*	**haz**	haced	**haga**	**hagan**
ir	*to go*	**ve**	id	**vaya**	**vayan**
poner	*to put (on), set*	**pon**	poned	**ponga**	**pongan**
salir	*to go out*	**sal**	salid	**salga**	**salgan**
ser	*to be*	**sé**	sed	**sea**	**sean**
tener	*to have, take*	**ten**	tened	**tenga**	**tengan**
venir	*to come (on)*	**ven**	venid	**venga**	**vengan**

¡Pon la silla bien, Juan!   ***Put** the chair straight, Juan!*
¡Niños, **venid**! Es la hora de comer   *Children, **come on**! It's lunch-time*

CHAPTER 13   WHAT HAVE YOU LEARNT?

A During a town-twinning visit to Spain, you shadow an assistant in the shopping centre's play-scheme for young children. Put the underlined verb in her instructions into the correct command form.

e.g. Alicia, <u>sacar</u> el boli de tu boca. TÚ → Alicia, **saca** el boli de tu boca.

En la guardería de niños

1	Alicia, ¡<u>sacar</u> el boli de tu boca! ¡Lo vas a tragar!	TÚ
2	Chicos, ¡<u>poner</u> las sillas bien, por favor!	VOSOTROS
3	¡Eh!, ¡<u>salir</u> de debajo de la mesa! No puedo ver lo que hacéis.	VOSOTROS
4	Paquito, ¡<u>dibujar</u> en la hoja de papel, y no en la mesa!	TÚ
6	¡<u>Tener</u> cuidado, chicas! Esta torre va a caer.	VOSOTRAS
7	¿Qué te pasa, Miguel? ¡<u>Venir</u> aquí!	TÚ

B While waiting for the assistant to finish at lunch-time, you read a notice in the staff rest-room about good salesmanship. Make up the adverb from the adjectives in brackets and insert them where indicated.

e.g. Escuchen a los clientes … → Escuchen a los clientes **atentamente**.

El arte de vender

1	Escuchen a los clientes …	(*atento*)
2	Sirvan a los clientes …	(*rápido*)
3	Hablen de nuestros productos ….	(*responsable*)
4	Hablen al cliente de los beneficios del producto ….	(*persuasivo*)
5	Expliquen las condiciones del contrato … y …	(*lento*) y (*claro*)
6	Si surge algún problema, intenten solucionarlo ….	(*diplomático*)
7	Si al fin y al cabo, el cliente no quiere comprar el producto, despídanse de él ….	(*educado*)

C You and your small party have been invited to spend the evening with the play-leader's family. She has written down the directions for the driver of your minibus. Write the verbs in brackets in the **usted** command form.

e.g. tomar – **tome** la carretera principal.

Al conductor del minibús …

Al salir del aparcamiento, (*tomar*) la carretera principal y (*seguir*) todo recto hasta los semáforos. Allí (*torcer*) a izquierda y (*subir*) la calle. Cuando llegue al hipermercado, (*coger*) la segunda calle a la izquierda. (*Tener*) cuidado porque hay una curva peligrosa inmediatamente después. (*Buscar*) el edificio Miraflores a la derecha. (*Aparcar*) el minibús debajo de los árboles, delante del edificio. Si tiene problemas, (*llamar*) al número 82.45.71.09.

UNIT

5

CHAPTER 14   WHAT DO YOU KNOW?

A You are interested in buying some new clothes. The shop assistant, Clara, explains
what is fashionable this year. Fill the gaps with the correct word from the list below.
e.g. ¿Qué se lleva … año?   →   ¿Qué se lleva **este** año?

La moda

¿Qué se lleva … año? Pues, … faldas largas están muy de moda. Hay que llevarlas
con uno de … jerseys largos y ajustados. ¿Le gusta … chaqueta de seda? Le va muy
bien. ¿Quiere probarla con … pantalón holgado? … colores van muy bien juntos. Los
probadores están allí, al fondo.

este   estos   estas   este   esta   estos

B You're not happy with the clothes she's suggested. In your conversation with her,
find the words which mean THIS ONE, THAT ONE, THOSE ONES, THESE ONES, THAT ONE
OVER THERE, THOSE ONES OVER THERE.
eg. **Ésta** = *this one*

¿No tiene otro?

CLARA   ¿Qué le parece? ¿Le gusta la chaqueta? **Ésta** es muy bonita.

TÚ   No me gusta mucho. Es un poco pequeña. ¿Puedo probarme ésa?

CLARA   ¿La roja? Sí. Pero le va bien el pantalón, ¿no?

TÚ   No sé … No me gusta el color. ¿Puedo ver aquél, en el escaparate?

CLARA   Muy bien. Se lo traigo en seguida.

TÚ   Y quiero zapatos también.

CLARA   ¿Le gustan éstos?

TÚ   Mm… ¿Ésos en azul marino – los tiene en treinta y ocho?

CLARA   Me parece que sí. Voy a ver … No, lo siento. Aquéllos sólo tenemos en
        cuarenta y cuarenta y dos.

TÚ   ¡Qué pena! Bueno, voy a probarme la chaqueta y el pantalón.

C Having finished your shopping, you head for a self-service café. As you wait in the
queue, you read the notice on the wall. Choose the correct alternative from the brackets.
e.g. Todos nuestros platos **se hacen** con …

Aviso importante

Todos nuestros platos (*se hace/se hacen*) con los mejores productos de España. (*Se
prepara/se preparan*) la comida con ingredientes frescos y cultivados biológicamente
donde sea posible. ¡Aquí (*se come/se comen*) sólo lo mejor! No (*se vende/se venden*)
bebidas alcohólicas, pero (*se puede/se pueden*) traer su propia botella de vino, y
beberla aquí.

Saying *this* and *that*

1 To say *this*, use **este**. To say *that* use **ese** if the person or object is not far away, and
aquel if you want to indicate 'over there':

¡Qué rabia! – **este** ordenador no funciona   *What a pain! – **this** computer isn't*
                                                working
¿y **ese** ordenador, cerca de ti?   *and **that** computer, near you?*
¿y **aquel** ordenador cerca de la puerta?   *and **that** computer (over there) near*
                                                the door?

2 **Este**, **ese** and **aquel** behave like ADJECTIVES. They have different forms, depending on
whether you're talking about masculine or feminine things and whether there is only
one of them (*this*, *that*) or more than one (*these*, *those*):

meaning		MASCULINE	FEMININE
here, near the speaker	*this*	**este**	**esta**
	these	**estos**	**estas**
there, near the listener	*that*	**ese**	**esa**
	those	**esos**	**esas**
over there, far from listener and speaker	*that*	**aquel**	**aquella**
	those	**aquellos**	**aquellas**

Esta camisa es muy pequeña   ***This** shirt is very small*
¿Me pasas **esos** pantalones?   *Can you pass me **those** trousers?*
¡**Aquellas** faldas son horribles! ***Those** skirts (over there) are horrible!*

3 *This*, *that*, *these* and *those* need to be repeated in Spanish before each noun, although
in English the second one is often left out:

Esta jarra y **este** plato no son caros   *This jug and plate are not expensive*
Esas botas y **esos** zapatos son baratos *Those boots and shoes are cheap*

4 When referring to something general, use **esto**, **eso**, and **aquello**:

¡**Esto** es fenemonal – no hay clases hoy! *This is great – no classes today!*
¡**Eso** es!   *That's it!*
Todo **aquello** en la guerra era terrible   *All **that** (stuff) in the war was terrible*

Saying *this one* and *that one*

5 To say *this/that one*, *these/those ones*, use the same forms as above, but give each an
accent on the first 'e':

¿Ese abrigo negro? no, prefiero **éste**   *That black coat? no, I prefer **this one***
Me gusta esta cinta – no me gusta **ésa**   *I like this tape – I don't like **that one***
Estos bolsos son más caros que **aquéllos**   *These bags are dearer than **those ones***

Help Yourself to Essential Spanish Grammar

Using **se**

6 English has several ways of indicating what people generally do:

In Great Britain, ***they*** *drink a lot of tea*	*One never knows/you never know, these days*
People *eat more sweet things now*	*As a nation,* ***we*** *don't do a lot of exercise*

7 Spanish often uses **se** with the verb in the third person (*s/he, they* form) to say what people generally do. Use the *s/he* form with singular nouns, and the *they* form with plural nouns:

En Gran Bretaña, **se bebe** mucho té	*In Great Britain,* ***we drink*** *a lot of tea*
Se compra menos fruta que antes	***People buy*** *less fruit than before*
Se venden corbatas aquí, ¿verdad?	***You sell*** *ties here, don't you?*
Se hablan castellano y gallego allí	***They speak*** *Spanish and Galician there*

8 Use **se** where English doesn't mention *who* is doing the action, e.g. *is made, is spoken, are served*:

La mejor paella **se hace** en Valencia	*The best paella* ***is made*** *in Valencia*
El mejor español **se habla** en Burgos	*The best Spanish* ***is spoken*** *in Burgos*
Las comidas **se sirven** después de la una	*Meals* ***are served*** *after one o'clock*

Positive command forms of reflexive verbs

9 To form the positive command form of reflexive verbs, the reflexive pronoun is added to the end of the verb. You may need an accent to maintain the stress pattern:

irse	*to go*	¡**Vete** a tu cuarto, Ana!	*Go to your room, Ana!*
sentar**se**	*to sit down*	¡**Siéntense** por favor!	*Please sit down!*

For reflexive pronouns, see p. 44. For stress and accents, see the Appendix, p. 148.

10 In the **vosotros** command form, the final -**d** is omitted, except in the verb -**irse** (*to go off, go away*):

callar**se**	*to be quiet*	¡**Callaos**, todos!	*Be quiet, everyone!*
ir**se**	*to go away*	¡**Idos**! ¡gamberros!	*Go away! louts!*

CHAPTER 14   WHAT HAVE YOU LEARNT?

A   You overhear a rebellious daughter telling her mother what she thinks of the clothes her mother wants to buy for her. Make the adjectives in brackets agree with the nouns they describe.

e.g. No me gusta nada (*este*) falda gris.   →   No me gusta nada **esta** falda gris.

De tiendas

No me gusta nada (*este*) falda gris. ¡Es demasiado larga! ¡Y (*ese*) jersey es horrible! Quiero algo de lana o de algodón. ¡Odio (*aquel*) zapatos! Todo el mundo lleva tacones altos este año. ¿Y (*ese*) medias? ¡Ni hablar! Quiero (*aquel*) sudadera negra y (*este*) vaqueros azules Levi's. ¡Me va muy bien (*ese*) camisa blanca a cuadros azules y (*aquel*) par de botas negras de cuero en el escaparate! ¡Y ya está!

B   You decide to buy some gifts from a market stall. In the following conversation with the stall-holder, Pepe, put the words in brackets into Spanish.

e.g. [These ones] son muy bonitos.   →   **Éstos** son muy bonitos.

El puesto de regalos

PEPE   ¿Le interesan los platos de cerámica? [THESE ONES] son muy bonitos.

TÚ   ¿Cuánto valen [THOSE ONES]?

PEPE   [THAT ONE] cuesta dos mil y [THAT ONE OVER THERE], tres mil quinientas.

TÚ   Son un poco caros. ¿Cuánto cuesta la taza azul?

PEPE   [THIS ONE] vale mil quinientas.

TÚ   Me gustan también las muñecas, [THOSE ONES OVER THERE].

PEPE   Cuestan mil pesetas. ¿Usted ve [THESE ONES], las pequeñas? Sólo ochocientas pesetas.

TÚ   Perfecto. Me llevo dos. Y un cenicero. Sí, [THAT ONE]. Gracias.

C   Your eye is caught by a series of small announcements in a shop window. Insert **te**, **se** or **os** in the gaps as appropriate.

e.g. ¡Hága... millonario!   →   ¡Hága**se** millonario!

Anuncios

1   ¡Hága... millonario! ¡Compre su billete de lotería aquí!

2   ¡Jóvenes! ¡Imagina... súper inteligentes, sacando buenas notas en vuestros exámenes! Clases particulares con profesor experimentado.

3   ¿Eres tímido/a? ¿Careces de confianza en ti mismo/a? Inscribe... en nuestro próximo cursillo "Todo a tu alcance".

4   ¡Atención, chicos/as de 15–18 años! ¿Queréis ganar un poco de dinero extra? ¡Presenta... el día 20 en la recepción del Hotel Finlandia.

5   ¡Señoras! ¿Se sienten cansadas y aburridas? ¡Transfórmen... en nuestro salón de belleza, El Rostro Bello!

UNIT

5

CHAPTER 15   WHAT DO YOU KNOW?

A The Menéndez family on holiday in Mexico are considering what to bring home as a present for their neighbours. Read the list of bargains and complete their sentences by inserting **más**, **menos** or **tan** into the gaps.

e.g. El póster es ... barato que el plato de cerámica.   →   El póster es **más** barato que el plato de cerámica.

¡Gangas estupendas!

Plato de cerámica	250 pesos	Flauta	175 pesos
Póster de Méjico	220 pesos	Cenicero	200 pesos
Abanico	130 pesos	Muñeca	200 pesos

SEÑOR El póster es ... barato que el plato de cerámica.

SEÑORA Sí, pero la cerámica es mejor. Es ... típica de Méjico.

SEÑORA ¿No te gustan las flautas? Son ... caras que la cerámica y también son muy típicas.

SEÑORA Sí, pero los platos son ... útiles que la cerámica. Las flautas son ideales para niños, pero para adultos no.

SEÑOR ¿Qué te parecen los abanicos? Son los ... baratos de todo.

SEÑORA No son ... típicos como las cosas hechas aquí en Méjico.

SEÑOR Las muñecas son bonitas. Y ... baratas que los pósteres.

SEÑORA ¿O un cenicero? Son ... baratos como las muñecas pero más útiles.

SEÑOR ¡Idiota! ¡Nuestros vecinos no fuman!

B The Menéndez children are aged between three and seventeen and unable to agree on what to do in the afternoon. Match up their suggestions (1–7) and reactions (a–g) correctly.

e.g. 1 ¡Yo quiero ir a la playa!   →   c ¡Nadar en el mar es aburrido!

¡Ni hablar!

1 ¡Yo quiero ir a la playa!   a ¿Haciendo turismo en un grupo? ¡No!
2 Me apetece ir al cine.   b ¿Comprar recuerdos otra vez? ¡No, gracias!
3 Quiero jugar al fútbol.   c ¡Nadar en el mar es aburrido!
4 ¡Vamos a las tiendas!   d ¡No – no voy a pasar toda la tarde bailando!
5 ¡Quiero ir a la discoteca!   e ¡Ver películas es muy pesado, mamá!
6 Quisiera ir de excursión.   f ¡Dormir es lo más aburrido de todo!
7 Podemos descansar   g Practicar deporte es para bebés como tú
  en nuestras camas.   Miguelito. ¡Yo no quiero!

Comparative (regular)

1 In English, we have several ways of comparing people or things:

*Is algebra **more** difficult **than** geometry?*   *I find Spanish easier **than** French*
*Málaga is **less** important **than** Seville*   *He is **as** big **as** me now*

2 In Spanish the COMPARATIVE forms are:

más ... que	*more ... than, -er ... than*
menos ... que	*less ... than, fewer ... than*
tan ... como	*as ... as*
tanto ... como	*as ... as*

Estoy **más** cansada hoy **que** ayer   *I'm **more** tired today **than** yesterday*
Hay **menos** chicas **que** chicos aquí   *There are **fewer** girls **than** boys here*
Este vino es **tan** bueno **como** el otro   *This wine is **as** good **as** the other one*
Tengo **tanto** dinero **como** tú   *I have **as** much money **as** you*

Remember that adjectives continue to agree in number and gender. See p. 20.

3 Remember to use subject pronouns in comparisons of people:

Soy tan alto como **tú**   *I'm as tall as **you***
Son tan depistados como **nosotros**   *They're as absent minded as **us***

See subject pronouns on p. 6

Superlative of regular adjectives

4 SUPERLATIVE forms of adjectives describe how something is the *tallest, most intelligent, best* etc. In Spanish, the superlative forms are **el más...**, **la más...**, **los más...**, **las más...** (depending on the number and gender of the thing or person described), followed by the adjective:

Este edificio es **el más** grande   *This building is **the biggest***
Esta calle es **la más** larga   *This street is **the longest***
Juan es **el menos** listo de los hermanos   *Juan is **the least** clever of the brothers*
Estas casas son **las más** bonitas   *These houses are **the prettiest***

If the superlative comes *after* the noun, omit the **el, la, los, las**:

los pisos **más** caros   *the most expensive flats*

The present participle

5 The PRESENT PARTICIPLE in English is the part of the verb which ends in *-ing*: *playing, writing*. It is also used after *when, while* and *by*:

eating quickly is bad for you	*when buying food, check the sell-by date*

6 In Spanish, PRESENT PARTICIPLES are formed as follows. Remove the infinitive ending (**-ar**, **-er**, **-ir**) to get the stem of the verb. Add **-ando** to the stem of **-ar** verbs, and **-iendo** to the stem of **-er/-ir** verbs:

bajar →	Baj**ando** la calle, se cayó	*Going down the street, he fell over*
comer →	Com**iendo** pulpo, devolvió	*While eating octopus, he was sick*
salir →	Sal**iendo** del bar, le vió	*When leaving the bar, she saw him*

7 The following common present participles are irregular:

leer	→ leyendo	*reading*	pedir	→ pidiendo	*asking for*
creer	→ creyendo	*believing*	reñir	→ riñiendo	*scolding*
ir	→ yendo	*going*	preferir	→ prefiriendo	*preferring*
oír	→ oyendo	*hearing*	sentir	→ sintiendo	*feeling*
dormir	→ durmiendo	*sleeping*	venir	→ viniendo	*coming*

Yendo al centro, vio un accidente	*Going to the centre, he saw an accident*
Prefiriendo el mar, se fue a Alicante	*Preferring the sea, he went to Alicante*

The present continuous

8 The PRESENT CONTINUOUS is used to emphasise what is happening now:

*Ana doesn't read much, does she? Well, **she is reading** in her room right now!*

9 The PRESENT CONTINUOUS in Spanish is very similar to English. You need part of the verb *to be* (**estar**) and the PRESENT PARTICIPLE (the "ing" word)

¡Marta – ven! – ¿Qué **estás haciendo**?	*Marta – come here! What **are you doing?***
¡**Estoy hablando** con Nuria! ¿Y Iñaki?	***I'm talking** to Nuria! What about Iñaki?*
¡Iñaki **está durmiendo** en el sofá!	*Iñaki **is sleeping** on the sofa!*

*For **estar**, see page 10.*

CHAPTER 15   WHAT HAVE YOU LEARNT?

A Señora Menéndez settles down in the park café to read a tourist brochure, while her husband looks after the children – supposedly! Write the verb in brackets in the required form of the present continuous.

e.g. Yoli está (*charlar*) ...   →   Yoli está **charlando** ...

¡Qué desastre de padre!

¿Dónde están los niños? Yoli está (*charlar*) con el camarero de la cafetería, Luis está (*subir*) a un árbol enorme, Miguelito está (*dormir*) en la hierba, Juanita está en la arena (*comer*) no sé qué, Merche está (*jugar*) sola en los columpios, Rafa está (*pedir*) un helado al dueño de la heladería ... ¿Y mi marido? ¡Está (*leer*) el periódico tranquilamente en un banco! ¡Qué desastre!

B The tourist brochure has some interesting facts on South America. Using the facts below, explain how each is the longest, tallest etc. in South America.

e.g. El río Amazonas es ... (*largo*).   →   El río Amazonas es **el más largo**.

América del Sur

1 El río Amazonas, Brasil/Perú, 6.439 kilómetros, es ...   (*largo*)
2 La montaña Aconcagua, Argentina, 6.960 metros, es ...   (*alto*)
3 El lago Titicaca, Bolivia/Perú, 8.287 metros cuadros, es ...   (*grande*)
4 El desierto de Atacama, Chile, es ...   (*seco*)
5 El país de Chile, sólo 180 kilómetros de anchura, es ...   (*estrecho*)
6 Los habitantes del Paraguay son ...   (*pobre*)
7 La ciudad de Méjico es ...   (*contaminado*)

C On their last evening, the Menéndez family dine out. Put the expressions in brackets into Spanish, completing the gaps in their conversation. Note that the appropriate Spanish adjectives are given for support.

Las especialidades mexicanas

LUIS	El guacamole es [MORE DELICIOUS THAN] la sopa.	[delicioso]
YOLI	Sí, pero las chimichangas son [MORE TYPICAL].	[típico]
MAMÁ	Miguelito no puede comerlas. Son [SPICER THAN] las enchiladas.	[picante]
PAPÁ	Sí. Me parece que las empanadas son [MILDER] para él.	[suave]
MERCHE	¿Los burritos son [AS GOOD AS] las empanadas, Yoli?	[bueno]
YOLI	Sí, son [TASTIER]. Y la salsa es [THE MOST DELICIOUS] de todas las salsas.	[rico, delicioso]
MAMÁ	Para mí, los pimientos fritos. Son [LESS SALTY THAN] los otros platos.	[salado]
PAPÁ	Pues, yo voy a pedir el plato [CHEAPEST]. ¡Como somos ocho, me va a costar un dineral!	[barato]

Help Yourself to Essential Spanish Grammar

Revision test 13–15

A Are you a good friend, or careless of your friends' feelings? Make adverbs from the adjectives in brackets and insert them where indicated.

e.g. Le dices … lo que opinas.   →   Le dices **francamente** lo que opinas.

¿Buen amigo o no?

1 Tu novio/a te acompaña a una fiesta. Lleva algo que no te gusta.
  a Le dices … lo que opinas.   *(franco)*
  b Le explicas … que la fiesta no es tan formal (o informal)
     y que sería mejor tal vez llevar otra cosa.   *(diplomático)*
  c Le piropeas …   *(alegre)*
2 Alguien te dice que tu novio/a sale con otro/a.
  a Cuestionas a tu novio/a …   *(abierto)*
  b Hablas … a alguien quien os conoce … los dos.   *(rápido) (bueno)*
  c No lo crees. Tu novio/a siempre se comporta … y …   *(sincero) (correcto)*

Now do the test to see if you are a good friend. Tick the sentences which describe your attitude and check your results.*

B You are putting together an advertisement for an organisation promoting distance learning. You have written it in the familiar **tú** form, but your editor feels it should be in the **usted** form. Rewrite it correctly.

e.g. Abre   →   Abra

Peluquería con vídeos

¡Abre los ojos! ¡Aprende peluquería! Es más sencillo de lo que parece. Invita a un grupo de amigas y mirad juntas el nuevo Curso de vídeos de GEP. Ésta es la mejor manera: mirando, sin horarios en casa. Conviértete en una auténtica profesional de la peluquería. Decídete y matricúlate en el nuevo curso, o solicita ahora información de cualquiera de nuestros cursos. Ponte en nuestras manos, ahora es el momento de aprender.

C Charo's tutor is not impressed with the quality of her recent work. Put the words in brackets into Spanish.

e.g. [THESE] deberes   →   **Estos** deberes …

La pobre Charo

TUTOR   ¡[THESE] deberes no son muy buenos, Charo!

CHARO   Es que no tuve mucho tiempo [THIS] semana. Tuve que …

TUTOR   ¡Excusas, excusas! [THAT] ejercicio está sin hacer todavía y [THESE] páginas son un desastre, llenas de errores.

CHARO   Hice todo [THAT] en casa, porque estaba ausente cuando se hizo en clase.

TUTOR   Hay que hacer el ejercicio número once otra vez, y [THAT ONE] también. Siéntate en una mesa. Sí, [THAT ONE OVER THERE].

D   A magazine item comparing food and drink in Spain and the United Kingdom catches your eye. Put the verbs in brackets into the correct form of the verb using **se**.
e.g. Primero (*notarse*)   →   Primero **se** nota

La comida española

¿Cuáles son las diferencias entre la comida española y la británica? Primero, (*notarse*) que (*usarse*) menos aceite y más grasa animal, aunque esto está cambiando. No (*comprarse*) tanto ajo allí como aquí, pero (*utilizarse*) en los platos mediterráneos que son muy populares. En el Reino Unido (*beberse*) muchos tés e infusiones de hierbas. Incluso en las estaciones de servicios en las autopistas (*servirse*) una gama enorme. (*Verse*) también en los supermercados muchos tipos de leche: de cabra, de oveja, de soja. Aquí en España, estas cosas sólo (*comprarse*) en tiendas especializadas.

E   The children near you on the plane are quarrelsome and the air-hostess is losing patience. Put the words in English into Spanish and insert them where indicated.
e.g. Yo soy más alta que…, Carlos.   →   Yo soy más alto que **tú**, Carlos.

Los niños pesados del avión

REME	Yo soy más alta que …, Carlos.	YOU
CARLOS	¡Qué va! Eres más baja que …	ME
NURIA	¡Yo soy más alta que … dos!	YOU (PLUR.)
FELIPE	Y Carlos no es muy fuerte. Yo soy más fuerte que …	HIM
REME	¡Y qué, Felipe! No eres tan inteligente como …	US
AZAFATA	¡Sentaos y callaos! Si no, voy a hablar a vuestros padres.	
NURIA	Me da igual. ¡Es usted más estricta que …!	THEM

F   An elderly passenger complains about the noise on her long-haul flight. Change the underlined verbs to the correct form of the PRESENT CONTINUOUS tense.
e.g. La azafata <u>lee</u>   →   La azafata **está leyendo**

En el vuelo

Hay mucha movida. La azafata <u>lee</u> un cuento a un grupo de niños rebeldes, y la mayória le <u>escucha</u>. Un padre detrás de mi asiento <u>riñe</u> a su hijo menor que quiere ir para ver lo que <u>pasa</u>. Las otras azafatas <u>van</u> y <u>vienen</u> de la cocina, y <u>hacen</u> mucho ruido. ¡Y nos quedan cinco horas todavía!

UNIT

6   Las vacaciones

A José had an eventful journey to Bilbao with Iñigo, who's returning to Spain. Choose the correct form of the verb in brackets to complete his postcard.

e.g. ... yo (*salí/saliste*) de casa a las ocho   →   ... yo **salí** de casa a las ocho

El viaje desastroso

El viernes, yo (*salí/saliste*) de casa a las ocho y (*llegó/llegué*) al aeropuerto dos horas más tarde. Allí, (*encontró/encontré*) a Iñigo y (*pasamos/pasáis*) una hora en el bar. Pero – ¡fíjate! – (*perdieron/perdimos*) el avión. Por fin, (*cogimos/cogieron*) un vuelo a las cinco. En la Oficina de Turismo (*reservaste/reservé*) un hotel en el centro para la noche: ¡qué ruidoso! Yo no (*durmió/dormí*) mucho. Por la mañana, Iñigo y yo (*desayunaron/desayunamos*) chocolate con churros en un café enfrente y (*escribieron/escribimos*) un montón de postales. Yo (*compré/compró*) una guía de Bilbao pero a lo contrario de lo que dice, ¡Bilbao no es ni turístico ni bonito!

B On Saturday, Iñigo uses the notes in his diary to write home. Read his notes, then choose the appropriate time phrase from the list below to fill the gaps.

e.g. Llegamos el viernes de ...   →   Llegamos el viernes de **la semana pasada**

La Primera Semana

viernes	Llegada.
fin de semana	¡Descanso total!
lunes	Mañana: alquilé coche. Viaje a San Vicente – precioso.
martes	¡Todo el día en la playa!
miércoles	¡Lluvia! Visita a Potes en la sierra – Fuente Dé.
jueves	¡Más lluvia! Mañana – Santillana. Tarde – visita a las cuevas.
viernes	Mañana – compras en Santander; 10.00 – discoteca.

Llegamos el viernes de .... El fin de semana, descansamos, pero ... alquilé un Seat Ibiza y fuimos hasta San Vicente. Un día, tomamos el sol en la playa y ... subimos a Potes en los Picos de Europa. Cogimos el teleférico a la cumbre Fuente Dé. Luego llovió ..., así que no fuimos a la playa el jueves ni el viernes. Me encantó la visita ... a las cuevas. Luego ... fuimos a las tiendas en Santander. Fuimos a una discoteca ... – ¡y me duelen los pies algo terrible hoy! Os escribo pronto – un abrazo, Iñigo.

> *el lunes por la mañana   anoche   la semana pasada*
> *durante dos días   ayer   hace tres días   anteayer*

The Preterite tense: regular verbs

1 The PRETERITE tense is used to:

say what happened	*I left the library at six*
say what didn't happen	*I didn't arrive home till late*
ask what happened	When *did you notice the broken window?*

2 To form the preterite tense, remove the **-ar**, **-er**, **-ir** endings from the infinitive. You then have the STEM of the verb, to which you add the preterite endings:

a Preterite forms of **-ar** verbs, e.g. **hablar** (*to speak*) → **habl-**

yo	habl**é**	*I spoke*	nosotros	habl**amos**	*we spoke*
tú	habl**aste**	*you spoke*	vosotros	habl**asteis**	*you spoke*
él	habl**ó**	*he spoke*	ellos	habl**aron**	*they spoke*
ella	habl**ó**	*she spoke*	ellas	habl**aron**	*they spoke*
usted	habl**ó**	*you spoke*	ustedes	habl**aron**	*you spoke*

b Preterite forms of **-er** and **-ir** verbs, e.g. **comer** (*to eat*) → **com-**
     vivir (*to live*) → **viv-**

yo	com**í**	*I ate*	nosotros	viv**imos**	*we lived*
tú	com**iste**	*you ate*	vosotros	viv**isteis**	*you lived*
él	com**ió**	*he ate*	ellos	viv**ieron**	*they lived*
ella	com**ió**	*she ate*	ellas	viv**ieron**	*they lived*
usted	com**ió**	*you ate*	ustedes	viv**ieron**	*they lived*

3 In English, we often use *did* or *didn't* as part of the preterite tense. There is no equivalent in Spanish:

¿No le habl**aste**?	***Didn't** you **talk** to him?*	¡Que sí, le habl**é**!	*Yes, I **did** talk to him*
¿Compr**ó** él la bici?	***Did** he **buy** the bike?*	No, no lo compr**ó**	*No, he **didn't** buy it*

4 The spelling of some regular verbs changes in order to keep the same sound.

a Verbs ending in -**zar**, -**car**, and -**gar** change in the **yo** form:

z - → **c**	cruzar	yo cru**cé**	*I crossed*
c - → **qu**	tocar	to**qué**	*I touched*
g - → **gu**	llegar	lle**gué**	*I arrived*

b   With verbs ending in **-aer**, **-eer**, **-oir**, and **-uir** change the **-i** to **-y** in the **él/ella/usted** and **ellos/ellas/ustedes** forms:

caer	él/ella/usted cayó	he/she/you fell
	ellos/ellas/ustedes cayeron	they/you fell
leer	él/ella/usted leyó	he/she/you read
	ellos/ellas/ustedes leyeron	they/you read
oir	él/ella/usted oyó	he/she/you heard
	ellos/ellas/ustedes oyeron	they/you heard
destruir	él/ella/usted destruyó	he/she/you destroyed
	ellos/ellas/ustedes destruyeron	they/you destroyed

Time phrases in the past

5   Phrases which often accompany the preterite tense are:

ayer	yesterday	el año pasado	last year
ayer (por la tarde)	yesterday (afternoon)	el otro día	the other day
anteayer	the day before yesterday	hace dos días	two days ago
anoche	last night	hace tres años	three years ago
la semana pasada	last week	durante dos siglos	for three centuries

Examples:

Ayer por la mañana, tomé el sol	*Yesterday morning*, I sunbathed
Anoche bailé en la discoteca hasta la una	*Last night*, I danced in the disco till one
Hace dos años, visitamos Marruecos	*Two years ago*, we visited Morocco

Pero and sino

6   There are two ways of saying *but* in Spanish: **pero** and **sino**. **Sino** is used only after a negative which suggests a contradiction:

| ¡Mi boli no es rojo, **sino** azul! | *My biro isn't red, but blue!* |
| ¡No fui yo, **sino** él! | *It wasn't me, but him!* |

Pero is used in all other cases:

| Tengo un boli, **pero** no sé dónde está | *I've got a biro, but I don't know where it is* |
| Ibiza es bonita, **pero** Menorca es tranquila | *Ibiza is pretty, but Menorca is quiet* |

CHAPTER 16 WHAT HAVE YOU LEARNT?

A José and Iñigo meet Raúl and Juanjo, who are enthusiastic about their recent three-month stay in Seville. Put the correct ending on the verb.

e.g. ¿Cómo … trabajo en Sevilla? *encontrar*

→ ¿Cómo **encontraste** trabajo en Sevilla?

¿Sevilla? ¡Es una maravilla!

JOSÉ	¿Cómo … trabajo en Sevilla, Raúl?	*encontrar*
RAÚL	Bueno, … Juanjo y yo en mayo. Juanjo … trabajo en los bares, y yo … un puesto en un café, como camarero.	*llegar, buscar conseguir*
JUANJO	Y por la noche, … los dos a los clubs y discotecas.	*salir*
RAÚL	Yo … la guitarra y Juanjo… flamenco para los turistas.	*tocar, bailar*
JUANJO	Para nosotros, fué estupendo. … a mucha gente.	*conocer*
RAÚL	Y los turistas nos … muchas cosas – vino, dinero.	*regalar*
JUANJO	Me … muy bien los ingleses – ¡… muchas fotos!	*caer*, sacar*
IÑIGO	¡Qué bien! A lo mejor, nos vamos nosotros.	

B José and Iñigo travel down to Seville, and find a leaflet written in 1992 as the Sevillanos prepared themselves for Expo. Put the English expressions into Spanish.

e.g. [For many years] → **Durante muchos años**

Un poco de historia

Sevilla ha cambiado mucho en los últimos años. [FOR MANY YEARS] era una ciudad famosa pero un poco descuidada – pero [TEN YEARS AGO] ocurrió algo que cambió la ciudad para siempre: empezaron a planificar la EXPO 1992. [YESTERDAY] Sevilla era antigua y turística – hoy es moderna e internacional. [FOR SIX CENTURIES] durmió Sevilla, envuelta en las memorias de su pasado glorioso – pero [LAST YEAR] se despertó y empezó a convertirse en un símbolo vibrante de un futuro brillante.

C On the coach, they overhear a Madrileño and a Sevillano arguing about the respective merits of their cities. Complete the gaps with **pero** or **sino**.

e.g. Bueno, Sevilla es bonita, … no es tan importante como Madrid.

→ Bueno, Sevilla es bonita, **pero** no es tan importante como Madrid.

¡Madrid es mejor!

M Bueno, Sevilla es bonita, … no es tan importante como Madrid.

S ¿Qué? Madrid es administrativo – ¡… no tiene nada de cultura!

M ¿Y Sevilla? Tiene flamenco y toros, … es todo. ¡Cosa de provincias!

S ¡Sevilla no es provincial, … internacional! Madrid es sucio y feo.

M Oye – no es feo Madrid, … precioso. Hay contaminación, sí – ¡… igual que en Sevilla!

---

* *caer* (in this context): *gustar*

UNIT

6

CHAPTER 17   WHAT DO YOU KNOW?

A Read about the climate in the Balearics. Match up the sentences correctly:

Las Baleares

Las islas Baleares tienen un clima mediterráneo. Formentera, con sus pocos árboles, tiene fama de tener más calor, y Mallorca más horas de sol. Las temperaturas en Menorca son más suaves, con neblina y riesgo de vientos. En todas las islas, hay la posibilidad de tormentas. Las temperaturas en la costa son más bajas que en el interior.

1 En verano en Menorca, hace …	a neblina.
2 En Mallorca, en verano hace …	b riesgo de tormenta.
3 En la isla menorquina, a veces hay …	c muchísimo calor.
4 En Formentera hace …	d mucho sol.
5 En todas las islas en verano hay …	e más viento que en las otras islas.

B Ramón, a journalist, interviews Catriona and Carlos about their life together in Menorca. Complete the gaps with **hay**, **hace** or **desde hace**.

e.g. ¿… cuánto tiempo viven aquí ?   →   ¿**desde hace** cuánto tiempo viven aquí?

Catriona y Carlos

RAMÓN   Catriona y Carlos, ¿… cuánto tiempo viven aquí en Menorca?

CARLOS   Catriona vino aquí … quince años – de Escocia, pero yo soy nativo.

RAMÓN   ¿Y … mucha gente como ustedes, en la isla?

CATRIONA   Bueno, en aquella época, no. Pero ahora … más.

RAMÓN   Usted habla muy bien el español. ¿Aprende … mucho tiempo?

CATRIONA   ¡Tuve que aprender! – ¡… quince años, casi nadie hablaba inglés aquí!

C Catriona tells her story. Choose the appropriate verb from the list below.

El romance

Yo … aquí a Menorca en 1980 cuando … dieciséis años. No … más que una maleta y veinte libras esterlinas en total. Claro, no … sobrevivir sin dinero, así que … un anuncio en el periódico. Me llamó una madre: … una señorita inglesa para enseñar inglés a su hijo, Carlos. Nos enamoramos y me casé con él en el año 1985.

tuve   puse   vine   pude   traje   quiso

Irregular preterite verbs

1   The following verbs have irregular stems in the preterite tense. They are a group
    sometimes known as the *pretérito grave*:

INFINITIVES		STEM
to walk	andar	**anduv-**
to fit	caber	**cup-**
to drive	conducir	**conduj-***
to say	decir	**dij-***
to be	estar	**estuv-**
to do, make	hacer	**hic-**
to have	haber	**hub-**

INFINITIVES		STEM
to be able to	poder	**pud-**
to put	poner	**pus-**
to want to	querer	**quis-**
to know	saber	**sup-**
to have	tener	**tuv-**
to bring	traer	**traj-***
to come	venir	**vin-**

2   Note, all these verbs have the same endings:

yo	**-e**	nosotros	**-imos**
tú	**-iste**	vosotros	**-isteis**
él	**-o**	ellos	**-ieron**
ella	**-o**	ellas	**-ieron**
usted	**-o**	ustedes	**-ieron**

¿**Condujiste** el coche nuevo ayer?   *Did you drive the new car yesterday?*
¡No! Lo **quiso** Manolo para ir a Madrid.   *No! Manolo **wanted** it to go to Madrid.*
Y no **pude** salir por la tarde ...   *And **I could** not go out in the evening ...*
... porque **vinieron** sus padres.   *... because his parents **came**.*

3   The preterite stem of **hacer** (*to do, to make*) is **hic-** but when followed by -o, in the
    él/ella/usted form, it changes to **hiz-**:

¿Pili, **hic**iste los deberes?   *Pili, did you do your homework?*
Bueno, **hic**e el inglés   *Well, I did the English*
¡pero mi novio **hiz**o el resto!   *but my boyfriend did the rest!*

4   **Dar** (*to give*) is irregular in the preterite tense. Note also that the verbs **ir** (*to go*) and
    ser (*to be*) share the same preterite forms.

DAR			
yo	**dí**	nosotros	**dimos**
tú	**diste**	vosotros	**disteis**
él	**dio**	ellos	**dieron**
ella	**dio**	ellas	**dieron**
usted	**dio**	ustedes	**dieron**

IR/SER			
yo	**fui**	nosotros	**fuimos**
tú	**fuiste**	vosotros	**fuisteis**
él	**fue**	ellos	**fueron**
ella	**fue**	ellas	**fueron**
usted	**fue**	ustedes	**fueron**

*note in the **ellos**, **ellas** and **ustedes** form these verbs have the ending **-eron**

Le **di** una copia de la foto de Ibiza.   *I gave him a copy of the photo of Ibiza.*
¿**Fue** a Ibiza? ¿Por quince días?   *Did he go to Ibiza? For a fortnight?*
Bueno, creo que **fue** sólo una semana.   *Well, I think it was only a week.*
   The preterite tense of irregular verbs is listed in full in the Appendix, page 130

Hay and hace

5   **Hay** means *there is* or *there are*:

Perdone, ¿**hay** un banco por aquí?   *Excuse me – **is there** a bank near here?*
Hay mil alumnos en mi instituto   ***There are** a thousand pupils in my school*

6   **Hace** is used to express time in terms of how long **ago** things happened:

hace dos días   *two days **ago***   **hace** cinco años   *five years **ago***

7   Both **hace ... que** and **desde hace**, with the present tense, express *how long for*:

¿**Desde hace** cuánto tiempo aprendes?/¿**Cuánto** tiempo **hace que** aprendes?
*And **how long** have you been learning **for**?*
Hace tres años **que** aprendo español/Aprendo español **desde hace** tres años
*I've been learning Spanish **for** three years*

8   **Hace** or **hay** can be used to describe the weather in the present tense:

hace buen tiempo	*the weather's good*	**hace** calor	*it's hot*
hace bueno	*it's fine*	**hace** frío	*it's cold*
hace mal tiempo	*the weather's bad*	**hace** sol	*it's sunny*
hace malo	*it's bad*	**hace** viento	*it's windy*
hay niebla	*it's foggy*	**hay** hielo	*it's icy*
hay neblina	*it's misty*	**hay** tormenta	*it's stormy*

¿Qué tiempo **hace** en el sur?   *What's the weather like in the south?*
Normalmente **hace** mucho sol y calor   *Normally it's very sunny and hot*
pero a veces **hay** tormenta por la noche   *but sometimes there's a storm at night*

9   **Hizo** is the preterite form of **hace** and **hubo** is the preterite form of **hay**:

Hizo buen tiempo el año pasado   *The weather **was** good last year*
Hubo una tormenta enorme   ***There was** an enormous storm*

CHAPTER 17   WHAT HAVE YOU LEARNT?

A   Mari Paz is not impressed by the weather on her holiday in Galicia, in the north-west
    of Spain. Insert either **hubo** or **hizo** in the gaps in her account of the weather.
    e.g. pero por la tarde, … mucho viento   →   pero por la tarde, **hizo** mucho viento.

Galicia

¡Qué tiempo más malo! Cuando llegué, hacía mucho sol y calor, pero por la tarde, …
mucho viento. Por la noche … una tormenta tremenda y llovió mucho. Luego …
neblina por toda la costa – se llama el 'orbayu' aquí – y no pudimos bañarnos,
porque … fresquito. Parece que … malo el verano pasado – ¡y que ya en agosto …
bastante frío para ponerse un jersey!

B   The bad weather is making Mari Paz and her friends on the campsite irritable. Put the
    verbs in brackets in the preterite tense, with the correct ending.
    e.g. ¿No (*traer*) tú agua ayer?   →   ¿No **trajiste** tú agua ayer?

En el camping

MARI PAZ   No hay ni pan, ni agua. ¡Paco! ¿No (*traer*) tú agua ayer?

PACO   Sí, (*ir*) a los lavabos y llené el cacharro con agua del grifo.

MARI PAZ   Pues, no queda. Mila, ¿no (*hacer*) tú la compra esta mañana?

MILA   No (*venir*) el camión con el pan. Me (*decir*) el dueño que es fiesta.

MARI PAZ   ¡Ay, no me (*dar*) cuenta! Tal vez haya un supermercado en Orense.

DAVID   ¿Tenemos dinero? Ayer Mila y yo no (*poder*) sacar dinero porque
        dejamos las tarjetas aquí en la recepción.

PACO   Y Mari Paz y yo (*estar*) toda la tarde sin comer, ¡porque no (*traer*)
       vosotros bastante pizza para todos!

MARI PAZ   ¡Yo (*tener*) hambre ayer, pero hoy va a ser peor todavía!

C   Paco is fed up. Express his thoughts in a different way, using the phrases given at the
    end of each complaint.
    e.g. Estamos aquí desde hace una semana.   →   **Hace una semana que** estamos aquí.

¡Estoy harto!

1   Estamos aquí desde hace una semana.   *hace … que*
2   Y hace cinco días que no vemos el sol.   *desde hace*
3   Hace dos días que no comemos bien, y tengo hambre.   *desde hace*
4   Conozco a Mari Paz desde hace cinco años.   *hace … que*
5   Pero hace tres días que Mari Paz está de muy mal humor.   *desde hace*
    ¡Estoy harto!

UNIT

6

CHAPTER 18   WHAT DO YOU KNOW?

A Señor Gonzalo is not only unhappy about his treatment in a smart hotel, but he has also lost his voice. Use his notes to explain, on his behalf, what's wrong to the manager. Change the underlined verbs from the *I* form to the *he* form.
e.g. <u>Leí</u> en la guía   →   **Leyó** en la guía

Las quejas del Señor Gonzalo

1 <u>Leí</u> en la guía que el hotel era excelente.
2 <u>Elegí</u> el hotel porque lo recomendó un amigo.
3 En la cafetería, <u>pedí</u> un té con leche – pero la leche era caliente.
4 <u>Me vestí</u> elegantemente, pero sin corbata – y no me dejaron entrar en el restaurante.
5 El vídeo no funcionó – pero <u>seguí</u> las instrucciones correctamente.
6 No <u>dormí</u> bien – el colchón era muy duro.

B The manager is apologetic, but protests the excellence of his hotel. Select the appropriate word from the list below, and fill in the gaps.
e.g. Lo siento que usted se encuentre … esta mañana. (*bad*)
    →   Lo siento que usted se encuentre **mal** esta mañana.

Lo siento mucho, pero …

1 Siento que se encuentre usted … esta mañana.	*bad*
2 Pero le aseguro que nuestro hotel no es ….	*bad*
3 Nuestros clientes dicen que este hotel es … que los otros.	*better*
4 El servicio aquí siempre es muy ….	*good*
5 Hay quien que opinan que es el … de la provincia.	*best*
6 ¡Lo que es cierto, es que no es el …!	*worst*

bueno   mejor   peor   malo   mejor   mal

C Señora Gonzalo is not impressed by the manager. Choose the correct alternative from the brackets as she argues her husband's case.
e.g. es bonita (*e/y*) interesante   →   es bonita **e** interesante

El libro de reclamaciones

Nos decidimos hacer un viaje por esta región de España porque es bonita (*e/y*) interesante. No queríamos un hotel (*o/u*) hostal barato y feo – y leímos que este hotel era muy antiguo (*e/y*) histórico. Siento decírselo, pero en su cafetería hay bichos – no sé si son cucarachas (*o/u*) hormigas – (*e/y*) el jardín está lleno de cardos (*e/y*) hierbas malas. ¿El mejor de la región? ¡Qué va! ¿Me trae el libro de reclamaciones, por favor?

Stem-changing preterite tense verbs

1 Some verbs which have a stem-change in the present, also have one in the preterite tense. It happens only in the third person (**él/ella/usted/ellos/ellas/ustedes**) and the endings are regular.

a Verbs with a stem-change **o** → **u**:

dormir	to sleep		
yo	dormí	nosotros	dormimos
tú	dormiste	vosotros	dormisteis
él	d**u**rmió	ellos	d**u**rmieron
ella	d**u**rmió	ellas	d**u**rmieron
usted	d**u**rmió	ustedes	d**u**rmieron

The other common verb with this pattern is **morir** (*to die*):

Los niños **durmieron** toda la noche   *The children slept all night*
Franco **murió** en el año 1975   *Franco died in the year 1975*

b Verbs with a stem change **e** → **i**:

pedir	to ask for		
yo	pedí	nosotros	pedimos
tú	pediste	vosotros	pedisteis
él	p**i**dió	ellos	p**i**dieron
ella	p**i**dió	ellas	p**i**dieron
usted	p**i**dió	ustedes	p**i**dieron

Other common verbs with this pattern:

divertir(se)	to enjoy oneself	**preferir**	to prefer	**sentir**	to feel
elegir	to choose	**reír**	to laugh	**servir**	to serve
herir	to wound	**reñir**	to scold	**sonreír**	to smile
mentir	to lie	**seguir**	to follow	**vestir(se)**	to dress

Examples:

Juan se divirtió mucho en la discoteca   *Juan enjoyed himself a lot at the disco*
pero los otros prefirieron quedarse en casa   *but the others preferred to stay at home*

c A few stem-changing verbs also change their third person endings from **-ió** to **-ó** to make them easier to pronounce:

reír(se)	to laugh	Carmen se r**ió** mucho	*Carmen laughed a lot*
sonreír	to smile	Nadie sonr**ió**	*No one smiled*
reñir	to scold	Mi madre me ri**ñó**	*My mother scolded me*

The preterite tense of stem-changing verbs is also given in the Appendix, page 130

Irregular comparative and superlative forms

2 The comparative and superlative forms of the following adjectives (**bueno/malo**) are irregular, and they do not need the normal **más** in front:

bueno	*good*	→	**mejor**	*better*	**(el) mejor**	*the best*
malo	*bad*	→	**peor**	*worse*	**(el) peor**	*the worst*

Esta bici es **mejor** que nada	*This bike is **better** than nothing*
Esta bici es la **mejor**	*This bike is **the best***
¡Tus deberes son **peores**!	*Your homework is **worse**!*
Tus deberes son **los peores** de la clase	*Your homework is **the worst** in the class*

3 **Mayor** means *older/oldest/elder/eldest*, and **menor** means *younger/youngest* when referring to people:

Mi hermano **mayor** tiene 18 años	*My **older** brother is 18*
Susana es **la mayor** de la familia	*Susana is the **eldest** in the family*
Ana es **la menor** de mis hermanas	*Ana is the **youngest** of my sisters*

Saying *very/extremely*

4 To say *very* or *extremely* in Spanish, add **-ísimo** to the end of adjectives. Remember that the adjective ending may need to change to agree in number and gender with the thing or person it describes:

el jamón es **buenísimo**	*the ham is **very good***
la clase es **aburridísima**	*the class is **extremely boring***
los platos son **carísimos**	*the dishes are **very expensive***
las torres son **altísimas**	*the towers are **very, very high***

Y and o

5 The word **y** (*and*) changes to **e** before words beginning with an **i** or an **hi** (but not an **hie**):

españoles **e** ingleses	geografía **e** historia	hay niebla **y** hielo

6 The word **o** (*or*) changes to **u** before words beginning with an **o** or **ho**:

hay siete **u** ocho salas en el cine	ponen películas violentas **u** horribles

CHAPTER 18   WHAT HAVE YOU LEARNT?

A Mario's night away with some friends didn't quite turn out the way he hoped. Put the verbs in brackets into the preterite tense, with the correct ending.

e.g. Carlos y yo no (*conseguir*) una mesa   →   Carlos y yo no **conseguimos** una mesa

El fin de semana

¡Es que fue un desastre! Belén, Tere, Carlos y yo no (*conseguir*) una mesa hasta las diez de la noche. Tere estaba enfadada con Carlos, y no (*sonreír*) ni una vez. ¡La música era tan fuerte, que nos (*impedir*) de hablar mucho! Así que, de conversación estimulante, nada. Los otros (*pedir*) pimientos rellenos, y yo merluza, pero el cocinero nuevo (*freír*) todo en tanto aceite que no nos gustó nada. Y luego el camarero (*servir*) un vino tinto de la casa tan desgradable que no lo pudimos beber. Belén (*sentirse*) tan mala, que volvimos todos al hotel. Allí, había una fiesta de boda – y como Carlos y Tere estaban en la planta baja, (*dormir*) muy poco. Belén me (*reñir*) toda la noche porque yo no (*pedir*) el libro de reclamaciones en el restaurante.

B Back home, Belén and Mario are having a post-mortem on the disastrous week-end. Replace the English word with the correct Spanish word.

e.g. De verdad, la comida no era muy...   →   De verdad, la comida no era muy **buena**.

Recordando lo ocurrido

BELÉN	De verdad, la comida no era muy ...	[good]
MARIO	¡Y el vino era ... que la comida!	[worse]
BELÉN	El hotel no me gustó nada. Era ... de mi vida.	[the worst]
MARIO	¡Qué va! El hotel no era ... – tenía cuatro estrellas.	[bad]
BELÉN	¿Y Carlos, tu ... amigo? Estaba de muy mal humor.	[best]
MARIO	Tu amiga Tere fue ... – ¡no sonrió en toda la tarde!	[worse]
BELÉN	¡De verdad, no fueron ... vacaciones del verano!	[the best]

C Read the advice about Spanish accommodation below; insert the correct word for *and* (**y**, **e**) and *or* (**o**, **u**).

e.g. en paradores ... hoteles de lujo   →   en paradores **u** hoteles de lujo

El alojamiento en España

1 Lo más caro es quedarse en paradores ... hoteles de lujo.   OR
2 Hay muchos campings de buena calidad ... precio en la costa.   AND
3 ¡Pero cuidado! Fondas ... hostales muy baratos pueden ser sucios.   OR
4 Los albergues juveniles son limpios ... higiénicos.   AND
5 En las sierras, hay refugios ... hospederías sencillas.   AND
6 Es mejor alojarse donde cumplen las normas municipales ... oficiales.   OR

Help Yourself to Essential Spanish Grammar

Revision test 16–18

A The adverts below are from young people seeking to exchange or sell music. Choose the correct alternative from within the brackets.

Vendo, Busco y Cambio

1 ¿Os gusta El Último de la Fila (*o/u*) os interesa material de Chris O'Donnell? Escribid urgentemente (*e/y*) mandad sello respuesta Marta, C/ Sta. Ana, SALOU.

2 Pósters, reportajes, entrevistas de cantantes, grupos (*e/y*) incluso actores. Tengo más de 700 videoclips. Escribe a Juan, C/ Font nº12 (*o/u*) a la revista.

3 ¡Hola! ¿Tenéis material de Take That (*e/y*) de East 17 que váis a tirar a la basura (*o/u*) se lo váis a dar a alguien? Yo os lo cambio por material de vuestras estrellas (*e/y*) ídolos: Keanu Reeves, Magneto, NKOTB. Escribe a Elsa, Aptdo. 251, MADRID.

B Amelia won a competition to see her favourite pop-star. Complete her account by choosing the appropriate verb, and giving it the correct ending.

e.g. yo … al acropuerto → yo llegué al aeropuerto

El concurso

Jueves. El viaje: yo … al aeropuerto con Ainhoa de Smash Hits a las once. ¡El avión no … hasta las cuatro! … revistas y … con Ainhoa. Viaje interminable.

llegar   salir   charlar   leer

Viernes. Turismo: Nueva York era impresionante. Por la mañana, … con Ainhoa a la cima del famoso Empire State Building – ¡qué vistas más maravillosas! Por la tarde, … un poco de compra, … un paseo en Central Park, y luego Ainhoa y yo … en un restaurante en el barrio chino – era riquísima, la comida.

dar   comer   subir   hacer

Sábado. La actuación: ¡qué ilusión! … dos horas en el estudio, viendo las preparaciones para la grabación para su nuevo disco. Cuando … a Janet, estaba yo muy emocionada – pero la más pequeña del clan de los Jackson era muy simpática. Ella … a saludarme personalmente y hablarme un ratito. Luego … a cantar – ¡Qué maravilla!

ver   pasar   empezar   venir

C Things are fraught in the Garfía household. Put the English expressions into Spanish and insert them in the gaps in the sentences.

¡No me toca a mí!

UNAI	¡Oye, Pili! Te toca a ti fregar hoy. Yo fregué …	YESTERDAY
PILI	¡Mamá – esto no es justo! Yo lavé los platos …	LAST NIGHT
UNAI	Y … cuando tú estabas en la cama, ¡yo planché!	YESTERDAY MORNING
PILI	¡Tus cosas que ensuciaste … jugando al fútbol!	THE OTHER DAY
UNAI	Planché tu ropa también - y … recogí toda la casa.	TWO DAYS AGO
MAMÁ	¡No me toca a mí! Yo hago los quehaceres …	FOR FIFTEEN YEARS

D Read the following information on how the weather affects us. First complete the gaps with **hace** or **hay**, and then match up the sentences correctly.
e.g. 1d Cuando hace buen tiempo, todo el mundo se siente mejor.

¿Cómo nos afecta el tiempo?

1 Cuando … buen tiempo	a los niños se comportan peor.
2 Si no … mucho sol en invierno	b se aumenta el riesgo de accidentes.
3 Cuando … mucho viento	c la gente se vuelve menos enérgica.
4 Cuando… tormentas eléctricas	d todo el mundo se siente mejor.
5 Si … neblina	e se sube la incidencia de fracturas.
6 Cuando …hielo	f mucha gente sufre de dolor de cabeza.
7 Cuando … frío	g la falta de luz afecta y deprime a mucha gente.

E Read the opinions below. Make the words in brackets agree if necessary.
e.g. Las (*mejor*) máquinas electrónicas   →   Las **mejores** máquinas electrónicas

¿Opinas tú igual?

1 Las (*mejor*) máquinas electrónicas se hacen en Japón.
2 El agua británica es la (*peor*) de Europa.
3 Los franceses hacen los (*mejor*) vinos de Europa.
4 Alemania fabrica los electrodomésticos (*mejor*) del mundo.
5 Los italianos son los (*peor*) conductores de coche en el mundo.
6 En cuanto a la comodidad, los automóviles Lada son los (*peor*).
7 Las chicas obtienen (*mejor*) resultados en los exámenes de GCSE que los chicos.
8 El (*mejor*) caviar del mundo viene de Rusia.
9 El índice de crímenes domésticos en Inglaterra es (*peor*) que en Irlanda del Norte.
10 Escocia hace los (*mejor*) whiskys del mundo.

F The Mexican group, Garibaldi, talk to Ana about their music. Put the verbs in the preterite tense with the correct ending, and insert them in the gaps.
e.g. ¿Cómo …? (*empezar*)   →   ¿Cómo **empezasteis**?

Garibaldi

ANA	'Garibaldi Caribe' es vuestro sexto album. ¿Cómo …?	*empezar*
CHARLY	La idea de 'Garibaldi' … de Oscar Gómez y Luis De Llano.	*ser*
VICTOR	Ellos … formar un grupo que cantara música mejicana	*querer*
	modernizada, e … una serie de audiciones en Méjico.	*hacer*
ANA	¿Oscar y Luis … a los que ahora forman parte del grupo?	*escoger*
VICTOR	No, sólo a cinco. Tres otros … y ya han sido reemplazados.	*irse*
CHARLY	Paola, Ingrid y Adrián … después de la fiesta de Acapulco.	*entrar*
ANA	¿Y la música de 'Garibaldi Caribe' – de dónde …?	*venir*
VICTOR	Nosotros … la música tropical con el tinte Garibaldi.	*mezclar*
ANA	El album … mucho éxito en Méjico – ¿va a pasar lo mismo aquí?	*tener*
CHARLY	La gente española nos … muy simpática en nuestra gira.	*caer*
	Nos … actuar en España hace tres años – ¡espero que sea igual!	*encantar*

¡Qué desastre!

A The Ruiz family are checking they have done everything in preparation for their holiday in London. Choose the correct verb for each gap from the lists given, and then write it in the perfect tense in the **yo** form.

e.g. Mamá: Yo he ... el coche   →   Mamá: Yo he **lavado** el coche

Los preparativos

Mamá: Yo he... el coche, he ... las pesetas en libras esterlinas, he ... las llaves con la vecina, y he... las plantas.

regar   cambiar   lavar   dejar

Papá: Yo he... un montón de ropa, he... los dormitorios, he ... a la agencia de viajes, y he... los billetes.

reservar   salir   planchar   recoger

Nacho: Yo he ... a la caja de ahorros, he... un poco de dinero, he... caramelos para el viaje – ¡y los he... casi todos ya!

comer   sacar   ir   comprar

B The Ruiz family make an overnight stop and begin to unpack – only to discover that their preparations were not as thorough as they had thought! Complete the sentences with the words for *it/them*: **lo**, **la**, **los** or **las**.

e.g. ¡Yo no ... tengo!   →   ¡Yo no **lo** tengo!

El momento de la verdad

MAMÁ ¿Quién tiene <u>el jabón</u>?

PAPÁ ¿Dónde están <u>las toallas</u>?

NACHO No encuentro <u>el walkman</u>.

PAPÁ ¿Y <u>los bañadores</u>?

MAMÁ ¿<u>La crema de sol</u> está allí?

NACHO ¿<u>Las revistas</u>, Mamá?

PAPÁ ¿No has traído <u>el talco</u>?

MAMÁ ¡No veo <u>los pasaportes</u>!

PAPÁ ¡Yo no ... tengo!

MAMÁ ¡... dejé encima de la cama!

MAMÁ ¿No ... tienes tú?

NACHO No ... veo, papá.

PAPÁ No ... tengo yo.

MAMÁ ... he dejado en el coche.

MAMÁ ¿Por qué no ... trajiste tú?

PAPÁ ¡Calma! ¡... tengo yo!

The regular perfect tense

1 The PERFECT TENSE explains what you **have** done or what **has** happened:

| **I have broken** my ankle | The ambulance **has arrived**. |

2 To form the perfect tense in Spanish, use the present tense of the verb **haber** and the PAST PARTICIPLE. The PAST PARTICIPLE is formed as follows:

verbs ending in -**ar**	comp**rar**	→	comp**rado**	(*to buy*)	→	(*bought*)
verbs ending in -**er**	com**er**	→	com**ido**	(*to eat*)	→	(*eaten*)
verbs ending in -**ir**	viv**ir**	→	viv**ido**	(*to live*)	→	(*lived*)

The present tense form of **haber** is as follows:

yo	**he**	nosotros	**hemos**
tú	**has**	vosotros	**habéis**
él, ella	**ha**	ellos, ellas	**han**
usted	**ha**	ustedes	**han**

He dejado mi chaqueta en el parque	*I've left my jacket in the park*
Ha comido demasiado	*He's eaten too much*
¿Qué **has perdido**?	*What have you lost?*

3 With reflexive verbs, the reflexive pronoun comes before **haber**:

Me he lavado las manos   *I've/I have washed my hands*

Direct objects and the pronouns **me, te** etc.

4 DIRECT OBJECTS are nouns which follow the verb directly. Below, **un boli**, **la bolsa** and **las camas** are DIRECT OBJECTS:

VERB	DIRECT OBJECT	VERB	DIRECT OBJECT
tengo	**un boli**	*I have*	***a ball-point pen***
perdiste	**la bolsa**	*you lost*	***the bag***
hacemos	**las camas**	*we make*	***the beds***

5 DIRECT OBJECT PRONOUNS are words like *it*, or *them*. You can use them instead of nouns and they allow us to refer to the same thing/person without always repeating the same word:

Yo tengo **un boli**	→	Yo **lo** tengo	*I've got **it***
Tú perdiste **la bolsa**	→	Tú **la** perdiste	*You lost **it***
Martín hace **las camas**	→	Martín **las** hace	*Martín makes **them***

Help Yourself to Essential Spanish Grammar

6 Here is a complete list of direct object pronouns:

me		me	nos	us	
you	*(familiar singular)*	**te**	**os**	*you*	*(familiar plural)*
him,	*(masculine)*	**le**	**les**	*them*	*(masculine)*
it	*(masculine)*	**lo**	**los**	*them*	*(masculine)*
her, it	*(feminine)*	**la**	**las**	*them*	*(feminine)*
you	*(formal singular)*	**le**	**les**	*you*	*(formal plural)*

¡Alicia **me** pegó, Mamá!   *Alicia hit **me**, Mum!*
El boli rojo – ¿**lo** has visto?   *The red biro – have you seen **it**?*
¿Dónde está la goma? ¿**la** tienes?   *Where's the rubber? have you got **it**?*

7 Use **los** for masculine things, and **les** for masculine people:

Los zapatos – ¿**los** quieres?   *The shoes – do you want **them**?*
¿Los hermanos? **les** vi ayer   *The brothers? I saw **them** yesterday*

8 Look at the position of direct object pronouns:

a In English, the direct object pronoun comes after the verb. In Spanish, it normally comes <u>before</u> the verb:

   Os ví ayer   *I saw **you** yesterday*   No **la** conozco   *I don't know **her***

b In the perfect tense, the direct object pronoun <u>must</u> come before whichever part of **haber** you are using:

   ¿Miguel? sí, **le** he visto   *Miguel? Yes, I've seen him.*

c In positive commands, add the direct object pronoun to the <u>end</u> of the verb. You may need an accent to keep the stress on the same syllable:

   Copia el cuadro – ¡haz**lo** ahora!   *Copy the grid – do **it** now!*
   ¡**Cópialo** correctamente!   *Copy **it** correctly!*

   For stress and accentuation, see the Appendix, p. 48

d When using two verbs together, either place the direct object pronoun at the beginning on its own, or add it to the end of the second verb:

   Le voy a ver / voy a ver**le**   *I'm going to see him*
   Lo está haciendo / está haciéndo**lo**   *He is doing it*

CHAPTER 19   WHAT HAVE YOU LEARNT?

A Are you prone to disaster on holiday? In the quiz below, put the verbs in brackets in the perfect tense.

e.g. Tú (*dejar*) la máquina fotográfica en el avión.   →   Tú **has dejado** la máquina fotográfica en el avión.

De vacaciones

1 Has llegado a España. En la recogida de equipaje, te das cuenta de que ...
a Tú (*dejar*) la máquina fotográfica en el avión.
b La línea aérea (*perder*) una de tus maletas – porque tú no (*atar*) bien la etiqueta de viaje.
c Tus maletas (*llegar*) juntas en estado perfecto.

2 Tu hotel está todavía en construcción. Un día, vuelves y ...
a (*Entrar*) muchas moscas porque tú no (*cerrar*) las persianas.
b Los obreros (*ensuciar*) el cuarto de baño lavándose las manos.
c La criada (*limpiar*) perfectamente la habitación porque la (*impresionar*) tú, intentando hablar español.

3 Al final de las vacaciones, vuelves al aeropuerto. Descubres que ...
a Tu avión (*salir*) ya, porque tú (*equivocarse*) de la hora.
b La agencia de viajes no (*rellenar*) correctamente tu billete de vuelta.
c Todo está en orden. Tú (*divertirse*) mucho.

Now do the quiz yourself. Choose the response which best describes what happens to you on holiday and check your results below.*

B Nuria doesn't have much luck when travelling. She greets her uncle at the airport with a tale of woe. Fill in the gaps with the correct direct object pronoun.

e.g. ¿No ... tienes ya?   →   ¿No **las** tienes ya?

Los desastres de Nuria

TÍO   ¡Nuria! ¿Qué tal? Pero ¿dónde están las maletas? ¿No ... tienes ya?
NURIA   ¡No, no tengo el equipaje! Iberia ... ha perdido entre Londres y aquí.
TÍO   ¡Qué rabia! Y tus padres, ¿dónde están? No ... veo.
NURIA   Pero, ¿no recibiste los recados de parte de Papá? ... mandó ayer.
TÍO   No recibí nada. Sólo una postal que ... mandó tu padre hace mucho.
NURIA   Mamá tuvo apendicitis. ... visité en el hospital ayer. Va mejor.
TÍO   ¡Dios mío! Bueno, puedes venir a mi casa, Nuria. ... llevo en coche.

Mayoría de c: todo te sale bien – ¡y tienes suerte!
* Mayoría de a: ¡debes organizarte mejor! Mayoría de b: ¡qué mala suerte tienes – quédate en casa!

Help Yourself to Essential Spanish Grammar

CHAPTER 20   WHAT DO YOU KNOW?

A The bad-tempered Dr. Marañón has arrived in his consulting room to find that his new nurse is untidy and disorganised. Fill in the gaps with the correct past participle from the list below.

e.g. 1 ¿No se ha ... usted los guantes para lavar los instrumentos?   →
  ¿No se ha **puesto** usted los guantes para lavar los instrumentos?

El médico malhumorado
1 ¿No se ha ... usted los guantes para lavar los instrumentos?
2 ¿Las recetas? ¡No, no las he ... todavía! Necesito mi boli. ¿Dónde está?
3 ¿El esparadrapo? No sé dónde está. No lo he ...
4 ¡Oye, hay que recoger todo bien! He ... estas tijeras en el suelo.
5 ¡No tengo sitio para hacer nada! ¡Alguien ha ... mi mesa de papeles!
6 ¿Quién ha ... mi correo? ¡Si dice 'privado', lo abro yo!
  abierto   cubierto   puesto   escrito   visto   descubierto

B The nurse makes a list of all the things she needs to have ready for the afternoon clinic. Choose the correct alternative from the brackets.

e.g. Los instrumentos (*esterilizado/esterilizados*) correctamente...   →
  Los instrumentos **esterilizados** correctamente...

Los preparativos
1 Los instrumentos (*esterilizado/esterilizados*) correctamente...
2 Las vendas (*preparados/preparadas*) ...
3 La mesa (*recogido/recogida*) bien ...
4 El estetoscopio (*puesto/puesta*) en su caja ...
5 Las jeringas (*envuelta/envueltas*) en su plástico ...
6 La cama (*cubierto/cubierta*) de una sábana limpia ...

C By now, Dr. Marañón has a headache. He talks through the arrangements for the afternoon clinic with his receptionist, Marta. Insert the following where appropriate: **a él, a ella, a mí, a nosotros, a usted, a ustedes**.

e.g. ¿Me da una aspirina ... también?   →   ¿Me da una aspirina **a mí** también?

El trabajo de la recepcionista
DOCTOR   Me duele la cabeza, Marta. ¿Me da una aspirina ... también?
MARTA   Claro, doctor. Y le traigo ... un buen café en seguida.
DOCTOR   Gracias. Y a la enfermera. Tráigale algo ....
MARTA   Viene el Dr. Gómez a las tres. Le he mandado ... las radiografías.
DOCTOR   Marta, ¡es usted un sol! ¿Nos ha dejado ... los documentos?
MARTA   Sí. Y les he dejado ... una lista de los pacientes de la tarde.

The irregular perfect tense

1 The following verbs have irregular past participles in the perfect tense:

to open	abrir	**abierto**	*open(ed)*
to cover	cubrir	**cubierto**	*covered*
to discover	descubrir	**descubierto**	*discovered*
to say, tell	decir	**dicho**	*said, told*
to describe	describir	**descrito**	*described*
to write	escribir	**escrito**	*written*
to fry	freír	**frito**	*fried*
to return	volver	**vuelto**	*returned*
to give back	devolver	**devuelto**	*given back*
to do, make	hacer	**hecho**	*done, made*
to die	morir	**muerto**	*dead*
to put, set	poner	**puesto**	*put, set*
to break	romper	**roto**	*broken*
to see	ver	**visto**	*seen*

Examples:

Hemos **hecho** una denuncia — *We've **done** a report*
¿Has **escrito** a la compañía de seguros? — *Have you **written** to the insurers?*
Sí, pero no han **dicho** nada — *Yes, but they haven't **said** anything*

Using past participles as adjectives

2 Past participles can also be used as adjectives. In this case they need to agree in number and gender with the noun they describe:

Prefiero la carne **hecha** — *I prefer meat well **done***
palabras **dichas** en broma — *words **said** in jest*

For agreement of adjectives, see p. 20.

Indirect objects and the pronouns **me**, **te** etc.

3 An INDIRECT OBJECT is a person or a thing affected by a verb and often has the word *to* or *for* in front of it in English. Below, **profesora** and **Juan** are INDIRECT OBJECTS:

VERB	INDIRECT OBJECT	VERB	INDIRECT OBJECT
escribí	a la **profesora**	*I wrote*	*to the **teacher***
compré	algo para **Juan**	*I bought something*	*for **Juan***

Help Yourself to Essential Spanish Grammar

Sometimes the words *to* and *for* are left out in English. If you want to check that an object is indirect, try <u>adding</u> *to* or *for* to see if it makes sense:

*He gave **Sra. Pérez** the letter*	*He gave the letter to **Sra. Perez***
*I bought my **brothers** a present*	*I bought a present for my **brothers***

4   As with direct objects (p. 86) you can replace an INDIRECT OBJECT by an INDIRECT OBJECT PRONOUN:

He gave **her** the letter	I bought **them** a present

5   Here is a complete list of the INDIRECT OBJECT PRONOUNS in Spanish:

me		**me**	**nos**	*us*	
you	*(familiar singular)*	**te**	**os**	*you*	*(familiar plural)*
him		**le**	**les**	*them*	*(masculine)*
her		**le**	**les**	*them*	*(feminine)*
you	*(formal singular)*	**le**	**les**	*you*	*(formal plural)*

Te mando una postal   *I'll send **you** a postcard*
¿Qué **le** dijiste?   *What did you say to **him**?*
Les escribo el fin de semana   *I'll write to **them** at the week-end*

> *For the use of indirect object pronouns with **gustar** and similar verbs, see p. 48*

6   If there is a risk of confusion when using **le** (*him, her, you*) or **les** (*them, you*), make your meaning clear by adding **a** and the correct subject pronoun:

Le di un regalo **a él**, pero no **a ella**   *I gave **him** a present, but not **her***
Les mando los detalles **a ustedes**   *I'm sending **you** the details*

> *For subject pronouns, see p. 6*

7   Spanish often uses both the indirect object and pronoun:

Le mandé flores a mi **novia**   *I sent flowers to my **girl-friend***

8   The position of indirect object pronouns is the same as direct object pronouns – before the main verb, or added to the end of the infinitive or command:

me dijo: ¡da**le** el boli en seguida!   he said to **me**: give **him** the biro straightaway!
voy a enviar**os** la revista   I'm going to send **you** the magazine

> *For the position of direct object pronouns, see p. 87*

CHAPTER 20   WHAT HAVE YOU LEARNT?

A Dr. Yolanda Soria and her husband Ignacio are going on holiday, but first they each
have a number of things to do. What do they mentally say as they look at the state of
their lists? Put their thoughts in the perfect tense.

e.g. poner el botiquín en el coche   →   **he puesto** el botiquín en el coche

Hay que …

Yolanda	Ignacio
poner el botiquín en el coche ✓	abrir una lata de atún ✓
decir adiós a mi suplente ✗	freír las patatas y la cebolla ✗
devolver mis llaves a la recepción ✗	romper seis huevos en un bol ✓
escribir una receta para la Sra. Muñoz ✓	hacer la tortilla ✗

B While he makes the omelette, Ignacio glances at the paper. The headlines do not
make comforting reading for those about to travel. Put the verb in brackets in its past
participle form, making it agree where necessary.

e.g. veinte heridos (*trasladar*) …   →   veinte heridos **trasladados** …

Sucesos

1 Accidente en la N630: veinte heridos (*trasladar*) al hospital.
2 Tres personas (*morir*) en un accidente de tráfico en Mieres.
3 Autobús francés (*precipitar*) al mar cerca de Estepona.
4 Mal estado de la carretera por lluvias (*caer*) anoche.
5 Dos cadáveres (*rescatar*) de un Seat en la Sierra de Gredos.
6 Una niña (*desaparecer*) en un accidente de helicóptero.

C Yolanda goes to the surgery to hand over to her locum, Señor Garay – only to find
it's so busy she has to lend him, and the receptionist Marta, a hand. Complete her
sentences below correctly with **le, te, les, me, nos, os**.

e.g. ¿El chico se ha roto el dedo? Hay que hacer… una radiografía.   →
¿El chico se ha roto el dedo? Hay que hacer**le** una radiografía.

En la clínica

1 ¿El chico se ha roto el dedo? Hay que hacer… una radiografía.
2 Marta – el señor Garay y yo tenemos sed. ¿Puedes preparar… un té?
3 ¿Las víctimas tienen quemaduras graves? Sería mejor no poner… nada.
4 Pero, ¿qué te pasa, chiquitita? ¡Tranquila! Voy a poner… una inyección.
5 Chicos – vosotros dos tenéis una insolación. Voy a dar… una crema.
6 ¡Ay! ¡Me he cortado el dedo con las tijeras! Debo poner… una tirita.

Help Yourself to Essential Spanish Grammar

UNIT

7

CHAPTER 21   WHAT DO YOU KNOW?

A Read the policeman's notes (below) on an accident, and match up the halves of the
sentences in his report.
e.g. 1 El testigo era …   →   c un Sr. Blasco y Beltrán.

El accidente

Nombre y posición del testigo: Sr. Blasco y Beltrán, en la terraza del Hotel Miramar
Hora: 11.15
Tiempo: viento, lluvia débil
Vehículos: Seat Ibiza, gris: Vespino, rojo
Número de personas: Seat – 4; Vespino – 1
Detalles del accidente: Vespino – pasar la cafetería, quiso evitar un coche
                                             mal aparcado
                                   Seat   – salir de una calle enfrente de la cafetería,
                                             chocar con el vespino. Joven caído en la
                                             carretera.

1 El testigo era …	a lloviendo un poco.
2 Estaba tomando un refresco …	b de una calle enfrente del hotel.
3 Hacía viento y estaba …	c un Sr. Blasco y Beltrán.
4 Un vespino rojo estaba …	d el Vespino y el joven se cayó al suelo.
5 El joven del vespino quiso evitar …	e pasando el hotel hacia las 11.15.
6 Un Seat estaba saliendo …	f en la terraza del Hotel Miramar.
7 El conductor del Seat …	g un coche mal aparcado.
8 El Seat chocó con …	h no vio el Vespino.

B Inside the Hotel Mirimar, the receptionist is besieged with requests from guests.
Complete the gaps with the correct pairs of pronouns from the list below.
e.g. 1 No funciona mi cámara. ¿… puede reparar?
    → No funciona mi cámara. ¿**me la** puede reparar?

¿En qué puedo servirle?
1 No funciona mi cámara. ¿… puede reparar?
2 Mis padres quieren lavar el coche, pero ¿… puede hacer usted?
3 Nuestra habitación no está arreglada todavía. ¿… arregla pronto?
4 Quiero mandar un fax. ¿… puede mandar usted?
5 Los zapatos de mi marido están muy sucios. ¿… puede limpiar?
6 ¿La habitación del Sr. Roldán no está lista? ¡Pero … prometí para las tres!

se lo   se la   me lo   me la   nos la   se los

The imperfect tense

1 The IMPERFECT TENSE is used to describe what *used to happen*, to say what *was happening*, and to describe what something *was* like:

> I *used to live* in Menorca. It *was* a very tranquil island.
> The holiday trade *was beginning* to expand at that time.

2 The regular IMPERFECT TENSE is formed from the infinitive as follows. Remove the final -**ar**, -**er**, and -**ir** endings and add the following endings:

	-AR trabajar	-ER comer	-IR vivir
yo	trabaj**aba**	com**ía**	viv**ía**
tú	trabaj**abas**	com**ías**	viv**ías**
él, ella, usted	trabaj**aba**	com**ía**	viv**ía**
nosotros	trabaj**ábamos**	com**íamos**	viv**íamos**
vosotros	trabaj**abais**	com**íais**	viv**íais**
ellos, ellas, ustedes	trabaj**aban**	com**ían**	viv**ían**

> Mi abuelo **vivía** cerca en aquella época   *My grandfather **was living** nearby then*
> **Comíamos** en su casa   *We **used to eat** in his house*

3 The following verbs are irregular in the imperfect tense:

	SER (*to be*)	VER (*to see*)	IR (*to go*)
yo	**era**	**veía**	**iba**
tú	**eras**	**veías**	**ibas**
él, ella, usted	**era**	**veía**	**iba**
nosotros	**éramos**	**veíamos**	**íbamos**
vosotros	**erais**	**veíais**	**ibais**
ellos, ellas, ustedes	**eran**	**veían**	**iban**

> El pueblo **estaba** un poco descuidado   *The village **was** a bit shabby*
> **Veía** los burros   *I **used to see** the donkeys*
> **Iban** al campo para trabajar   ***They were going** to the fields to work*

The imperfect continuous

4 The IMPERFECT CONTINUOUS is used to emphasise what was happening:

> *I **was listening** to the radio when I heard a loud explosion*

5 To form the IMPERFECT CONTINUOUS you need the imperfect tense of the verb **estar** (*to be*) and the PRESENT PARTICIPLE:

El coche **estaba saliendo** del garaje   *The car **was coming out** of the garage*
Estábamos comiendo en aquel momento   *We **were eating** at that moment*

For the present participle, see page 67.

Using the preterite and the imperfect tenses together

6 Use the guide below to help you select the correct past tense. The PRETERITE tense describes an action that occurred at a fixed time in the past. The IMPERFECT and IMPERFECT CONTINUOUS can both be used to say what was happening:

PRETERITE	to say what happened
IMPERFECT	to describe, to set the scene, to say what was happening
IMPERFECT CONTINUOUS	to emphasise what was happening

Porque **hacía** frío, **fuimos** en coche   *Because it **was** cold, **we went** by car*
Estaba preparando la cena cuando   *He **was preparing** the evening meal when*
se desmayó   *he fainted*

Direct and indirect object pronouns together

7 When using direct and indirect object pronouns together, the indirect object pronoun comes first:

Me lo dijo en secreto   *He told **me it** in secret*
¿La carta? **te la** envié hace dos días   *The letter? I sent **it to you** two days ago*

8 If both the pronouns begin with the letter **l**, the indirect object pronoun changes to **se**:

Se lo explicó claramente	*He explained **it to her** clearly*	(le lo)
¿La bolsa? ¡**se la** di a él!	*The bag? I gave **it to him**!*	(le la)
Se lo dije a ellos ayer	*I told **it to them** yesterday*	(les lo)

9 In sentences with a main verb and an infinitive, or with a positive command, place the indirect and direct pronouns either before the main verb, or on the end of the infinitive. Note the need for an accent, to keep the stress pattern:

¿Las sandalias? **Me las** quiero probar / Quiero prob**ár**melas. Dá**melas**

For direct and indirect object pronouns, see p. 87, 91

CHAPTER 21   WHAT HAVE YOU LEARNT?

A The grandmother of the family you're staying with reminisces about her home in bygone days. Put the underlined verbs in the imperfect tense.

e.g. <u>se hace</u> → **se hacía**

Guipúzcoa antigua

En los caseríos vascos antiguos, la vida de la familia <u>se hace</u> en la cocina. Allí <u>está</u> el hogar o 'llar', donde mi madre <u>enciende</u> el fuego que <u>es</u> la única calefacción. De día, mi madre y yo <u>preparamos</u> la comida. Por la noche, toda la familia <u>se reúne</u> allí también. Mi hermana mayor <u>cose</u> la ropa y mi madre <u>enseña</u> a mis hermanos a leer. Cuando <u>nos vamos</u> a la cama, mi padre <u>coloca</u> algunas brasas en un calentador de cobre, y con eso <u>suele</u> calentar el interior de nuestras camas … Una vida tranquila, ¡pero dura!

B Suddenly, you hear the screeching of brakes and rush outside. Celia and Jorge explain what happened. Put the verbs (in brackets) in the imperfect or imperfect continuous tense as necessary.

e.g. *ver* → **estaba viendo**

El accidente

CELIA   Yo (*ver*) la tele cuando oí el ruido de los frenos.

JORGE   Pero yo (*estar*) fuera. (*Barrer*) la acera delante de la casa.

CELIA   Mientras (*acercarse*) a la esquina, el conductor miró hacia atrás.

JORGE   La señora (*cruzar*) la calle cuando le atropelló el coche.

CELIA   La visibilidad (*ser*) buena cuando se produjo el accidente.

JORGE   Aunque (*hacer*) frío, no (*haber*) hielo en la carretera.

CELIA   Una chica guapa le (*llamar*) la atención – ¡qué estúpido!

C The medical services arrive on the scene. Read their instructions, and put the English expressions into Spanish, inserting them in the appropriate spaces.

e.g. ¡Páse…lo! → **¡Pásemelo!**

Asistencia medical

1 ¡Rápido – el botiquín! ¡Páse…lo!   [TO ME]

2 La señora necesita oxígeno. Sí, dé…lo en seguida.   [TO HER]

3 ¿Agua, señora? Lo siento, no … la puedo dar.   [TO YOU]

4 Ese vendaje – ¿… lo abre, por favor?   [FOR US]

5 La camilla – búsca…la. Está en la ambulancia.   [FOR ME]

6 ¿Esa venda? – dé…la a mis compañeros allí.   [TO THEM]

7 ¿Un analgésico? Dé…lo por inyección.   [TO HIM]

Revision test 19–21

A Carmina who is going on holiday with you and your Spanish host family is fussing about the final arrangements. Put the sentences in English into Spanish.

e.g. ANDREU HAS RETURNED IT → Andreu **lo ha devuelto**

Hay que ...

CARMINA   Se debe devolver el vídeo al videoclub.

TÚ   [ANDREU HAS RETURNED IT.]

CARMINA   Es imprescindible escribir al hotel con la fecha de nuestra llegada.

TÚ   [SR. AND SRA. VELÁZQUEZ HAVE WRITTEN.]

CARMINA   Hay que hacer la maleta grande.

TÚ   [HAVEN'T YOU DONE IT?]

CARMINA   Ah sí, es verdad. Pero debo cerrarla con llave.

TÚ   [WE HAVE LOCKED IT.]

CARMINA   Necesito poner mis gafas de sol en una de las maletas.

TÚ   [I'VE PUT THEM IN THE SMALL SUITCASE.]

CARMINA   Entonces, ¿por qué estamos esperando aquí? ¡Vamos al coche!

B Do you adore clothes, are you mildly interested in them, or do you hate the whole process of choosing what to wear? Insert **te**, **lo**, **la**, **le**, **os**, **los**, **las** as appropriate in the following sentences.

e.g. ... gastas en seguida en tu tienda de ropa favorita.   → **Las** gastas en seguida en tu tienda de ropa favorita.

¿Te gusta la ropa?

1 Te tocan cincuenta mil pesetas en la lotería:
   a ... gastas en seguida en tu tienda de ropa favorita.
   b llamas a tu amigo/a, y ... invitas a ayudarte a gastar la mitad.
   c no gastas el dinero – ... ahorras todo.

2 Cuando vas a una tienda de ropa con un/a amigo/a:
   a Eliges muchas prendas, y te ... pruebas todas.
   b Eliges una prenda que te gustaría llevar, y te ... pruebas.
   c ... pasas mal en las tiendas de ropa. Esperas a tu amigo/a fuera.

3 Tu amigo/a recibe dos entradas gratis para un desfile de modas:
   a tu amigo/a ... invita a acompañarle, porque sabe que te va a gustar.
   b lo pensáis, pero a ti y a tu amigo/a no ... interesa mucho. No vais.
   c tu amigo no ... dice nada. Sabe que es inútil.

4 Te invitan a un baile de disfraces:
   a sacas todas las cosas de tu guardarropa, y pasas todo el día probándote....
   b llamas a tu amigo/a y ... discutís por teléfono.
   c lees la invitación, y ... echas a la basura.

Now do the test to find out what your attitude to clothes is. Tick the sentences which best describe you and check your results.*

*Una mayoría de a: te encanta la ropa, y es algo importante para ti. Una mayoría de b: te interesa la ropa, pero no excesivamente. Una mayoría de c: la ropa te es indiferente.

C   Antonio has set up his own business as a Mister Fix-it-Quick. Rephrase the queries from clients below, putting the pronouns in the alternative position.

e.g. ¿Me la puede reparar para el lunes?   →   ¿Puede **reparármela** para el lunes?

En el Servicio Súper Rápido

1   La máquina no funciona. ¿Me la puede reparar para el lunes?
2   He rasgado el dobladillo[1] de este pantalón. ¿Usted me lo puede coser?
3   Esta falda de mi madre está sucia. ¿Se la puede limpiar usted?
4   Los faros del coche no funcionan. ¿El mecánico me los puede mirar hoy?
5   Nos hacen falta más llaves para el coche. ¿Nos las puede cortar aquí?
6   Les voy a dejar mi reloj. Necesita una pila nueva.

D   At the scene of an accident, Gabi and Tere try to make sense of what happened. Put the verbs in brackets into the imperfect, the imperfect continuous or the preterite tense as necessary.

e.g. Yo (*salir*) de la tienda   →   Yo **salía/estaba saliendo** de la tienda

¿Qué pasó exactamente?

GABI   Yo (*salir*) de la tienda, cuando (*oír*) el chirriar[2] del coche gris.
TERE   El coche (*ir*) muy rápido – demasiado rápido para las condiciones.
GABI   Pero la joven de la moto (*tener*) la culpa también. (*Hablar*) con su pasajero cuando (*ponerse*) rojos los semáforos.
TERE   Es verdad. Los dos jóvenes no (*prestar*) atención.
GABI   Parece que el conductor del coche no (*ver*) la moto cruzando la calle.
NACHO   ¡Qué ruido más horrible cuando el coche (*chocar*) con la moto!
GABI   ¿Has visto con qué fuerza (*caerse*) el joven de delante?
TERE   Sí. Y el coche (*resbalarse*) y (*pararse*) contra aquel árbol grande.
NACHO   Por el hielo, supongo. (*Haber*) hielo en la carretera.
TERE   Y lluvia también encima. (*Llover*) hace poco, ¿te acuerdas?

E   Dani, with the help of his two excited nephews, is deciding to whom he is going to give which Christmas presents. Put the correct pronouns into the gaps as necessary: you may need one or two.

e.g. ¿Mis abuelos? … voy a regalar este jarro   →   ¿Mis abuelos? **Les** voy a regalar este jarro

Los regalos de Navidad

1   ¿Mis abuelos? … voy a regalar este jarro.
2   Las entradas para el teatro, … … doy a mis padres.
3   ¡Tranquilos, chicos! O el hueso para el perro, ¡… … regalo a vosotros!
4   ¿Qué … voy a dar a mi hermano? ¡Nada!
5   La botella de perfume, … … regalo a mi hermana.
6   El vale-regalo del Corte Inglés – … … doy a mi tía.
7   ¿Y tú, Felipe? ¿Qué te gustaría? Ah, ¡el regalo 'misterio', … … doy a ti!
8   ¿La caja de turrón? ¡… … guardo para mí!

---

[1] *el dobladillo*: hem
[2] *el chirriar*: the screeching of brakes

Help Yourself to Essential Spanish Grammar

El mundo de hoy y del futuro

CHAPTER 22   WHAT DO YOU KNOW?

A Raúl tells his visitor, Gabi, about the changes in his local area. Fill in the gaps with the relevant past participle from the list below.

e.g. Aquí habían **construido**.

¡Cómo ha cambiado la zona!

RAÚL   Ya ves los cambios. Aquí habían … la compañía de tabaco una fábrica.

GABI   Y ahora hay un polideportivo – ¡qué bien! La compañía habiá … también un lago artificial al mismo tiempo, ¿no?

RAÚL   Sí, pero estaba siempre … Ahora la nueva administración hace un parque precioso, con fuentes y todo. ¿Ves dónde están esas casas bonitas?

GABI   Sí. El ayuntamiento había … tierra a la compañía para pisos, ¿no?

RAÚL   Sí – unos pisos enormes y muy feos. Pero la nueva administración los ha …

GABI   Habían … en aquella época mucho bosque también, ¿verdad?

RAÚL   Sí, pero están plantando un jardín botánico. Y van a construir un central comercial enorme.

GABI   ¿Allí dónde la companía de tabacos había … unas tiendas pequeñas para los obreros?

RAÚL   Precisamente. La zona ha … mucho, ¿verdad?

> cambiado   quitado   dado   hecho   construido
> contaminado   montado   desmontado

B Andres and Pilar are looking around an exhibition of 'Housing for the Future', and commenting on what they see. What are the original nouns or adjectives from which the words in italics come?

e.g. ¡Andres, mira la *casita*!   →   ¡Andres, mira la **casa**!

La exposición

1 ¡Andres, mira la *casita*!

2 ¿Ves el *jardincito*? ¡Qué mono es!

3 ¡Qué feo es ese *rinconcillo*!

4 ¿Y el *hotelucho* enfrente? No me gustaría vivir enfrente de esto.

5 ¡Qué *balconazo*! Hay sitio para toda la familia.

6 Mira el invernadero – ¡qué *chiquito*!

7 ¿Has visto el *garajote*? Allí caben tres coches, por lo menos.

8 ¡Qué *grandona* es la entrada!

The pluperfect tense

1   The PLUPERFECT TENSE explains what you *had* done or what *had* happened:

> *I **had arranged** for him to come at twelve; by half past, he still **had** not **arrived***

2   To form the PLUPERFECT tense use the imperfect tense of the verb **haber** and any past participle. The imperfect tense of **haber** is as follows:

yo	**había**	nosotros	**habíamos**
tú	**había**	vosotros	**habíais**
él, ella	**había**	ellos, ellas	**habían**
usted	**había**	ustedes	**habían**

Yo **había** visitado la región con ella — *I **had visited** the region with her*
Nunca **había visto** tanta contaminación — *She **had** never **seen** so much pollution*
Habían construido una central eléctrica — *They **had constructed** a power station*

For past participles, see p. 86 and p. 90

To have just ... **acabar de**

3   **Acabar de**, followed by the inifinitive, means *to have just done something*. It is used in two tenses only – the present and the imperfect:

PRESENT	**Acabo de** dejar un recado	*I **have just** left a message*
	Acabamos de salir de clase	*We **have just** come out of class*
IMPERFECT	Mi gato **acababa de** morir	*My cat **had just** died*
	Mis primos **acababan de** llegar	*My cousins **had just** arrived*

Diminutives and augmentatives

4   A DIMINUTIVE ending is added to a noun or adjective to make that person or object smaller, rather like *pig* and *piglet* in English.

5   DIMINUTIVES often carry an emotional overtone as well. Some have a favourable or positive meaning, some an unfavourable or negative meaning, and some can be both. To form a diminutive, take off the ending of the word and add the following endings:
e.g. abue**la** → abue**lita**

ENDING	MEANING	EXAMPLES
-(c)ito / -(c)ita	positive	dear, sweet, nice
-(c)illo / -(c)illa	positive/negative	cute, pleasant
-ucho / -ucha	negative	horrible, miserable

mi abuela	*my grandmother*	mi abue**lita**	*my **dear** grandma*
la casa	*the house*	la cas**ucha**	*the miserable little house*

6 DIMINUTIVE adjectives can be made masculine, feminine, singular or plural by applying the normal rules for adjective agreement:

| pequeño → ella es pequeñita | joven → ellos son jovencitos |

For the rules for adjective agreement, see p. 20

7 Insert the letter **c** if you want to add the diminutive **ito/illo** to a word ending in **-e**, **-n**, or **-r**: e.g. pobre → pobre**c**ito /a

| baja, pobre | Es bajita, la pobre**c**ita | *She's a bit on the short side, poor little thing* |

8 When adding a DIMINUTIVE, there may be spelling changes to keep the same sound:

| un chico → un chi**qui**to |

9 Nouns and adjectives which have an accent lose it when a diminutive is added:

| un **árbol** → un **arb**ol**ito** | un rat**ón** → un rat**oncito** |

10 You may need to look at the rest of the sentence for clues as to whether the DIMINUTIVE has a positive or negative meaning:

| ligero
light | Me gusta este vino liger**illo**
*I like this **pleasantly light** wine* |
| el hombre
the man | Ese hombre**cillo** era muy descortés
*That **horrid little** man was very rude* |

11 An AUGMENTATIVE ending is added to a noun or adjective to make that person or object bigger. It is formed in the same way as a diminutive and can also carry an emotional meaning:

ENDING	MEANING	EXAMPLES
-ón/-ona	neutral/positive/negative	very big
-azo/-aza	neutral/positive/negative	really, extremely
-ote/-ota	negative	great, huge, whopping

grande	*big*	grand**ón**	*very big*
simpática	*nice*	simpatic**ona**	*extremely nice*
gordo	*fat*	gord**ote**	*a real fatty*

CHAPTER 22   WHAT HAVE YOU LEARNT?

A A journalist writes about a local lake, which has suffered years of ecological neglect.
Write the correct form in the pluperfect tense of the verb in brackets.
e.g. *perjudicar*   →   **habíamos perjudicado**

El desastre ecológico

Nosotros, los habitantes de esta zona tan preciosa, (*perjudicar*) el equilibrio ecológico
de nuestro lago, sin saberlo. Durante los años setenta y ochenta, los veraneantes
(*ensuciar*) las playas artificiales, la comunidad pesquera (*despoblar*) el lago de los
peces nativos, y yo mismo (*contribuir*) a este desastre ecológico, como niño,
cogiendo flores silvestres. Hablé con el alcalde, Ramón Hernández Ferrol y le
pregunté:
– ¿Qué medidas (*tomar*) usted para proteger la naturaleza de este lugar?
– Pues, al principio, ningunas. Nosotros de aquí no (*darse*) cuenta de su importancia
ecológica. En aquella época, nadie (*hace*r) ningún estudio.
– Parece que un investigador científico de Guadalajara (*escribir*) un artículo sobre la
posibilidad de un desastre ecológico – ¿no lo (*estudiar*) ustedes?
– Lo (*leer*) nosotros, que nos interesábamos en la naturaleza, sí. Pero el Concejo
Municipal, desgraciadamente, no...

B Pedro explains how the various members of his family try not to waste – or do waste
– resources and energy. Rewrite his sentences, replacing the underlined verbs with
the correct form and tense of **acabar de** as appropriate.
e.g. Yo <u>he cerrado</u> el agua   →   Yo **acabo** de cerrar el agua

El padre consciente
1 Yo <u>he cerrado</u> el agua: José <u>había abierto</u> el grifo antes de salir.
2 Sara y José <u>han llevado</u> las bolsas y botellas de plástico para reciclar.
3 Yo <u>había comprado</u> botellas de vidrio – José se queja porque pesan mucho.
4 Mi mujer <u>ha apagado</u> las luces en los cuartos que los niños <u>habían encendido</u> hace
poco. Es que cuesta mucho la electricidad.
5 <u>Hemos bajado</u> la temperatura de la calefacción, para no gastar energía.
6 Hoy <u>he escrito</u> al periódico para apoyar su campaña de ahorrar energía.

C At a meeting of the Ecology Action Group, some participants are more interested in
looking at the opposite sex than in the issues at hand! Decide whether the comments
you overhear are favourable or unfavourable.

¿Favorable o no?
1 ¡Psst! ¡Miguel, mira la jovencita allí!
2 Ese liderillo me fastidia, ¿sabes?
3 ¡Qué grandota es esa miembro del comité! ¡A la derecha! ¿No ves?
4 El chico que habla ahora – ¡qué talentazo tiene!
5 ¿Has visto el chico detrás de mí? ¡Qué guapetón es!

Help Yourself to Essential Spanish Grammar

UNIT

8

CHAPTER 23   WHAT DO YOU KNOW?

A The company which makes Tamagotchis wrote the following pre-launch article. It describes how the company hopes the toy will prove to be a world-wide craze. Choose the correct verb from the two offered in brackets.

e.g. **llegará** a nuestras tiendas

El Tamagotchi

Dentro de muy poco, (*llegarán/llegará*) a vuestras tiendas un nuevo tipo de juguete – el tamagotchi. El prototipo (*estará*, *estaré*) listo dentro de muy pocos meses, y (*venderán/venderé*) hasta veinte millones de ejemplares sólo dentro del Japón, en nuestro opinión. En la propaganda publicitaria, el tamagotchi mismo (*explicará/explicaré*):

'Yo soy una mascota virtual. (*Podré/Podrás*) vivir muchos años, como los animales domésticos. (*Seré/serás*) como tu amigo o amiga. Tú (*tendrás/tendremos*) que cuidarme y mostrarme cariño – si no, (*moriré/morirá*)'.

B A journalist broods on the appearance of the Spanish health fanatic. Fill in the gaps in his article by choosing the correct word from the list below.

e.g. el **tener** buena salud.

El hombre del siglo veintiuno

Yo no soy – y nunca seré – un hombre del siglo veintiuno. Veo su imagen típica por todas partes. El ... buena salud es su pasión, y ... ejercicio su hobby favorito. Miembro del lobby anti-tabaco, no aguanta el ... en lugares públicos y según él, comprar cigarrillos o cigarros es ... sus pocas pelas[1] a la basura.

fumar   tener   tirar   hacer

Tampoco le gusta ... – ni las bebidas fuertes como el whisky, ni los refrescos inofensivos como la limonada. Y no permite tampoco el pasatiempo favorito de millones de españoles: el ... la tarde del sábado delante de la tele viendo el fútbol. En cuanto a ... gastrónomo ¡ni hablar! El ... es para vivir, y no al revés. Su misión es la misma que los fanáticos religiosos: ... en seres sanos, delgados y (por último) tan tristes como él.

comer   beber   pasar   convertirnos   ser

---

[1] *sus pocas pelas*: the little bit of money that one has.

The future tense

1 The FUTURE TENSE describes what you *will* or *shall* do, or *won't* do in the future:

> *I shall explain* it all in my new book
> *There will be* widespread chaos when the comet hits the Earth
> Many people *won't (will not)* know what has hit them

2 To form the FUTURE TENSE, add the future endings to the whole of the infinitive. Note that the endings are the same for -**ar**, -**er**, and -**ir** verbs:

	-AR trabajar	-ER comer	-IR vivir
yo	trabajar**é**	comer**é**	vivir**é**
tú	trabajar**ás**	comer**ás**	vivir**ás**
él, ella, usted	trabajar**á**	comer**á**	vivir**á**
nosotros	trabajar**emos**	comer**emos**	vivir**emos**
vosotros	trabajar**éis**	comer**éis**	vivir**éis**
ellos, ellas, ustedes	trabajar**arán**	comer**án**	vivir**án**

En el futuro, **trabajaremos** desde casa   *In the future, **we will work** from home*
La gente **comerá** productos biológicos   *People **will eat** organic products*
Vivirán en comunidades pequeñas   *They **will live** in small communities*

3 Some common verbs have irregular stems, but regular endings:

MEANING	INFINITIVE	FUTURE	MEANING	INFINITIVE	FUTURE
to fit (into)	caber	**cabré**	*to wish, want to*	querer	**querré**
to say, tell	decir	**diré**	*to know*	saber	**sabré**
to have/be	haber	**habré**	*to go out*	salir	**saldré**
to do, make	hacer	**haré**	*to have*	tener	**tendré**
to be able to	poder	**podré**	*to be worth*	valer	**valdré**
to put (on)	poner	**pondré**	*to come*	venir	**vendré**

Se lo **diré** a mi padre mañana   *I shall **tell** my father tomorrow*
Habrá inundaciones   *There **will be** floods*
Mis amigos **vendrán** en verano   *My friends **will come** in summer*

4 Compound verbs of **poner** and **tener** – like **componer** (*to compose*) and **detener** (*to stop*) – behave like their 'parent' verbs:

Compondrá un nuevo concierto   *She **will compose** a new concerto*
No la **detendré**   *I will not **stop** her*

5 The future tense is also used when estimating, guessing or supposing:

¡Son las once de la noche! – ¿Dónde **estarán** los chicos?
It's eleven at night! – I wonder where the boys are?
¿Cuántos años tiene el presidente? **Tendrá** unos sesenta y cinco años.
How old is the president? He must be getting on for sixty-five.

Verbal nouns

6 A verbal noun ends in *-ing* in English: *reading, smoking,* and *drinking* are all
examples of verbal nouns. In Spanish, use the infinitive:

Leer te abre otros mundos   *Reading opens up other worlds to you*
Fumar veinte cigarillos es estúpido   *Smoking twenty cigarrettes is stupid*

Put the word **el** (*the*) in front of the infinitive to indicate '*the whole business of ...*' or
'*the concept of ...*':

Odio **el ladrar** de los perros por la noche – me vuelve loca
*I hate **the barking** of dogs at night – it drives me mad*

El fumar en lugares públicos es algo que no aguanto
Smoking in public places is something I can't stand

Again and usually

7 *Again* is often expressed by **otra vez** or **de nuevo**. **De nuevo** often has the meaning
from the beginning/from scratch:

Tengo que hacerlo **otra vez**   *I have to do it **again***
Empezaré **de nuevo** mañana   *I'll start **again** (**from scratch**) tomorrow*

The appropriate part of the verb **volver a** can also be used to express *again*:

Volveré a hacerlo mañana   *I'll do it **again** tomorrow*

8 *Usually* or *used to ...* is frequently expressed using the appropriate part of the verb
soler + infinitive. It is used in the present and imperfect tenses only:

PRESENT	**Suele salir** los viernes	*He usually goes out on Fridays*
IMPERFECT	**Solíamos ir** a Marbella	*We used to go to Marbella*

CHAPTER 23   WHAT HAVE YOU LEARNT?

A Are you optimistic, pessimistic or quietly confident about the state of the world in the first decades of the new millennium? Read the quiz, and put the verbs in brackets in the correct form of the future tense.

e.g. ofrecer → **ofrecerá**

El mundo futuro

El comercio

a Internet (*ofrecer*) nuevas oportunidades para comprar y vender.

b Las compañías internacionales (*dominar*) el comercio mundial.

c Con la crisis en el mercado de dinero, las unidades monetarias europeas no (*valer*) nada.

El trabajo

a La tecnología (*hacer*) posible el pleno empleo.

b (*Poder*) trabajar mucho más desde nuestras casas.

c Sólo los ricos (tener) trabajo – los demás (*vivir*) en la miseria.

El transporte

a Los expertos (*inventar*) una nueva forma de energía barata y limpia.

b El transporte privado no (*ser*) rentable: (*costar*) mucho más que hoy.

c No (*haber*) un sistema de transporte público. Y con la falta de seguridad ciudadana, ni tú ni yo no (*querer*) ir a ningún sitio.

Now do the quiz by ticking the statement which most applies to you in each section and check your results below*.

B In the future, Miki will work from home. Read about his morning and rewrite the sentences, replacing the underlined words with the correct part of **soler** or **volver a**.

e.g. Normalmente, Miki se levanta … → Miki **suele** levantarse …

Una vista al mundo del trabajo

1 Normalmente, Miki se levanta cuando el despertador electrónico lo juzga necesario.

2 El robot-cocinero, por regla general, prepara el desayuno.

3 Por lo general, Miki no lava los platos – el lavavajillas lo hace.

4 Normalmente descarga su correo electrónico primero.

5 Trabajadores como él pasa en general toda la mañana delante del ordenador.

6 A la una, los aparatos-robot hacen la comida otra vez.

7 Miki no trabaja otra vez por la tarde: nadie trabaja más de veinte horas a la semana. Él y sus amigos normalmente salen o van al cine.

*Mayoría de a: eres súper optimista – ¿pero eres realista? Mayoría de b: tienes confianza en el futuro (¡tocando madera!). Mayoría de c: eres muy pesimista – ¿no tienes ninguna fe en el prójimo?

Help Yourself to Essential Spanish Grammar

UNIT

8

CHAPTER 24   WHAT DO YOU KNOW?

A Felipe is enthusiastic about ecological matters and quizzes his parents. Select the
correct alternative from the brackets to complete his questions.

e.g. ¿Mamá, ... el nuevo profesor de ecología?

→   ¿Mamá, **conoces** el nuevo profesor de ecología?

¿Qué sabéis?

1	¿Mamá, ... el nuevo profesor de ecología?	*(conoces/sabes)*
2	Es un señor muy interesante. ... mucho de la ecología.	*(sabe/conoce)*
3	¿... que España está muy atrasada, ecológicamente?	*(conocíais, sabíais)*
4	Yo no ... mucho de todo esto, pero quiero aprender.	*(sé, conozco)*
5	¿... alguna organización en que me pueda inscribir?	*(sabemos, conocemos)*

B Over lunch, Felipe lectures the family and their guest, Señor Gutiérrez, telling them
what they would have to do if he were Minister for Ecology. Complete the gaps in
his sentences with the words from the list below.

e.g. Tú, mamá, ... productos biológicos en envases más ecológicos.

→   Tú, mamá, **utilizarías** productos biológicos en envases más ecológicos.

Si fuera yo Ministro ...

1 Tú, mamá, ... productos biológicos en envases más ecológicos.
2 Dentro de casa, nosotros todos ... mucha energía.
3 Usted, señor, no ... uno de estos cochazos que gastan tanta gasolina.
4 ¡Vosotros dos, mamá y papá, ... menos papel!
5 Mis hermanas ... evitar los aerosoles – hay un montón en el cuarto de baño.
6 ¡Yo, por lo menos, ... de una manera responsable!

  compraría   deberían   actuaría   consumiríais   utilizarías   ahorraríamos

C As Felipe's father heads for the supermarket, he is waylaid by his son who tells him
what not to do when out shopping. Fill in the gaps with the appropriate part of the
verb from the list below.

e.g. no ... la compra ...   →   no **hagas** la compra ...

¡No seas irresponsable!

Papá, cuando vayas al supermercado, no ... la compra de una manera irresponsable.
No ... productos con muchas químicas, no ... cosas en envases de plástico, y no ...
bolsas de plástico – llévate la cesta grande de mamá. En el coche, no ... rápidamente,
porque eso usa mucha gasolina. Si vas a lavar el coche, no ... un lavado de coches
automático – usan demasiada agua. Y por favor, no ... a tu amigo, el Señor
Gutiérrez, a casa para comer – ¡me fastidia este hombre, con sus ideas capitalistas!

  busques   pidas   compres   hagas   elijas   conduzcas   traigas

Help Yourself to Essential Spanish Grammar

Conocer, saber

1 The verb **conocer** means *to know* (*people, places, organisations*). When used with people, remember to use **a** after it:

No **conozco** el norte   *I don't **know** the north*
¿**Conoces a** María Martínez?   ***Do you know** María Martínez?*

For the personal **a**, see p. 52

2 The verb **saber** means *to know* (*facts*), or *to know how to*:

¿Toca la guitarra? ¡lo **sabía** ya!   *He plays the guitar? **I knew** that already!*
No sé nadar   *I don't **know how to** swim*

The conditional tense

3 The CONDITIONAL TENSE describes what you *would* or *would not* do:

> ***I would buy** chemical-free foods*
>
> ***Would you** not **consider** taking a year out from college?*

4 To form the CONDITIONAL TENSE, add the following endings to the whole of the infinitive. Note that the endings are the same for -**ar**, -**er**, and -**ir** verbs:

	-AR trabajar	-ER comer	-IR vivir
yo	trabajar**ía**	comer**ía**	vivir**ía**
tú	trabajar**ías**	comer**ías**	vivir**ías**
él, ella, usted	trabajar**ía**	comer**ía**	vivir**ía**
nosotros	trabajar**íamos**	comer**íamos**	vivir**íamos**
vosotros	trabajar**íais**	comer**íais**	vivir**íais**
ellos, ellas, ustedes	trabajar**ían**	comer**ían**	vivir**ían**

No **trabajaría** nunca en una fábrica   *I would never **work** in a factory*
Comería sólo pollo y pescado   *He would **eat** only chicken and fish*
Viviría en la costa   *I would **live** on the coast*

5 Some common verbs have irregular stems, (formed in the same way as irregular future stems) but regular endings:

Tendrías mas oportunidades allí   *You **would have** more opportunities there*
Los niños **podrían** visitarnos   *The children **would be able to/could** visit us*

For irregular future stems, see p. 104

Help Yourself to Essential Spanish Grammar

6 Note that **quisiera** is often used to express *I would like* instead of the conditional form (**querría**) of **querer** (*to want/wish to*):

   Quisiera saber qué haría usted   *I would like to know what you would do*

Telling someone not to do something

7 The NEGATIVE COMMAND form tells someone NOT to do something. It is formed as follows: take the **yo** form of the present tense, remove the final -**o** and add the following endings:

	-AR	-ER	-IR
	trabajar	comer	vivir
present tense **yo** form → remove the final -**o**	trabaj**o** → trabaj-	com**o** → com-	viv**o** → viv-
tú	no trabaj**es**	no com**as**	no viv**as**
usted	no trabaj**e**	no com**a**	no viv**a**
vosotros	no trabaj**éis**	no com**áis**	no viv**áis**
ustedes	no trabaj**en**	no com**an**	no viv**an**

TÚ	Marta, **¡no comas** tan rápido!	*Marta, don't eat so fast!*
VOSOTROS	¡No **trabajéis** tanto, chicos!	*Don't work so much, lads!*
USTED	¡Señor, **no coma** eso!	*Sir, don't eat that!*
USTEDES	¡Señores – **no trabajen** allí!	*Gentlemen, don't work there!*

8 Verbs which are irregular in the **yo** form, and stem-changing verbs, still follow the same pattern as above in the negative command form. Some examples are:

INFINITIVE		YO	NEGATIVE COMMAND	MEANING
to do	hacer	hago	**¡No haga** eso!	*Don't do that!*
to play	jugar	juego	**¡No juegas** allí!	*Don't play there!*

   For the irregular present tense and stem-changing verbs, see p. 35 and p. 38

9 The following common verbs are irregular in the negative command form:

	IR *to go*	SABER *to know*	SER *to be*	ESTAR *to be*	HABER *to have*	DAR *to give*
tú	**vayas**	**sepas**	**seas**	**estés**	**hayas**	**des**
usted	**vaya**	**sepa**	**sea**	**esté**	**haya**	**dé**
vosotros	**vayáis**	**sepáis**	**seáis**	**estéis**	**hayáis**	**deis**
ustedes	**vayan**	**sepan**	**sean**	**estén**	**hayan**	**den**

Felipe, ¡no **seas** así!   *Felipe, don't be like that!*
Chicas, ¡no me **deis** la lata! *Girls, don't give me any hassle!*

CHAPTER 24　WHAT HAVE YOU LEARNT?

A Celia reads the comments from the company's teleworkers on the noticeboard at work. She mentally rehearses the arguments for and against working from home. Put the underlined verbs into the conditional tense.

e.g. Trabajo desde casa …　→　**Trabajaría** desde casa …

Me imagino que …

1 Trabajo desde casa, pero voy a una oficina central un día a la semana.
2 Me pongo en contacto todos los días con mi jefe o jefa.
3 Me mandan información por medio del correo electrónico.
4 Hago mi trabajo más rápido y mejor.
5 Lo mejor es que estás en casa para los niños.
6 Lo peor es que tienes que organizar el día de otra manera.
7 Puede haber muchas interrupciones: los niños, los vecinos …
8 Hay días cuando no sales. A veces te sientes un poco aislada.

¿Les interesa la posibilidad? Hablen con su gerente.

B Before Christmas, a newspaper runs an article on avoiding the consumerism of recent years, and gives recommendations for parents and children. Put the verbs in brackets into the correct negative command form:

e.g. No (*regalar*) un animal …　→　No **regalen** un animal …

Para una Navidad anti-consumidora

A ustedes, los padres …

1 No (*regalar*) un animal doméstico a su niño: 'adopten' un animal de un zoo.
2 No (*eligir*) un árbol natural: sería mejor comprar un abeto artificial.
3 No (*dar*) mucha importancia a los regalos: ayuden a sus niños a pensar en la bondad de la gente, y no en el dinero que hayan gastado.
4 No (*ir*) a los centros comerciales con sus hijos en los diez días antes de Navidad – ellos necesitan un descanso del bombo publicitario[1].

A vosotros, los niños …

1 No (*dar*) mucho trabajo a vuestros padres – ¡les sobra!
2 No (*ser*) ingratos si no recibís los regalos que queríais.
3 No (*calcular*) el coste de los regalos y no (*hacer*) comparaciones.
4 No (*olvidarse*) de decir 'gracias', o llamar por teléfono, a todos los que os hayan regalado algo.

---

[1] el bombo publicitario: *hype*.

Revision test 22–24

A The account of the lives of young girls sold to witch doctors in parts of Africa has shocked Spain. Read the account of Ketima's life and put the verbs into the pluperfect tense.

e.g. *cometer* → Un miembro masculino de la familia **había cometido** un crimen.

Ketima

1 Un miembro masculino de la familia ... un crimen. *(cometer)*
2 Para evitar una maldición, los padres ... su hija Ketima al brujo. *(entregar)*
3 Ketima ... que trabajar dieciocho horas por día, cuidando la casa. *(tener)*
4 El brujo la ... una de sus esclavas – condenada a un infierno diario. *(hacer)*
5 Abusada, Ketima ... luz[1] a un hijo, cuando tenía sólo doce años. *(dar)*
6 Después de cuatro años, la pobre Ketima ... mala. *(ponerse)*
7 El brujo, que le ... el espíritu, la llevó al desierto cercano. *(romper)*
8 Allí, a solas, sufriendo horriblemente, ... Ketima. *(morir)*

Pero su muerte no ha sido en vano. Hoy en día, misioneros 'compran' a los brujos las niñas vendidas por sus familias, y les ofrecen una nueva vida.

B A British girl is asked what she thinks of the facilities in her holiday resort. Put the English phrases into Spanish. Use the diminutives and augmentatives -**ito**, -**cillo**, -**ucho**, -**ote**, making them agree where necessary.

e.g. IT'S A HORRIBLE LITTLE FLAT! → ¡Es un **pisucho**!

¿Qué opinas?

– ¿No le gusta el piso?
IT'S A HORRIBLE LITTLE FLAT!
– ¿Pero tiene jardín, no?
IT'S A MISERABLE LITTLE GARDEN.

– ¿No le gusta la playa?
IT'S VERY SMALL[2]
– ¿Y el vigilante de la playa?[3]
HE'S REALLY, REALLY NICE!

C To find out what will happen to you next year, select the appropriate verbs from the lists below and put them in the future tense.

e.g. *mejorar* → Tu rendimiento escolar **mejorará** con respecto al ...

Tu horóscopo

Estudios Tu rendimiento escolar ... con respecto al año pasado. En periodo de exámenes ... todo a tu favor, y ... concentrarte en el estudio, aunque durante el resto del año ... por momentos de despiste.

tener   mejorar   pasar   poder

Amor ... un importante dilema – si abres los ojos ... que alguien piensa en ti más de lo normal. Intenta ir paso a paso y te ... bien las cosas. Si no tienes pareja, este año ... tu media naranja.[4]

salir   encontrar   resolver   ver

---

[1] dar luz a: *to give birth to*
[2] chico/a: *small*
[3] el vigilante: *lifeguard*
[4] media naranja: *better half, partner*

Help Yourself to Essential Spanish Grammar

Dinero En la primera mitad del año, te … dinero de los sitios más insospechadas. Cuidado – tus amigos te … dinero y si no se les das, te … sufrir.
Tú no … que hacer: pero familiares te ayudarán.

saber   pedir   llover   hacer

D A South American counsellor on a chat-show gives his views on maintaining good relationships. Put the expressions in English into Spanish.

e.g. LISTENING → **Escuchar** es importante

Las relaciones con los demás
¿Para las buenas relaciones, qué es lo más importante?
 – [LISTENING] es más importante que hablar.
   ¿No es importante [THE CONCEPT OF COMMUNICATING] también?
 – Sí. Pero [THE WHOLE BUSINESS OF TALKING], como medio de comunicación, está sobreestimado. [EXPLAINING] tu punto de vista implica no [PAYING ATTENTION] al otro.
   ¿Qué otras maneras hay de comunicarse?
 – ¡Hay muchas! [SMILING], [LOOKING] compasivo, [TOUCHING] el hombro o la mano – todas estas cosas demuestran tu cariño y tu solicitud.
   ¿[THE WHOLE BUSINESS OF KNOWING] cómo mantener buenas relaciones es muy complejo, entonces?
 – Sí. [GETTING TO KNOW] a otra persona es una aventura sin fin.

E A group of young Spaniards prepare questions on green issues to ask a visiting politician. Put the underlined verbs into the conditional tense.

e.g. Quiero → **Quisiera**

Los políticos y los intereses 'verdes'
1 Quiero saber lo que van ustedes a hacer para el medio ambiente.
2 ¿Qué hace usted para apoyar el movimiento 'verde'?
3 ¿Cómo podemos nosotros, los jóvenes, ayudar?
4 ¿Qué medidas recomienda usted para limpiar nuestras ciudades?
5 ¿Qué dice usted a la crítica que su partido apoya a los empresarios?
6 ¿Cómo contestan los ministros a la acusación de ser indiferente?

F Read the following recommendations for 'shopaholics', and put the underlined words into the negative command form.

e.g. comprar → **No compres**

No debes …
 … comprar a locas – haz una lista, y sólo compra las cosas en tu lista.
 … salir con amigos todos los fines de semana. ¡Ver la tele no cuesta nada!
 … ir, tú y tus amigos, a las boutiques – ¡ellos te animarán a comprar!
 … ser súper generosa y prestar dinero a todo el mundo.
 … estar todo el día en el centro comercial – busca otras cosas que hacer.
 … permitirte más de una hora en un almacén grande.
 … hacer la compra en el supermercado cuando tienes hambre.

Los acontecimientos

Unit 9 contains material which the syllabuses required for those aiming at the very highest grades at GCSE and Standard grade.

You will be expected to understand some of the grammar points in listening and reading tasks in the examination.

Each chapter starts with grammar explanations. Read through them carefully before doing the Practice exercises which follow.

The Revision test at the end of the unit will offer you an opportunity for additional practice.

The subjunctive

1 The SUBJUNCTIVE is a form of the verb which is common in Spanish. It is sometimes described as a *mood*. It is not a tense: it has a number of tenses of its own. The tenses you have learnt so far have all been part of the *indicative mood*.

2 The SUBJUNCTIVE often implies uncertainty: if there is a possibility that an action <u>may not</u> take place, then you need a subjunctive tense. If it is certain that the action has taken place or will take place, then you use a tense from the *indicative mood*. Compare the examples below:

INDICATIVE MOOD	
*Ana **cleans** the car on Tuesdays* *Ana **cleaned** the car on Sunday* *I **want** to clean the car today*	These are facts There is no doubt about them

SUBJUNCTIVE MOOD	
*When Juan **arrives**, he can clean up* *I'm ordering Juan **to do** it* *I also want Juan **to tidy** his room*	Juan might not arrive – I don't know but he might not do it! He might tidy it – but he might not!

The present subjunctive

3 You have already met parts of the PRESENT SUBJUNCTIVE when you learnt the negative command form (p. 109). The PRESENT SUBJUNCTIVE is formed from the **yo** form of the present tense. Remove the final -**o** ending from the present tense and add the following endings to the stem of the verb. You will notice that apart from the *yo* form -**ar** verbs take -**er** verb endings, and -**er/ir** verbs take -**ar** endings:

	-AR	-ER	-IR
present tense **yo** form → remove the final -**o**	trabajar trabaj**o** → trabaj-	comer com**o** → com-	vivir viv**o** → viv-
yo	trabaj**e**	com**a**	viv**a**
tú	trabaj**es**	com**as**	viv**as**
él, ella, usted	trabaj**e**	com**a**	viv**a**
nosotros	trabaj**emos**	com**amos**	viv**amos**
vosotros	trabaj**éis**	com**áis**	viv**áis**
ellos, ellas, ustedes	trabaj**en**	com**an**	viv**an**

e.g. Espero que llegu**en** a tiempo.   *I hope they arrive on time.*
No quiero que salg**as**.   *I don't want you to go out.*
Dudo que ella teng**a** la culpa.   *I doubt that she is to blame.*

4 The following verbs are irregular in the present subjunctive:

	IR *to go*	SABER *to know*	SER *to be*	ESTAR *to be*	HABER *to have*	DAR *to give*
yo	vaya	sepa	sea	esté	haya	dé
tú	vayas	sepas	seas	estés	hayas	dés
él, ella, usted	vaya	sepa	sea	esté	haya	dé
nosotros	vayamos	sepamos	seamos	estemos	hayamos	demos
vosotros	vayáis	sepáis	seáis	estéis	hayáis	deis
ellos, ellas, ustedes	vayan	sepan	sean	estén	hayan	den

For other verbs which are irregular in the present subjunctive see p. 130

The subjunctive with verbs of *telling, ordering, wanting*

5 After verbs of telling, ordering or wanting someone else to do something, use the present subjunctive. In English, we often use the infinitive:

ORDERING	¡Le mando a Juan que lo **haga**! *I'm ordering Juan to do it!*
TELLING	¡Te digo que **termines** los deberes ahora! *I'm telling you to finish your homework now!*
WANTING	Quiero que Juan **recoja** su habitación también *I also want Juan to tidy his room*

6 The list below contains the common verbs of telling, ordering and wanting:

aconsejar*	*to advise*	permitir*	*to permit, allow*
decir	*to tell*	persuadir	*to persuade*
dejar	*to allow*	preferir	*to prefer*
hacer*	*to make, cause*	prohibir	*to forbid*
impedir	*to prevent*	querer	*to want, wish*
insistir (en)	*to insist (that)*	recomendar*	*to recommend*
mandar*	*to order*	rogar	*to request*
pedir	*to ask*	sugerir	*to suggest*

The asterisked verbs above can also be followed by an infinitive instead of **que +** subjunctive. Compare the examples below:

Mi madre no me permite **que vaya**
Mi madre no me permite **ir**   *My mother doesn't allow me to go*

Él me recomienda **estudiar** más
Él me recomienda **que estudie** más   *He recommends me to study more*

CHAPTER 25   PRACTICE

A The mother of Mariluz is anxious about her daughter's proposed trip to the disco in
   her boyfriend's new car. The underlined verbs are in the subjunctive. Give their
   infinitive form.
   e.g. <u>estés</u> → **estar**

En la carretera
1 Insisto en que <u>estés</u> otra vez en casa antes de las doce.
2 Para decir la verdad, Mariluz, prefiero que no <u>vayas</u> con él en el coche.
3 Os ruego que no <u>bebáis</u> alcohol – beber y conducir son incompatibles.
4 No quiero que <u>haya</u> algún accidente.
5 Tampoco quiero que <u>seáis</u> detenidos por la policía.
6 ¡Y prefiero que no <u>déis</u> positivo en la prueba del alcohol!
7 Os aconsejo que <u>tengáis</u> cuidado …

B On the way back from the disco, Mariluz and her boyfriend Roberto are stopped by
   the police. Put the verbs in brackets into the correct form of the subjunctive.
   e.g. (*parar*) Señor, le pido que **pare** el motor.

El momento de la verdad
GUARDIA 1   Señor, le pido que (*parar*) el motor.
GUARDIA 2   Y señora, le ruego que (*bajar*) del coche.
GUARDIA 1   Insisto en que (*someterse*) usted, señor, a la prueba de alcohol.
MARILUZ   Quiero que (*llamar*) ustedes a mi familia. Son las doce ya.
GUARDIA 1   En un momento, señorita. Prefiero que (*hacer*) nosotros la prueba en
            seguida.
GUARDIA 2   Señor, la prueba resulta positiva. Le digo que no (*conducir*) el coche y
            que me (*dar*) usted las llaves.
MARILUZ   ¡Ay, qué vergüenza! Mamá nos va a matar …

C In the police-station, Mariluz and her parents are given advice. Rewrite the
   policeman's comments, using the infinitive instead of the subjunctive.
   e.g. … les aconsejo que lleven a su hija …   →   … les aconseja **llevar** a su hija …

En la comisaría
1 Señores, les aconsejo <u>que lleven</u> a su hija ahora a casa.
2 Le permitimos que <u>pase</u> la noche en casa, pero …
3 … le mando a ella que <u>vuelva</u> aquí mañana para completar su declaración.
4 Les aconsejo que no le <u>hagan</u> muchas preguntas. Está muy cansada.
5 Le recomiendo que no <u>salga</u> con un chico que bebe tanto.
6 Bueno, les permitimos ahora que <u>se vayan</u> a casa. Hasta mañana.

Further uses of the subjunctive

1 The present subjunctive is used after the following phrases. Expressions of time only need the subjunctive when referring to future time:

FUTURE TIME		PURPOSE	
cuando	*when*	**para que**	*so that*
mientras	*while*	**a fin de que**	*in order that*
en cuanto (que)	*as soon as*	**sin que**	*without*
hasta que	*until*	**con tal que**	*provided that*
después (de) que	*after*	**a menos que**	*unless*
antes (de) que	*before*	**aunque**	*even if*

Cuando llegue Juan, puede limpiarlo   *When Juan **arrives**, he can clean it*
Voy a ver la tele **hasta que venga**   *I'm going to watch TV **until** she **comes***
Traeré el coche **para que** lo **vean**   *I'll bring the car **so that** they **can see** it*

2 The subjunctive is also used after verbs of emotion. Common verbs are:

sentir (que)	*to be sorry (that)*
temer (que), **tener miedo** (de que)	*to fear (that), to be afraid (that)*
estar contento / enfadado (de que)	*to be happy/angry (that)*
alegrarse de (que)	*to be pleased (that)*
sorprenderse (que)	*to be surprised (that)*

Siento que no **venga** Paco   *I'm sorry that Paco **isn't coming***
Estoy contento de que **estés** aquí   *I'm glad that **you are** here*

3 The subjunctive is needed with expressions of doubt or uncertainty, possibility, disbelief and necessity. Some examples are:

Dudo que venga Ana	***I doubt** that Ana will come*
Es posible que llegue tarde	***It's possible** that she will arrive late*
No creo que telefonee	***I don't think** she will phone*
Es necesario que coja el avión	***She needs** to catch the plane*

Que, quien(es)

4 The English words *who, which, that,* are expressed by **que** in Spanish:

La señora **que** vive enfrente es inglesa   *The lady **who** lives opposite is English*
La máquina **que** compré no funciona   *The camera **that** I bought doesn't work*

5 After short prepositions like **a** (*to*), **con** (*with*), **de** (*of*), use **que** (meaning *which*) with things/objects:

El asunto a **que** me refiero ...   *The matter **to which** I am referring ...*
Este es el trapo con **que** limpié   *This is the cloth **with which** I cleaned*
El hotel, **del que** te hablé ...   *The hotel, **about which** I told you ...*

6 After short prepositions, use **quien** (*singular*) or **quienes** (*plural*) with people. These are translated as *who, whom* in English:

La chica **a quien** me refiero …	*The girl,* **who** *I am referring to* …
Éste es el señor **con quien** hablé	*This is the man* **with whom** *I spoke*
Los chicos, **de quienes** te hablé …	*The boys,* **about whom** *I told you* …

Para and Por

7 **Para** conveys the idea of *intention/destination/purpose*:

IDEA		
destination	Salimos **para** la discoteca	We set out *for* the disco
intention	La coca-cola es **para** él	The Coca-Cola is *for* him
purpose	Estudia **para** enfermero	He's studying *to be* a nurse
'given that'	Es amable, **para** un guardia	He's kind, *for* a policeman
in order to	Voy allí **para** estudiar	I'm going there *in order to* study
specific future time or date	Estaré listo **para** las nueve Lo quiero **para** mañana	I'll be ready *for* nine o'clock I want it *for* tomorrow

8 **Por** conveys the idea of *through/because of/on behalf of*:

IDEA		
through/along	Siga **por** la calle	*Carry on* **along** *the street*
for/because of	Le admiro **por** su energía	*I admire her* **for** *her energy*
'to get'	Voy abajo **por** leche	*I'm going down* **for** *milk*
by	Fue construido **por** mi padre	*It was built* **by** *my father*
by (means of)	Mándalo **por** fax	*Send it* **by** *fax*
in exchange for	¿Mil libras **por** el reloj?	*A hundred pounds* **for** *the watch?*
per	cien kilómetros **por** hora	*a hundred kilometres* **per** *hour*
as, for	Pasa **por** nativa	*She passes* **as/for** *a native*
indefinite time, duration, place	Viví allí **por** mucho tiempo ¿Hay un banco **por** aquí?	*I lived there* **for** *a long time* *Is there a bank* **around** *here?*

9 In Spanish the phrase **estar para** means *to be about to, to be ready to/for*, and **estar por** means *to be in the mood to, to be inclined to*:

Estoy para la cama	*I'm ready for bed*
No tengo tiempo – **estoy para** salir	*I haven't got time –* *I'm about* *to go out*
¿Estás por salir?	*Are you in a mood to go out?*
No estoy por escuchar excusas	*I don't feel inclined to listen to excuses*

CHAPTER 26   PRACTICE

A Quino believes in UFOs. Decide why the underlined verbs in his sentences are in the
subjunctive. Do they indicate *future time*, *purpose* or *emotion*?
e.g. ... a los seres extraterrestres cuando los <u>vea</u>.   →   **future time**.

Creo en extraterrestres
1   Yo daré la bienvenida a los seres extraterrestres cuando los <u>vea</u>.
2   Vigilo el cielo cada noche para que <u>sea</u> yo el primero en verles.
3   No me sorprende que <u>haya</u> más experiencias de encuentros cercanos.
4   En cuanto <u>lluegue</u> el milenio, habrá más visitas de OVNIs.
5   Me alegro de que <u>visiten</u> la tierra, porque nos hace falta su inteligencia.
6   Nos ayudarán – a menos de que les <u>maten</u> las fuerzas armadas.

B Read about the use and abuse of hypnosis with those who claim to have been
abducted by aliens, and choose the correct word in brackets.
e.g. La hipnosis ha sido utilizada **por** ufólogos ...

La hipnosis
La hipnosis ha sido utilizada (*para/por*) ufólogos[1] como un método (*por/para*) sacar a
la luz la verdad sobre los contactos con extraterrestres. En muchos relatos de
abducción (*por/para*) seres extraños, los abducidos experimentan una investigación.
Algunos cambian esta invasión de su espacio físico y mental (*por/para*) un aumento
en su capacidad intelectual. Pero (*por/para*) otros, la experiencia es desagradable. La
hipnosis la reanima; pero precisamente (*para/por*) esta capacidad de despertar
sentimientos, es peligrosa. No es que las víctimas están (*para/por*) exagerar: pero
(*para/por*) ganar fama, el hipnotizador puede influir en los recuerdos o sugerir cosas
– y estas 'sugerencias' pasan (*por/para*) verdaderas experiencias dentro de un OVNI[2].

C A sceptical researcher has done his own investigations. Insert **que, quien** or **quienes**
into his findings.
e.g. Hipnoticé 16 voluntarios, a **quienes** di la instrucción.

Las abducciones imaginarias
Hipnoticé 16 voluntarios, a ... di la instrucción ... tenían que imaginar una
experiencia de abducción. Una 'víctima de una verdadera abducción', con ... hablé,
describió lo que le pasó. Mi libro, en el ... doy más detalles, explicará ... los dos
tipos de experiencia casi no diferían.

---

[1] ufólogo: *a researcher into UFOs*.
[2] OVNI (– Objeto Volante No Identificado) : *UFO*

Two verb expressions

1 When two verbs are put together, the second one goes into the INFINITIVE. The following verbs are all followed by the INFINITIVE. The second one is often translated in English with *to*…:

deber	*must, ought to*	**poder**	*to be able to*
decidir	*to decide to*	**querer**	*to want to*
esperar	*to hope to*	**saber**	*to know how to*
necesitar	*to need to*	**tener que**	*to have to*

Debo llamar a casa   *I must/ought to ring* home
Ella espera ver a Fernando allí   *She hopes to see* Fernando there

2 Verbs of *liking*, *preferring* and *hating* are also used with the INFINITIVE. In English, the second verb often ends in *-ing*:

Me gusta **bailar**   *I like dancing*
Prefiero **leer**   *I prefer reading*
Odio **patinar**   *I hate skating*

3 Some two-verb expressions are linked by a PREPOSITION. e.g. **a, de, en, con, por**.
   a The following common verbs are linked to the infinitive by **a**:

aprender a	*to learn to*	**invitar a**	*to invite to*
ayudar a	*to help to*	**ir a**	*to be going to*
decidirse a	*to decide to*	**pararse a**	*to stop to*
empezar a	*to begin to*	**ponerse a**	*to begin to*
enseñar a	*to teach to*	**volver a**	*to return, to .. again*

For a more detailed list of verbs and their prepositions see Section 5 in the Appendix, p. 147.

aprendo a nadar   *I'm learning to* swim
empezó a trabajar en junio   *he started working* in June

   b The following common verbs are linked to the infinitive by **de**:

acordarse de	*to remember to*	**olvidarse de**	*to forget to*
alegrarse de	*to be pleased to*	**parar de**	*to stop -ing*
cansarse de	*to get tired -ing*	**terminar de**	*to finish -ing*
dejar de	*to stop -ing*	**tratar de**	*to try to*

me acordé de reservar un asiento   *I remembered to reserve a seat*
¡**deja de** fastidiar a tu hermano!   *stop annoying your brother!*

c   The following verbs are linked by **con**, **en**, **por**:

amenezar con	*to threaten to/with*	**pensar en**	*to think of -ing*
soñar con	*to dream of -ing*	**tardar en**	*to take a long time -ing*
insistir en	*to insist on*	**empezar por**	*to begin by*
interesarse en/por	*to be interested in*	**terminar por**	*to end up -ing*

Le **amenazó con** decírselo a su padre   ***He threatened to*** *tell her father*
Me intereso en viajar   ***I'm interested in travelling***
Empezó por explicar el tema   ***She began by explaining*** *the theme*

Cuyo – whose

4   **Cuyo** is equivalent to the English word *whose*. Being an adjective, it agrees in number and gender with the noun which follows it:

la señora, **cuyo padre** conozco   *the lady,* ***whose father*** *I know*
Miguel, **cuya hija** vive cerca   *Michael,* ***whose daughter*** *lives nearby*
el chico, **cuyos amigos** odio   *the boy,* ***whose friends*** *I hate*
Felipe, **cuyas maletas** tengo aquí   *Felipe,* ***whose suitcases*** *I have here*

El cual – which

5   After longer prepositions (like **delante de**, **encima de**, **alrededor de**), the word in Spanish for *which* is **el cual**, **la cual**, **los cuales**, or **las cuales**:

el día durante **el cual** se murió mi abuelo, pasó lentamente
the day during ***which*** *my grandfather died, passed slowly*
¿ves **la** tienda, delante de **la cual** está la parada de autobuses?
do you see the shop, ***which*** *has the bus-stop in front of it?*
los pisos, encima de **los cuales** hay un restaurante, son caros
the flats, on top of ***which*** *there is a restaurant, are expensive*
las casas, alrededor de **las cuales** hay jardines preciosos, cuestan un dineral
the houses, around ***which*** *there are lovely gardens, cost a fortune*

Note that **de** in front of **el cual**, becomes **del cual**:

el museo, detrás **del cual** vivo yo   *the museum, behind* ***which*** *I live*

CHAPTER 27   PRACTICE

A   The Sunday supplement contains a series of humorous definitions. Insert the correct part of **cuyo** before the underlined words.

e.g. **cuyo** <u>tamaño</u>

Antología del disparate

El diamante: piedra preciosa, <u>tamaño</u> depende de su precio.
Gobierno: manera de arreglar las cosas, <u>formas</u> principales son dos – buenas y malas.
Examen: tres horas de tortura legal, <u>intención</u> es demostrar la ignorancia.
Profesor: figura decorativa en un aula, <u>rostro</u> se parece al humano.
Deberes: el poner de tareas imaginarias, <u>función</u> es tranquilizar a los padres.
Día escolar: período interminable, <u>minutos</u> son dos veces más largos que durante las vacaciones.

B   Match up correctly the two halves of the 'Stages of Man' which appeared in a school magazine.

e.g. 1 El bebé empieza ... d por salir con la suya[1]

Las etapas de la vida

1 El bebé empieza ...	a con ser adulto
2 El niño insiste ...	b niño otra vez
3 El adolescente sueña ...	c en ir a lo suyo[2]
4 El adulto se cansa ...	d por salir con la suya[1]
5 El anciano quiere ser ...	e de ser adulto

C   A Madrid newspaper reports a worrying phenomenon. Insert **el cual**, **del cual**, **de la cual**, **de los cuales** or **de las cuales** correctly in the gaps.

e.g. hablamos de los *skins*, detrás **de los cuales**

Los skins[3]

Hoy, hablamos de los *skins*, detrás ... andan adolescentes de sólo 14 años, atraídos por el halo de misterio y terror que inspiran. Tribu urbana, delante ... el público tiembla de miedo, sus miembros inician una campaña de terror en Castellón. Las plazas centrales, alrededor ... se reunen grupos antagonistas, ya son zonas prohibidas para la mayoría de la población. La violencia del mes pasado – durante ... murieron once jóvenes inocentes – se extiende más allá de Barcelona y Madrid. El odio tradicional (entre los *skins* y los homosexuales), ... hablaremos más tarde, sigue provocando las agresiones.

---

[1] Salir con la suya: *to get one's own way*

[2] Ir a lo suyo: *to do one's own thing*

[3] Los skins: *skin-heads*

Help Yourself to Essential French Grammar

The imperfect subjunctive

1 The imperfect subjunctive is formed as follows. Take the **ellos/ellas** form of the preterite tense (e.g. **trabajaron**), remove the ending -**ron**, then add either of the following sets of endings:

yo	**-ra**	**-se**
tú	**-ras**	**-ses**
él, ellas, usted	**-ra**	**-se**
nosotros	**-ramos**	**-semos**
vosotros	**-rais**	**-seis**
ellos, ellas, ustedes	**-ran**	**-sen**

Examples:

PRETERITE **ellos** FORM	REMOVE **-ron**	IMPERFECT SUBJUNCTIVE	
trabajaron	trabaja-	yo	**trabajara/trabajase**
comieron	comi-	nosotros	**comiéramos/comiésemos**
vivieron	vivie-	ellos	**vivieran/viviesen**

See p. 72 and p. 76 for the formation of the preterite tense

2 The imperfect subjunctive is needed where the subjunctive mood is required (e.g. after verbs of telling, ordering, wanting, verbs of emotion and after **cuando** in certain circumstances) and where the first verb is in the imperfect, the preterite or the conditional tense:

MAIN/FIRST VERB		IMPERFECT SUBJUNCTIVE VERB
IMPERFECT	yo **quería** *I wanted*	que Raúl **saliese** conmigo *Raúl to go out with me*
PRETERITE	mi padre me dijo *my father told me*	que no le **viera** más *not to see him again*
CONDITIONAL	tú no permitirías *you would not allow*	que **viniera** Raúl a la casa, ¿no? *Raúl to come to the house, would you?*

For a more detailed explanation of when the subjunctive mood is required, see p. 114
and p. 117

The passive

3 In THE PASSIVE, an action is done *to* someone or something *by* someone or something else. These examples, in English, will help you:

PASSIVE	ACTIVE
John **was hit by** the car.	*The car hit John.*
He **is being taken** to hospital **by** the doctor.	*The doctor is taking him to hospital.*
The card **will be signed by** the whole class.	*The whole class will sign the card.*

4 Although *by* often appears in PASSIVE sentences, it is not always necessary:

> *the house **was built** very quickly, and the firm **was sued** for damages*

5 You will notice that the passive is made up of two things in English: part of the verb *to be* (e.g. *was, is being, will be*) and the past participle (*hit, taken, signed*). The same, in the appropriate tense, is true in Spanish:

	PART OF *TO BE*	PAST PARTICIPLE
Juan	**fue**	**atropellado**
Juan	*was*	*knocked down*
la tarjeta	**será**	**firmado**
the card	*will be*	*signed*

6 Note that the past participle behaves like an adjective and agrees in number and gender with the noun to which it refers:

> **el** dinero fue robad**o**   **los** árboles fueron plantad**os**
> **la** casa fue construíd**a**   **las** flores fueron cogid**as**

7 The two verbs *to be* in Spanish – **ser** and **estar** – are both used with the passive. Use **ser** to indicate an action which is completed, and **estar** to describe the state or condition which results from that action. Study the following examples,

SER + PART PARTICIPLE (*action*)	ESTAR + PAST PARTICIPLE (*state*)
casas **son destruidas** cada día	las casas **están destruidas** y vacías
*homes **are destroyed** every day*	*the houses **are destroyed** and empty*
el instituto nuevo **fue abierto** ayer	el instituto **estuvo abierto** todo el verano
*the new school **was opened** yesterday*	*the school **was open** all summer*

8 **Por** is used in Spanish where English uses *by*:

> las casas son destruidas **por** las tropas   *the houses are destroyed **by** the troops*

9 The passive can be replaced by the **se** form of the verb

Las casas son destruidas por las tropas	las tropas destruyen las casas

see p.44 for the forms of se.

Help Yourself to Essential Spanish Grammar

CHAPTER 28   PRACTICE

A Read the article about Luisa and her possible involvment in drugs. Put the verbs in
brackets in the correct form of the present or imperfect subjunctive as required.
e.g. La policía trata el caso como si (*ser*) un accidente … → La policía trata el
caso como si **fuera/fuese** un accidente …

Luisa y la droga
Hace varios meses, la jovencita Luisa murió: cayó entre dos vagones de metro. La
policía trata el caso como si (*ser*) un accidente, pero la madre quiere que (*investigar*)
los hechos. "En mi opinión, fue relacionado con la droga", dice. "Mi hija pertenecía a
un grupo que tomaba drogas y a veces parecía como si (*estar*) despistada, y no sabía
lo que hacía. El líder es el culpable, en mi opinión: mandó a mi hija que (*ponerse*) a
robar cosas, y que (*buscar*) a otros para ayudarle. Luisa temía que los lideres la
(*matar*). Le pidió a un amigo que se uniese/se uniera con el grupo para que ella
(*poder*) seguir viviendo". La madre de Luisa tiene dos mensajes. A los padres de
jóvenes que viven así dice: 'Díganles que (*abandonar*) la droga y que (*volver*) a casa.
Y a los jóvenes dice "Un compañero o una compañera que se mete en la droga está
en peligro. Os recomiendo que (*hablar*) con los padres de vuestro amigo o amiga. Es
necesario que los padres (*saber*) en que están metidos sus hijos".

B Abandoned tourist complexes in Menorca are being demolished, and public green
spaces created in their place. Read the story of Cala Blanca and put the sentences into
the passive.
e.g. Una compañía alemana construyó el complejo turístico … → El complejo
turísto fue construído por una compañía alemana …

La demolición de 21 apartamentos en Cala Blanca
1 Una compañía alemana construyó el complejo turístico hace diez años.
2 Vendió la propiedad a una compañia británica poco después.
3 El dueño actual abandonó los edificios hace tres años.
4 La Consellería de Turismo inició las actuaciones de '**esponjamiento**'.
5 El año pasado, derribaron tres de los bloques.
6 El Ayuntamiento recuperó un solar de 1.500 metros.
7 Terminaron la construcción de un parque público la semana pasada.

Revision test 25–28

A Andrés answers his fussing parents as they wait for the arrival of his friends who are taking him on a week's snowboarding course. Put the verbs in brackets into the correct part of the present tense, using the subjunctive if necessary.
e.g. Cuando yo pract**ico** el snowboard…

El pobre Andrés

1 Cuando yo (*practicar*) el snowboard, ¡siempre llevo la ropa adecuada, Mamá!
2 Vale – en cuanto (*venir*) Paco, él te mostrará el equipo[1].
3 Os ruego que no me (*llamar*) por teléfono cada noche.
4 ¿Por qué? ¡Porque los demás me toman el pelo[2] y no quiero que lo (*hacer*)!
5 Claro que os mandaré una postal. Siempre os escribo cuando (*estar*) fuera.
6 Sí, me pondré una crema de sol. ¡Aunque no (*salir*) el sol, me la pondré!
7 ¡Mamá, por favor – no me (*dar*) más consejos! ¡Ah, ya viene Paco!
8 Bueno, me alegro de que (*estar*) aquí, Paco. ¿Nos vamos ya?
9 Mamá, ¡insisto en que (*quedarse*) aquí! No necesito besos, abrazos y lágrimas delante de los demás. Bueno, adiós …

B A group of students explain why they have been advised not to go straight to university. Answer the questions, using the infinitive to avoid the subjunctive.
e.g. ¿Qué mandan a Gabriel sus padres? Sus padres le mandan …
   → Sus padres le mandan **ganar** dinero …

Nos aconsejan …

Gabriel	Mis padres mandan que gane dinero, porque ellos no quieren pagarlo todo.
Ronaldo	Mis resultados hacen imprescindible que repita el año.
Conchi	Me aconseja mi padre que no vaya a la universidad en seguida.
Pili	Las autoridades permiten que pospongamos el ingreso en la universidad.
Moustapha	Mi madre recomienda que trabaje o viaje durante un año, antes de estudiar.
Carolina	Nuestros profesores aconsejan que vivamos un tiempo, o temporada en el extranjero.

1 ¿Qué mandan a Gabriel sus padres? Sus padres le mandan …
2 ¿Qué pasa con Ronaldo? Sus resultados hacen imprescindible …
3 ¿Qué aconseja el padre de Conchi? Le aconseja …
4 A los estudiantes como Pili, ¿qué permiten las autoridades? Les permiten …
5 ¿Qué recomienda la madre de Moustapha? Le recomienda …
6 ¿Qué aconsejan a Carolina sus profes? Le aconsejan …

---

[1] el equipo: *the equipment*
[2] tomar el pelo a uno: *to take the mickey*

Help Yourself to Spanish Grammar

C Don Quijote is one of the most famous figures in Spanish literature. Read about him below, and insert in the gaps the correct part of **que**, **quien**, **el cual** or **cuyo**. Remember to make them agree where necessary.
e.g. La Mancha, **que** es un territorio…

Don Quijote

La Mancha, … es un territorio de la parte central de España, está unida al nombre de Don Quijote, … aventuras son ya cosas de leyenda. El autor del libro, Cervantes, a … tantos admiran por su perspicacia y su ironía, describe lo que pasa a un señor … pierde el juicio a causa de dormir poco y leer demasiados libros de caballería. En la Plaza de España de Madrid está su estatua, al lado … aparece su fiel escudero, Sancho Panza. La aventura de los molinos de viento, … confundió Don Quijote con gigantes y con … quería luchar, sigue siendo la más famosa de las historias.

D Cruz is spending a few days with her friend, Eva. Read their conversation as they prepare to go out, and insert the correct Spanish word in the gaps.
e.g. ¿A qué hora salimos **para** el centro comercial?

Cruz y el fax

CRUZ	¿A qué hora salimos … el centro comercial?	[FOR]
EVA	¿Si estamos listos … las diez y media?	[FOR]
CRUZ	Vale. Oye, quiero mandar esta carta … fax.	[BY]
	¿Hay una oficina … allí donde me lo harían?	[AROUND]
EVA	Sí. Pero es caro. … mandar un fax, te costará	[IN ORDER TO]
	unas ochocientas pesetas. ¿Es … hoy?	[FOR]
CRUZ	Sí, es urgente. ¡Pero ochocientas … un fax!	[FOR]
EVA	Pues, mira. Voy abajo … café. Si quieres, voy	[TO GET]
	a casa de mi amiga al lado. Ella te lo hará.	
CRUZ	¡Estupendo! Muchas gracias … tu ayuda.	[FOR]

E The elderly Señora Aguirre is determined to go out, in spite of the objections of her niece. Put the phrases in brackets into Spanish:
e.g. I'VE DECIDED TO GO OUT   →   **He decidido salir/Me he decidido a salir**

Cosa de ancianas

NURIA ¿Qué haces, tía? ¿Por qué te pones el abrigo?
SRA.   [I'VE DECIDED TO GO OUT].
NURIA Pero, ¿adónde vas? ¡Son las cinco de la tarde!
SRA.   Voy a un merienda-baile. [I LOVE DANCING].
NURIA ¡Pero no puedes ir sola!
SRA.   ¿Dónde está el teléfono? [I OUGHT TO CALL A TAXI].
NURIA ¡Pero no vas a conocer a nadie!
SRA.   Conozco a Federico. [I HOPE TO SEE HIM THERE].
NURIA Pero, tía, siéntate. Me parece que ponen una buena película …
SRA.   ¡[I HATE WATCHING TV]! ¡Es cosa de ancianas! Bueno, me voy.

F Señor Iturbide talks about the difficulties of caring for his wife, who has Alzheimer's disease. Insert **a**, **de**, **con**, **en**, **por** or nothing, as necessary.

e.g. A veces, se olvida … cuidarse   →   A veces, se olvida **de** cuidarse

Mi mujer tiene la enfermedad de Alzheimer

A veces, se olvida … cuidarse de sí misma, y yo necesito … cuidarla físicamente. Muchas veces insiste … hacer cosas que, físicamente, son muy difíciles. Empieza … vestirse, por ejemplo, pero termina … no poder hacerlo. Tarda mucho … hacer cosas que antes hacía rápidamente. Deja … hacer cosas de repente sin darse cuenta de los peligros – por ejemplo, no se acuerda … que haya encendido el gas en la cocina. Se decide … salir a horas imprevistas, o piensa … acostarse a las diez de la mañana, porque no sabe qué hora es. Puede amenazarme … violencia porque no me reconoce, y porque se siente frustrada y no entiende por qué. Pero es mi mujer, y quiero… ayudarla. Trato … ser positivo, y optimista, pero no es fácil.

Help Yourself to Essential Spanish Grammar

Appendices

1 A quick reference guide to tenses in the verb tables

The present tense
It explains what happens or is happening now. In English, examples are *I go*, *I am going*, *I do go*.

The present participle
The part of the verb which ends in *-ing* in English: *sleeping*, *reading*, and *eating* are all present participles. It is also used with the present and imperfect tenses of the verb **estar** in Spanish to form the PRESENT CONTINUOUS TENSE (p. 67) and the IMPERFECT CONTINUOUS (p. 94).

The past participle
The part of the verb which often ends in *-ed* or *-en* in English: *waited*, *chosen*, and *fixed* are all past participles. It is also used with the present and imperfect tenses of the verb **haber** to form the PERFECT TENSE (p. 86) and the PLUPERFECT TENSE (p. 100).

The preterite tense
It explains what happened, indicating actions which have finished and are no longer happening. Equivalent examples in English are *I went*, *she bought* and *we saw*.

The imperfect tense
It explains what was happening, or used to happen over a period of time. In English, examples are *he was cooking* or *she used to run*.

The positive command form
This tells someone what to do: *hurry up!*, *run!* and *start!* are all positive commands in English.

The negative command form
This tells someone what NOT to do: *don't hurry!*, *don't run!* and *don't start!* are all negative command forms.

The future tense
It explains what *will* or *shall* happen: examples in English are *I shall go*, *it will rain* and *we will swim*.

The conditional tense
It explains what *would* happen: examples in English are *I would like*, *I would go*, *I would have*.

The present subjunctive
This is a form of the present tense which is used after certain verbs: see p. 114. It has no direct equivalent in English.

2 Verb tables

INFINITIVE PRESENT PARTICIPLE PAST PARTICIPLE		PRESENT	PRETERITE	IMPERFECT

a Regular verbs ending in -ar, -er, -ir

hablar *to speak or talk* hablando hablado	yo tú él, ella, Ud. nosotros vosotros ellos, ellas, Uds.	hablo hablas habla hablamos habláis hablan	hablé hablaste habló hablamos hablasteis hablaron	hablaba hablabas hablaba hablábamos hablabais hablaban
comer *to eat* comiendo comido	yo tú él, ella, Ud. nosotros vosotros ellos, ellas, Uds.	como comes come comemos coméis comen	comí comiste comió comimos comisteis comieron	comía comías comía comíamos comíais comían
vivir *to live* viviendo vivido	yo tú él, ella, Ud. nosotros vosotros ellos, ellas, Uds.	vivo vives vive vivimos vivís viven	viví viviste vivió vivimos vivisteis vivieron	vivía vivías vivía vivíamos vivíais vivían

b Irregular verbs

andar *to walk, to go* andando andado	yo tú él, ella, Ud. nosotros vosotros ellos, ellas, Uds.	ando andas anda andamos andáis andan	anduve anduviste anduvo anduvimos anduvisteis anduvieron	andaba andabas andaba andábamos andabais andaban
caber *to fit* cabiendo cabido	yo tú él, ella, Ud. nosotros vosotros ellos, ellas, Uds.	quepo cabes cabe cabemos cabéis caben	cupe cupiste cupo cupimos cupisteis cupieron	cabía cabías cabía cabíamos cabíais cabían
caer *to fall* cayendo caído	yo tú él, ella, Ud. nosotros vosotros ellos, ellas, Uds.	caigo caes cae caemos caéis caen	caí caíste cayó caímos caísteis cayeron	caía caías caía caíamos caíais caían

POSITIVE COMMANDS	NEGATIVE COMMANDS	FUTURE	CONDITIONAL	PRESENT SUBJUNCTIVE
		hablaré	hablaría	hable
habla	no hables	hablarás	hablarías	hables
hable	no hable	hablará	hablaría	hable
		hablaremos	hablaríamos	hablemos
hablad	no habléis	hablaréis	hablaríais	habléis
hablen	no hablen	hablarán	hablarían	hablen
		comeré	comería	coma
come	no comas	comerás	comerías	comas
coma	no coma	comerá	comería	coma
		comeremos	comeríamos	comamos
comed	no comáis	comeréis	comeríais	comáis
coman	no coman	comerán	comerían	coman
		viviré	viviría	viva
vive	no vivas	vivirás	vivirías	vivas
viva	no viva	vivirá	viviría	viva
		viviremos	viviríamos	vivamos
vivid	no viváis	viviréis	viviríais	viváis
vivan	no vivan	vivirán	vivirían	vivan
		andaré	andaría	ande
anda	no andes	andarás	andarías	andes
ande	no ande	andará	andaría	ande
		andaremos	andaríamos	andemos
andad	no andéis	andaréis	andaríais	andéis
anden	no anden	andarán	andarían	anden
		cabré	cabría	quepa
cabe	no quepas	cabrás	cabrías	quepas
quepa	no quepa	cabrá	cabría	quepa
		cabremos	cabríamos	quepamos
cabed	no quepáis	cabréis	cabríais	quepáis
quepan	no quepan	cabrán	cabrían	quepan
		caeré	caería	caiga
cae	no caigas	caerás	caerías	caigas
caiga	no caiga	caerá	caería	caiga
		caeremos	caeríamos	caigamos
caed	no caigáis	caeréis	caeríais	caigáis
caigan	no caigan	caerán	caerían	caigan

INFINITIVE PRESENT PARTICIPLE PAST PARTICIPLE		PRESENT	PRETERITE	IMPERFECT
conocer *to know* *to get to know* conociendo conocido	yo tú él, ella, Ud. nosotros vosotros ellos, ellas, Uds.	conozco conoces conoce conocemos conocéis conocen	conocí conociste conoció conocimos conocisteis conocieron	conocía conocías conocía conocíamos conocíais conocían
dar *to give* dando dado	yo tú él, ella, Ud. nosotros vosotros ellos, ellas, Uds.	doy das da damos dais dan	di diste dio dimos disteis dieron	daba dabas daba dábamos dabais daban
decir *to say, tell* diciendo dicho	yo tú él, ella, Ud. nosotros vosotros ellos, ellas, Uds.	digo dices dice decimos decís dicen	dije dijiste dijo dijimos dijisteis dijeron	decía decías decía decíamos decíais decían

divertir(se) (*to enjoy oneself*): see **preferir**

INFINITIVE		PRESENT	PRETERITE	IMPERFECT
dormir *to sleep* durmiendo dormido	yo tú él, ella, Ud. nosotros vosotros ellos, ellas, Uds.	duermo duermes duerme dormimos dormís duermen	dormí dormiste durmío dormimos dormisteis durmieron	dormía dormías dormía dormíamos dormíais dormían
estar *to be* estando estado	yo tú él, ella, Ud. nosotros vosotros ellos, ellas, Uds.	estoy estás está estamos estáis están	estuve estuviste estuvo estuvimos estuvisteis estuvieron	estaba estabas estaba estábamos estabais estaban
haber *to have (with past participle only)* habiendo habido	yo tú él, ella, Ud. nosotros vosotros ellos, ellas, Uds.	he has ha hemos habéis han	hube hubiste hubo hubimos hubisteis hubieron	había habías había habíamos habíais habían

POSITIVE COMMANDS	NEGATIVE COMMANDS	FUTURE	CONDITIONAL	PRESENT SUBJUNCTIVE
		conoceré	conocería	conozca
conoce	no conozcas	conocerás	conocería	conozcas
conozca	no conozca	conocerá	conocería	conoczca
		conoceremos	conoceríamos	conozcamos
conoced	no conozcáis	conoceréis	conoceríais	conozcáis
conozcan	no conozcan	conocerán	conocerían	conozcan
		daré	daría	dé
da	no des	darás	daría	des
dé	no dé	dará	daría	dé
		daremos	daríamos	demos
dad	no deis	daréis	daríais	deis
den	no den	darán	darían	den
		diré	diría	diga
di	no digas	dirás	dirías	digas
diga	no diga	dirá	diría	diga
		diremos	diríamos	digamos
decid	no digáis	diréis	diríais	digáis
digan	no digan	dirán	dirían	digan

POSITIVE COMMANDS	NEGATIVE COMMANDS	FUTURE	CONDITIONAL	PRESENT SUBJUNCTIVE
		dormiré	dormirías	duerma
duerme	no duermas	dormirás	dormirías	duermas
duerma	no duerma	dormirá	dormiría	duerma
		dormiremos	dormiríamos	durmamos
dormid	no durmáis	dormiréis	dormiríais	durmáis
duerman	no duerman	dormirán	dormirían	duerman
		estaré	estaría	esté
está	no estés	estarás	estarías	estés
esté	no esté	estará	estaría	esté
		estaremos	estaríamos	estemos
estad	no estéis	estaréis	estaríais	estéis
estén	no estén	estarán	estarían	estén
		habré	habría	haya
		habrás	habría	hayas
not used	*not used*	habrá	habría	haya
		habremos	habríamos	hayamos
		habréis	habríais	hayáis
		habrán	habrían	hayan

INFINITIVE PRESENT PARTICIPLE PAST PARTICIPLE		PRESENT	PRETERITE	IMPERFECT
hacer *to do, make* haciendo hecho	yo tú él, ella, Ud. nosotros vosotros ellos, ellas, Uds.	hago haces hace hacemos hacéis hacen	hice hiciste hizo hicimos hicisteis hicieron	hacía hacías hacía hacíamos hacíais hacían
ir *to go* yendo ido	yo tú él, ella, Ud. nosotros vosotros ellos, ellas, Uds.	voy vas va vamos vais van	fui fuiste fue fuimos fuisteis fueron	iba ibas iba íbamos ibais iban
jugar *to play* jugando jugado	yo tú él, ella, Ud. nosotros vosotros ellos, ellas, Uds.	juego juegas juega jugamos jugáis juegan	jugué jugaste jugó jugamos jugasteis jugaron	jugaba jugabas jugaba jugábamos jugabais jugaban
oír *to hear* oyendo oído	yo tú él, ella, Ud. nosotros vosotros ellos, ellas, Uds.	oigo oyes oye oímos oís oyen	oí oíste oyó oímos oísteis oyeron	oía oías oía oíamos oíais oían
poder *to be able to* pudiendo podido	yo tú él, ella, Ud. nosotros vosotros ellos, ellas, Uds.	puedo puedes puede podemos podéis pueden	pude pudiste pudo pudimos pudisteis pudieron	podía podías podía podíamos podíais podían
poner *to put, set, lay* poniendo puesto	yo tú él, ella, Ud. nosotros vosotros ellos, ellas, Uds.	pongo pones pone ponemos ponéis ponen	puse pusiste puso pusimos pusisteis pusieron	ponía ponías ponía poníamos poníais ponían

Help Yourself to Essential Spanish Grammar

POSITIVE COMMANDS	NEGATIVE COMMANDS	FUTURE	CONDITIONAL	PRESENT SUBJUNCTIVE
		haré	haría	haga
haz	no hagas	harás	harías	hagas
haga	no haga	hará	haría	haga
		haremos	haríamos	hagamos
haced	no hagáis	haréis	haríais	hagáis
hagan	no hagan	harán	harían	hagan
		iré	iría	vaya
ve	no vayas	irás	irías	vayas
vaya	no vaya	irá	iría	vaya
		iremos	iríamos	vayamos
id	no vayáis	iréis	iríais	vayáis
vayan	no vayan	irán	irían	vayan
		jugaré	jugaría	juegue
juega	no juegues	jugarás	jugarías	juegues
juegue	no juegue	jugará	jugaría	juegue
		jugaremos	jugaríamos	juguemos
jugad	no juguéis	jugaréis	jugaríais	juguéis
jueguen	no juegen	jugarán	jugarían	jueguen
		oiré	oiría	oiga
oye	no oigas	oirás	oirías	oigas
oiga	no oiga	oirá	oiría	oiga
		oiremos	oiríamos	oigamos
oíd	no oigáis	oiréis	oiríais	oigáis
oigan	no oigan	oirán	oirían	oigan
		podré	podría	pueda
		podrás	podrías	puedas
not used	*not used*	podrá	podría	pueda
		podremos	podríamos	podamos
		podréis	podríais	podáis
		podrán	podrían	puedan
		pondré	pondría	ponga
pon	no pongas	pondrás	pondrías	pongas
ponga	no ponga	pondrá	pondría	ponga
		pondremos	pondríamos	pongamos
poned	no pongáis	pondréis	pondríais	pongáis
pongan	no pongan	pondrán	pondrían	pongan

INFINITIVE PRESENT PARTICIPLE PAST PARTICIPLE		PRESENT	PRETERITE	IMPERFECT
preferir to prefer prefiriendo preferido	yo tú él, ella, Ud. nosotros vosotros ellos, ellas, Uds.	prefiero prefieres prefiere preferimos preferís prefieren	preferí preferiste prefirió preferimos preferisteis prefirieron	prefería preferías prefería preferíamos preferíais preferían
querer to want, wish to queriendo querido	yo tú él, ella, Ud. nosotros vosotros ellos, ellas, Uds.	quiero quieres quiere queremos queréis quieren	quise quisiste quiso quisimos quisisteis quisieron	quería querías quería queríamos queríais querían
saber to know sabiendo sabido	yo tú él, ella, Ud. nosotros vosotros ellos, ellas, Uds.	sé sabes sabe sabemos sabéis saben	supe supiste supo supimos supisteis supieron	sabía sabías sabía sabíamos sabíais sabían
salir to go out saliendo salido	yo tú él, ella, Ud. nosotros vosotros ellos, ellas, Uds.	salgo sales sale salimos salís salen	salí saliste salió salimos salisteis salieron	salía salías salía salíamos salíais salían
ser to be siendo sido	yo tú él, ella, Ud. nosotros vosotros ellos, ellas, Uds.	soy eres es somos sois son	fui fuiste fue fuimos fuisteis fueron	era eras era éramos erais eran
tener to have teniendo tenido	yo tú él, ella, Ud. nosotros vosotros ellos, ellas, Uds.	tengo tienes tiene tenemos tenéis tienen	tuve tuviste tuvo tuvimos tuvisteis tuvieron	tenía tenías tenía teníamos teníais tenían

POSITIVE COMMANDS	NEGATIVE COMMANDS	FUTURE	CONDITIONAL	PRESENT SUBJUNCTIVE
		preferiré	preferiría	prefiera
prefiere	no prefieras	preferirás	preferirías	prefieras
prefiera	no prefiera	preferirá	preferiría	prefiera
		preferiremos	preferiríamos	prefiramos
preferid	no prefiráis	preferiréis	preferiríais	prefiráis
prefieran	no prefieran	preferirán	preferirían	prefieran
		querré	querría	quiera
quiere	no quieras	querrás	querrías	quieras
quiera	no quiera	querrá	querría	quiera
		querremos	querríamos	queramos
quered	no queráis	querréis	querríais	queráis
quieran	no quieran	querrán	querrían	quieran
		sabré	sabría	sepa
sabe	no sepas	sabrás	sabrías	sepas
sepa	no sepa	sabrá	sabría	sepa
		sabremos	sabríamos	sepamos
sabed	no sepáis	sabréis	sabríais	sepáis
sepan	no sepan	sabrán	sabrían	sepan
		saldré	saldría	salga
sal	no salgas	saldrás	saldrías	salgas
salga	no salga	saldrá	saldría	salga
		saldremos	saldríamos	salgamos
salid	no salgáis	saldréis	saldríais	salgáis
salgan	no salgan	saldrán	saldrían	salgan
		seré	sería	sea
sé	no seas	serás	serías	seas
sea	no sea	será	sería	sea
		seremos	seríamos	seamos
sed	no seáis	seréis	seríais	seáis
sean	no sean	serán	serían	sean
		tendré	tendría	tenga
ten	no tengas	tendrás	tendrías	tengas
tenga	no tenga	tendrá	tendría	tenga
		tendremos	tendríamos	tengamos
tened	no tengáis	tendréis	tendríais	tengáis
tengan	no tengan	tendrán	tendrían	tengan

Help Yourself to Essential Spanish Grammar

INFINITIVE PRESENT PARTICIPLE PAST PARTICIPLE		PRESENT	PRETERITE	IMPERFECT
traer *to bring* trayendo traído	yo tú él, ella, Ud. nosotros vosotros ellos, ellas, Uds.	traigo traes trae traemos traéis traen	traje trajiste trajo trajimos trajisteis trajeron	traía traías traía traíamos traíais traían
valer *to be worth* valiendo valido	yo tú él, ella, Ud. nosotros vosotros ellos, ellas, Uds.	valgo vales vale valemos valéis valen	valí valiste valió valimos valisteis valieron	valía valías valía valíamos valíais valían
venir *to come* viniendo venido	yo tú él, ella, Ud. nosotros vosotros ellos, ellas, Uds.	vengo vienes viene venimos venís vienen	vine viniste vino vinimos vinisteis vinieron	venía venías venía veníamos veníais venían
ver *to see* viendo visto	yo tú él, ella, Ud. nosotros vosotros ellos, ellas, Uds.	veo ves ve vemos veis ven	vi viste vio vimos visteis vieron	veía veías veía veíamos veíais veían
volver *to return* volviendo vuelto	yo tú él, ella, Ud. nosotros vosotros ellos, ellas, Uds.	vuelvo vuelves vuelve volvemos volvéis vuelven	volví volviste volvió volvimos volvisteis volvieron	volvía volvías volvía volvíamos volvíais volvían

(**devolver** (*to return*), **resolver** (*to resolver*), **envolver** (*to wrap up*): like **volver**)

POSITIVE COMMANDS	NEGATIVE COMMANDS	FUTURE	CONDITIONAL	PRESENT SUBJUNCTIVE
		traeré	traería	traiga
trae	no traigas	traerás	traerías	traigas
traiga	no traiga	traerá	traería	traiga
		traeremos	traeríamos	traigamos
traed	no traigáis	traeréis	traeríais	traigáis
traigan	no traigan	traerán	traerían	traigan
		valdré	valdría	valga
val	no valgas	valdrás	valdrías	valgas
valga	no valga	valdrá	valdría	valga
		valdremos	valdríamos	valgamos
valed	no valgáis	valdréis	valdríais	valgáis
valgan	no valgan	valdrán	valdrían	valgan
		vendré	vendría	venga
ven	no vengas	vendrás	vendrías	vengas
venga	no venga	vendrá	vendría	venga
		vendremos	vendríamos	vengamos
venid	no vengáis	vendréis	vendríais	vengáis
vengan	no vengan	vendrán	vendrían	vengan
		veré	vería	vea
ve	no veas	verás	verías	veas
vea	no vea	verá	vería	vea
		veremos	veríamos	veamos
ved	no veáis	veréis	veríais	veáis
vean	no vean	verán	verían	vean
		volveré	volvería	vuelva
vuelve	no vuelvas	volverás	volverías	vuelvas
vuelva	no vuelva	volverá	volvería	vuelva
		volveremos	volveríamos	volvamos
volved	no volváis	volveréis	volveríais	volváis
vuelvan	no vuelvan	volverán	volverían	vuelvan

c Regular stem-changing verbs

INFINITIVE		PRESENT	PRETERITE	IMPERFECT
PRESENT PARTICIPLE				
PAST PARTICIPLE				

e > ie

cerrar	yo	cierro	cerré	cerraba
to close	tú	cierras	cerraste	cerrabas
	él, ella, Ud.	cierra	cerró	cerraba
cerrando	nosotros	cerramos	cerramos	cerrábamos
cerrado	vosotros	cerráis	cerrasteis	cerrabais
	ellos, ellas, Uds.	cierran	cerraron	cerraban

Similar verbs: comenzar   *to begin*   helar   *to freeze*
              despertar(se)   *to wake up*   merendar   *to have an afternoon snack*
              empezar   *to begin*   negar   *to deny*

e >i

servir	yo	sirvo	serví	servía
to serve	tú	sirves	serviste	servías
	él, ella, Ud.	sirve	sirvió	servía
sirviendo	nosotros	servimos	servimos	servíamos
servido	vosotros	servís	servisteis	servíais
	ellos, ellas, Uds.	sirven	sirvieron	servían

Similar verbs: competir   *to compete*   repetir   *to repeat*
              despedir(se)   *to say good-bye*   pedir   *to ask for*
              impedir   *to prevent*   vestir(se)   *to get dressed*

o >ue

probar	yo	pruebo	probé	probaba
to try	tú	pruebas	probaste	probabas
	él, ella, Ud.	prueba	probó	probaba
probando	nosotros	probamos	probamos	probábamos
probado	vosotros	probáis	probasteis	probabais
	ellos, ellas, Uds.	prueban	probaron	probaban

Similar verbs: acordar(se)   *to remember*   aprobar   *to pass (exams)/to approve*
              acostar(se)   *to go to bed*   contar   *to count, tell*
              almorzar   *to have lunch*   costar   *to cost*

u >ue

The only common verb in this group is **jugar** (*to play*). Since it also has other changes, as well as the stem-change, you will find it in full under 'Irregular verbs' on page 134.

The following stem-changing verbs also have other irregular parts. You will find them, in full, in the section 'Irregular verbs' p. 130:

dormir (*to sleep*); **morir** (*to die*); **poder** (*to be able to*); **preferir** (*to prefer*); **querer** (*to wish to, to want to*); **volver** (*to return*)

POSITIVE COMMANDS	NEGATIVE COMMANDS	FUTURE	CONDITIONAL	PRESENT SUBJUNCTIVE
		cerraré	cerraría	cierre
cierra	no cierres	cerrarás	cerrarías	cierres
cierre	no cierre	cerrará	cerraría	cierre
		cerraremos	cerraríamos	cerremos
cerrad	no cerréis	cerraréis	cerraríais	cerréis
cierren	no cierren	cerrarán	cerrarían	cierren

recomendar   *to recommend*   encender   *to light, switch on*
sentar(se)   *to sit down*   entender   *to understand*
                             perder   *to lose*

		serviré	serviría	sirva
sirve	no sirvas	servirás	servirías	sirvas
sirva	no sirva	servirá	serviría	sirva
		serviremos	serviríamos	sirvamos
servid	no sirváis	serviréis	serviríais	sirváis
sirven	no sirvan	servirán	servirían	sirvan

		probaré	probaría	pruebe
prueba	no pruebes	probarás	probarías	pruebes
prueba	no pruebe	probará	probaría	pruebe
		probaremos	probaríamos	probemos
probad	no probéis	probaréis	probaríais	probéis
prueban	no prueben	probarán	probarían	prueben

encontrar   *to find*   mover   *to move*
mostrar   *to show*   soñar   *to dream*

3 Special uses of certain verbs

The following verbs are used in special ways.

1 Caer, caer bien/mal

Caer means *to fall*. **Caer bien** means *to seem nice*; **caer mal** is *not to seem nice*:

¡cuidado, el cuadro va a **caer**!	*watch out, the picture is going **to fall**!*
me **cae bien**, ese chico	*I **like** that boy/**he seems nice** to me*
me **cae mal**, tu amigo nuevo	*I **don't like** your new friend*

2 Dar

The verb **dar** (*to give*) is used in a number of expressions: **dar un paseo** (*to go for a walk*), **dar a** (*to open onto*), **dar con** (*to run into, to bump into*), **dar de** (*to give food or drink to*), and **dar por** (*to think, to consider*) and many more:

doy un paseo	*I'm going for a walk*
da a la calle	*it opens onto the street*
di con él ayer	*I bumped into him yesterday*
le **di de** comer	*I gave him something to eat*
le **di por** muerto	*I gave him up for dead*

Note also the following colloquial expressions:

¿qué más da?	*what difference does it make? so?*
me da lo mismo/me da igual	*it's all the same to me, I don't mind*

3 Dejar, dejar de

The verb **dejar** means *to leave*, and **dejar de** means *to stop* or *to fail* (*to do something*):

dejé mi monedero en el taxi	*I left my purse in the taxi*
dejé de fumar hace poco	*I stopped smoking a while ago*
dejé de hacer mis deberes	*I failed to do my homework*

4 Ir, irse

The verb **ir** means *to go* to a particular place; **irse** means *to go away* or *to be off*:

voy a la piscina	*I'm going to the swimming pool*
me **voy** – ¡adiós!	*I'm off – goodbye!*

5 Jugar, tocar

To play a game or sport is **jugar**. *To play* an instrument is **tocar**:

juego al tenis   *I play tennis*
toco la guitarra   *I play the guitar*

6 Llegar de/a

Llegar de means *to arrive from*, and **llegar a** is *to arrive at*. On its own, **llegar** also has the meaning *to reach*. **Llegar a** followed by an infinitive means *to manage to* or *to become*:

el tren **llega de** Burgos a las dos   *the train **arrives from** Burgos at two*
¿a qué hora **llega a** Miranda?   *when **does it arrive at** Miranda?*
esta cuerda no **llega**   *this piece of rope doesn't **reach***
un día **llegaré a ser** la directora   *one day **I'll manage/get to be** the director*

7 Llevar, llevarse bien/mal

Llevar, on its own, means *to wear*, *to carry* or *to take*. When followed by the present participle, it means *have been -ing*. **Llevarse bien/mal (con)** is *to get on well/badly (with)*.

¿qué **llevas** a la fiesta?   *what **are you wearing** to the party?*
no puedo **llevar** esa maleta   *I can't **carry** that suitcase*
te **llevo** a la estación, si quieres   *I'll **take** you to the station, if you like*
llevo dos años **viviendo** en Madrid   *I **have been living** in Madrid for two years*
se **lleva bien** con mis padres   *he **gets on well** with my parents*
me **llevo** muy **mal** con ella   *I **get on** very **badly** with her*

8 Pasar, pasarlo bien/mal

Pasar means both *to happen* and *to spend* (*time*). **Pasarlo bien/mal** is *to have a good/bad time*:

¿qué **pasa** aquí?   *what's **happening/going on** here?*
paso dos horas al día estudiando   *I **spend** two hours a day studying*
¿**lo pasaste bien**?   *did you **have a good time**?*
lo pasamos muy **bien**   *we **had a** really **good time***

It can also means *to pass* – **pásame** la sal.

9 Pensar en/pensar de

Both **pensar en** and **pensar de** mean *to think about*. **Pensar de** is often used to indicate opinion, and **pensar en** suggests thinking deeply about something:

pienso en mis próximas vacaciones   *I'm **thinking about** going on my next holiday*
¿qué **piensas de** eso?   *what do you **think about** that?*
   *what's **your opinion of** that?*

10 Poner, ponerse, ponerse a

Poner means *to put*; it can also mean *to switch on* or *turn on*. **Ponerse** means *to put on* or *wear*, and can also mean to *become* (*without wishing to*). **Ponerse a** means *to start*:

pon la leche en el frigorífico	**put** the milk in the fridge
pon la radio, si quieres	**turn** the radio on, if you want
¿qué **te pones** para ir a la fiesta?	what **are you wearing** to the party?
¿por qué **te pones** rojo?	why **are you going** red?
cada vez que le veo **me pongo a** reír	every time I see him, **I start** to laugh

11 Quedar(se), quedar en, con

Both **quedar** and **quedarse** mean *to stay, to remain*. **Quedar** can also mean *to have …* *left*. **Quedar en** and **quedar con** mean *to agree to/about, to arrange*:

quedé dos semanas	**I stayed** two weeks
¿dónde **te quedas**?	where **are you staying**?
sólo **me quedan** cien pesetas	**I have** only a hundred pesetas **left**
¿**quedamos en** eso, entonces?	**are we agreed about** that then?
¿**en** qué **quedamos**?	**what's the arrangement**?
quedé con Manuel a las ocho	**I arranged** with Manuel for us to meet at eight

12 Servir para, servir de, servirse de

Servir para and **servir de** both mean *to be of use as/for* or *to serve as*. **Servirse de** means *to make use of* or *help oneself to*:

no **sirve para** nada	it's no **use for** anything
sirve de mesa	it's **used as** a table/it **serves as** a table
¿usted quiere **servirse de** algo?	would you like to **help yourself to** something?

13 Tener, tener que ver

Common expressions with **tener** can be found on p. 161. Other uses include the following: **tener** can mean *to be the matter with*; **tener que ver** means *to have to do with*:

¿qué **tiene** ella?	what **is the matter with** her?
no **tiene** nada **que ver** contigo	**it has** nothing **to do** with you

14 Volver, devolver

Volver means to *return* or *to come back*; **devolver** means *to return* or *to give back*:

¿a qué hora **vuelves**?	what time **are you coming back**?
¿me **devuelves** las llaves?	can you **give** me **back** the keys?

4 List of common reflexive verbs

See section 10.1, p. 44, on forming and using reflexive verbs.

abrocharse	*to fasten*
aburrirse	*to be bored*
acercarse	*to draw near to*
acordarse (de)	*to remember (about)*
acostarse	*to go to bed*
afeitarse	*to shave*
agotarse	*to exhaust oneself*
ahogarse	*to drown*
alegrarse (de)	*to be pleased (about)*
alejarse (de)	*to move away (from)*
alojarse (en)	*to stay (in)*
arreglarse	*to tidy oneself up*
asomarse (de)	*to lean out (of)*
asustarse	*to be frightened*
atreverse (a)	*to dare to*
bañarse	*to have a bath, to bathe (in sea or pool)*
caerse	*to fall (down)*
callarse	*to be quiet*
cansarse (de)	*to tire (of), get tired (of)*
casarse (con)	*to get married (to)*
cepillarse	*to brush oneself*
cortarse	*to cut oneself*
cuidarse	*to look after onself*
darse cuenta (de que)	*to realise*
darse prisa	*to hurry up*
defenderse (en)	*to defend, to manage, to keep going*
despedirse (de)	*to say goodbye (to)*
despertarse	*to waken up*
dirigirse (a)	*to go towards*
divertirse	*to enjoy oneself*
divorciarse	*to get divorced*
dormirse	*to fall asleep*
ducharse	*to have a shower*
enamorarse	*to fall in love with*
encontrarse	*to be situated, to find oneself, to meet*
enfadarse	*to get angry*
entenderse bien/mal (con)	*to get on well/badly with*
entretenerse	*to be entertained*
equivocarse	*to make a mistake, to be wrong*
esconderse	*to hide*
ganarse la vida	*to earn one's living*

Help Yourself to Essential French Grammar

interesarse (en)	*to be interested in*
hacerse	*to become*
hacerse daño	*to hurt oneself*
hallarse = encontrarse	*to find (oneself)*
informarse	*to find out, to get information*
irse	*to go away, to go off*
lavarse	*to wash*
lavarse los dientes	*to brush one's teeth*
levantarse	*to get up, stand up*
limpiarse los dientes	*to clean one's teeth*
llamarse	*to be called*
llevarse bien (con)	*to get on well (with)*
maquillarse	*to put on make-up*
mejorarse	*to get better, to improve*
mojarse	*to get wet*
moverse	*to move*
pararse	*to stop*
pasearse	*to go for a stroll*
peinarse	*to brush or comb one's hair*
ponerse	*to put on (clothes), to start to*
ponerse en camino	*to set out*
presentarse	*to introduce oneself, to apply for (a job)*
preguntarse	*to wonder*
preocuparse (de)	*to be worried (about)*
probarse	*to try on*
quedarse (en)	*to stay (in)*
quejarse (de)	*to complain (about)*
quemarse	*to burn oneself*
quitarse (la ropa)	*to take off (one's clothes)*
romperse	*to break (one's leg, arm etc.)*
sentarse	*to sit down*
sentirse (mal)	*to feel (ill)*
servirse (a)	*to help oneself (to)*
verse	*to see each other*
vestirse	*to get dressed*

Help Yourself to Essential Spanish Grammar

5 Verbs with prepositions

Some verbs are followed by a preposition linking them to a noun or pronoun. These are listed below.

Verbs which are followed by a preposition linking them to another verb are explained on page 120.

a These verbs are followed by prepositions in English, but not in Spanish:

buscar	*to look for*
escuchar	*to listen to*
esperar	*to wait for*
mirar	*to look at*
pagar	*to pay for*
pedir	*to ask for*

b The following verbs are followed by **a**:

acercarse a	*to approach*
asistir a	*to be present at*
jugar a	*to play*
oler a	*to smell of*
parecerse a	*to look like*
quitar a	*to take away from*
robar a	*to steal from*
saber a	*to taste of*
subir a	*to get on (a train, bus)*
tomar a uno por	*to take someone for*

c The following verbs are followed by **de**:

acordarse de	*to remember (about)*
bajar de	*to get off (a train, bus)*
cambiar de	*to change (train, bus)*
depender de	*to depend on*
despedirse de	*to say goodbye to*
pensar de	*to think of (opinion)*
quejarse de	*to complain*
reírse de	*to laugh at/about*
salir de	*to leave (a place)*

6 Stress and accents

It is worth learning the rules for stress and accents. Once you know them, you will be able to pronounce new words correctly, and will understand where to write accents.

a STRESS means the natural emphasis we put on part of a word. The letters in bold in the English examples below show where the normal stress falls:

dictionary **exer**cise **pen**cil

b In the examples above, you can see that the stress falls on the first part of the word, or on the first SYLLABLE. Words have one or more syllables:

1 syllable	book
2 syllables	pen - cil
3 syllables	ex - er - cise
4 syllables	dic - tion - ar - y

c In Spanish, the normal rules for stress are:

WORD ENDING IN ...	a vowel, -n, -s	a consonant (except -n, -s)
STRESS FALLS ON ...	next to last syllable	last syllable
EXAMPLES	a**mi**go, naran**ja**da, ana**li**zan, disco**te**cas	borra**dor**, ciu**dad**, pa**pel**, princi**pal**, ar**roz**

d Where there are two vowels together, the following rules apply:

  i The vowels **a**, **e**, **o** are called strong vowels. Pronounce each one separately, as if they are two syllables, and stress the first one:

  le-o **fe**-a ja-**le**-o

  ii The vowels **i**, **u** are called weak vowels. Run their sounds together to make one syllable, and stress the sound of the second one:

  fu**i**-mos ru**i**-do

  iii Where a strong and a weak vowel come together, run their sounds together to make one syllable and stress the sound of the strong one:

  oi-ga a-**cei**-te **ai**-re

e Where a word is not pronounced according to the normal rules of stress above, then you need an accent above a letter. An accent tells you to stress that letter or syllable:

má-qui-na an-**dén** con-ti-**nú**-a fru-te-**rí**-a **lá**-piz

f There are some common words which have different meanings with and without accents. In these cases the accent does not indicate stress, but meaning:

de	*of*	**dé**	*give (command)*
el	*the*	**él**	*he*
mi	*my*	**mí**	*me*
si	*if*	**sí**	*yes*
tu	*your*	**tú**	*you*
te	*you*	**té**	*tea*
solo	*alone*	**sólo**	*only*

7 Word order

There are some differences between Spanish and English word order:

a The person or thing doing the action in a sentence is called THE SUBJECT. In the example below, THE SUBJECT is my boyfriend and **rings** is the verb.
In English THE SUBJECT comes before the verb:

*My boyfriend **rings** me every day*

b In Spanish, it can be the other way round: the verb may come *before* THE SUBJECT. Compare the two Spanish versions below with the example above:

VERB BEFORE SUBJECT	me **llama** mi novio todos los días
SUBJECT BEFORE VERB	mi novio me **llama** todos los días

c The same applies whether THE SUBJECT is a person or thing. Look at the two possible Spanish versions below of the sentence '*the train arrived very late*':

VERB BEFORE SUBJECT	**llegó** muy tarde el tren
SUBJECT BEFORE VERB	el tren **llegó** muy tarde

d After direct speech, the verb always comes before THE SUBJECT:

– ¿Qué me dices? – **preguntó** Juan a su hermana
*'What are you telling me?' Juan **asked** his sister*

8 Prepositions

a Common, shorter, prepositions are listed below:

a	*to, at (see also p. 30)*
de	*from, of (see also p. 11)*
con	*with*
contra	*against*
desde	*from*
durante	*during*
en	*in, at (see also p. 35)*
entre	*between*
hacia	*about (time)*
hasta	*as far as, until*
para	*for (see also p. 118)*
por	*along, by (see also p. 118)*
tras	*behind, after, across, beyond*

b The following prepositions are followed by **de**. See p. 11 for further explanations and uses:

a la derecha de	*on the right of*
a la izquierda de	*on the left of*
al lado de	*next to, beside*
al final de	*at the end of*
al fondo de	*at the bottom of*
alrededor de	*around*
a través de	*across*
cerca de	*near (to)*
debajo de	*below, under*
detrás de	*behind*
delante de	*in front of*
dentro de	*inside*
encima de	*on top of, above*
enfrente de	*opposite*
en medio de	*in the middle of*
fuera de	*out (of)*
lejos de	*far (from)*

9 Useful linking words (conjunctions)

Linking words, or CONJUNCTIONS, are used to link two sentences, or parts of a sentence, together.

a   You should be familiar with the following common conjunctions:

donde	*where*
no sólo ... sino también	*not only ... but also*
o/u	*or (see p. 81)*
pero/sino	*but (see p. 73)*
si	*if*
sin embargo	*however*
y/e	*and (see p. 81)*

b   Here is a list of useful common conjunctions used to describe *when* something happens:

al (+infinitive)	*on (-ing)*
al musmo tiempo que	*at the same time as*
antes de	*before*
aunque	*although*
como	*as, since*
cuando*	*when, whenever*
desde que	*since*
después de	*after*
en cuanto*	*as soon as*
luego	*then*
mientras*	*while, whereas*
todas las veces	*whenever*

c   Here are some common conjunctions used to describe *why* something happens:

a causa de	*because of*
debido a	*due to, owing to*
por/con motivo de	*because of, owing to*
porque	*because*
puesto que	*given that, because*
ya que	*given that, because*

---

*After these conjunctions, the verb – in certain circumstances – needs the subjunctive: see p. 117

Help Yourself to Essential Spanish Grammar

10 Countries, regions and continents

Here is a list of countries, continents and regions of Spain.

a Countries:

Most countries are feminine and singular in Spanish. Those marked (*m*) are masculine, and those marked (*pl*) are plural.

In addition, it is usual with some countries to put **el**, **la**, **los** or **las** in front when talking about them: this is indicated before the relevant country:

Alemania	*Germany*
Argentina	*Argentina*
América	*America**
Australia	*Australia*
Austria	*Austria*
Bélgica	*Belgium*
el Brasil (*m*)	*Brazil*
Bolivia	*Bolivia*
el Canadá (*m*)	*Canada*
Chile (*m*)	*Chile*
China	*China*
Colombia	*Colombia*
Dinamarca	*Denmark*
el Ecuador (*m*)	*Ecuador*
Escocia	*Scotland*
España	*Spain*
los Estados Unidos (*m*) (*pl*)	*United States of America*
Francia	*France*
Gales (*m*)	*Wales*
Gran Bretaña	*Great Britain*
Grecia	*Greece*
Holanda	*Holland*
la India	*India*
Inglaterra	*England*
Irlanda del Norte	*Northern Ireland*
Irlanda del Sur	*Southern Ireland, Eire*
Italia	*Italy*
el Japón (*m*)	*Japan*
Luxemburgo (*m*)	*Luxembourg*
Marruecos (*m*)	*Morocco*
Méjico (*m*)	*Mexico*
Noruega	*Norway*
Nueva Zelanda	*New Zealand*
Pakistán (*m*)	*Pakistan*

*Depending on the context, it may mean North America, South America, or the whole continent.

Help Yourself to Essential Spanish Grammar

el Paraguay (*m*)	*Paraguay*
el Perú (*m*)	*Peru*
Portugal (*m*)	*Portugal*
el Reino Unido (*m*)	*United Kingdom*
Rusia	*Russia*
Suecia	*Sweden*
Suiza	*Switzerland*
Tunicia	*Tunisia*
el Uruguay (*m*)	*Uruguay*
Venezuela	*Venezuela*

b Continents:

África	*Africa*
América del Norte	*North America*
América del Sur	*South America*
Antillas (*pl*)	*West Indies*
Asia	*Asia*
Australasia	*Australasia*
Europa	*Europe*

c Some regions of Spain:

Andalucía	*Andalusia*
Castilla	*Castille*
Cataluña	*Cataluña*
Ceuta y Melilla	*Ceuta and Meilla**
Galicia	*Galicia*
el País Vasco (*m*)	*the Basque country*
Islas Baleares (*pl*)	*Balearic Islands***
Islas Canarias (*pl*)	*Canary Islands*

* Ceuta and Melilla are Spanish provinces on the tip of North Africa and are part of Spain.
** These islands comprise Mallorca, Menorca, Ibiza and Formentera.

Help Yourself to Essential Spanish Grammar

11 Numbers
Numbers 1–1000

0	cero	40	cuarenta	80	ochenta	
1	uno	41	cuarenta y uno	82	ochenta y uno	
2	dos	42	cuarenta y dos	82	ochenta y dos	
3	tres	43	cuarenta y tres	83	ochenta y tres	
4	cuatro	44	cuarenta y cuatro	84	ochenta y cuatro	
5	cinco	45	cuarenta y cinco	85	ochenta y cinco	
6	seis	46	cuarenta y seis	86	ochenta y seis	
7	siete	47	cuarenta y siete	87	ochenta y siete	
8	ocho	48	cuarenta y ocho	88	ochenta y ocho	
9	nueve	49	cuarenta y nueve	89	ochenta y nueve	
10	diez	50	cincuenta	90	noventa	
11	once	51	cincuenta y uno	91	noventa y uno	
12	doce	52	cincuenta y dos	92	noventa y dos	
13	trece	53	cincuenta y tres	93	noventa y tres	
14	catorce	54	cincuenta y cuatro	94	noventa y cuatro	
15	quince	55	cincuenta y cinco	95	noventa y cinco	
16	dieciséis	56	cincuenta y seis	96	noventa y seis	
17	diecisiete	57	cincuenta y siete	97	noventa y siete	
18	dieciocho	58	cincuenta y ocho	98	noventa y ocho	
19	diecinueve	59	cincuenta y nueve	99	noventa y nueve	
20	veinte	60	sesenta			
21	veintiuno	61	sesenta y uno			
22	veintidós	62	sesenta y dos			
23	veintitrés	63	sesenta y tres			
24	veinticuatro	64	sesenta y cuatro			
25	veinticinco	65	sesenta y cinco			
26	veintiséis	66	sesenta y seis			
27	veintisiete	67	sesenta y siete			
28	veintiocho	68	sesenta y ocho			
29	veintinueve	69	sesenta y nueve			
30	treinta	70	setenta	100	cien/cientos*	
31	treinta y uno	71	setenta y uno	200	doscientos	
32	treinta y dos	72	setenta y dos	300	trescientos	
33	treinta y tres	73	setenta y tres	400	cuatrocientos	
34	treinta y cuatro	74	setenta y cuatro	500	quinientos	
35	treinta y cinco	75	setenta y cinco	600	seiscientos	
36	treinta y seis	76	setenta y seis	700	setecientos	
37	treinta y siete	77	setenta y siete	800	ochocientos	
38	treinta y ocho	78	setenta y ocho	900	novecientos	
39	treinta y nueve	79	setenta y nueve	1000	mil	

*Notes

The number 100 on its own is **cien**. Followed by another number, it becomes **ciento**.

Note the different position in Spanish of the word **y** (*and*) in larger numbers: ciento treinta **y** uno: *a hundred **and** thirty-one*

Numbers 1000–1,000,000

2000	dos mil	8000	ocho mil
3000	tres mil	9000	nueve mil
4000	cuatro mil	10.000	diez mil
5000	cinco mil	100.000	cien mil
6000	seis mil	1.000.000	un millón
7000	siete mil	2.000.000	dos millones *etc.*

Note that to divide a larger number clearly, Spanish uses a full-stop where English uses a comma:

Spanish	English
10.000	10,000
350.000	350,000

Spanish uses a comma in decimals where English uses a point:

Spanish	English
3,75	3.75
6,5	6.5

12 Years

After the date 1000, years are expressed in terms of *thousands* (**mil**) rather than hundreds, as in English:

742	setecientos cuarenta y dos	*seven hundred and forty-two*
1910	**mil novecientos** diez	**nineteen hundred** *and ten*

Others expressions related to date are as follows:

a. de J.C (antes de Jesucristo)	*B.C.*
d. de J.C (después de Jesucristo)	*A.D.*
en el siglo diez	*in the tenth century*
durante los años 80	*in/during the 80s*
en el año 1980 y tantos	*in 1980 something*

13 Telling the time
a On the hour:

¿qué hora es?	*what time is it?*
es la una	*it's one o'clock*
son las dos/tres etc.	*it's two/three o'clock etc.*

b Use **medianoche** and **mediodía** to express midnight or midday:

es medianoche	*it's midnight*
es mediodía	*it's midday*

c How to express *a quarter past, half past, a quarter to*:

es la una y cuarto	*it's a quarter past one*
son las dos y media	*it's half past two*
son las tres menos cuarto	*it's a quarter to three*
son las cuatro y cuarto	*it's a quarter past four*

See chapters 8 and 10, p. 35 and p. 44 for further details on talking about the time.

14 Useful expressions of time
The list below contains useful expressions of time:

¿qué hora es?	*what's the time*
¿tienes hora?	*have you got the time?*
yo tengo (las ocho veinte)	*I make it (twenty past eight)*
son un poco más de las (siete)	*it's a little after (seven)*
es (la una) y pico	*it's a little after (one)*
serán (las diez)	*it'll be about (ten)*
a eso de (las cinco)	*about (five)*
en punto	*on the dot*
a las (diez) a más tardar	*by (ten) at the latest*
desde (las dos) hasta (las cuatro)	*from (two) until/till (four)*
entre (la una) y (las dos)	*between (one) and (two)*
antes del mediodía	*before midday*
después del medianoche	*after midnight*

15 The 24-hour clock

Telling the time by the 24-four hour clock is more common in Spanish than in English:

1 h	la una	la una de la madrugada	*1 a.m.*
2 h	las dos	las dos de la madrugada	*2 a.m.*
3 h	las tres	las tres de la madrugada	*3 a.m.*
4 h	las cuatro	las cuatro de la madrugada	*4 a.m.*
5 h	las cinco	las cinco de la mañana	*5 a.m.*
6 h	las seis	las seis de la mañana	*6 a.m.*
7 h	las siete	las siete de la mañana	*7 a.m.*
8 h	las ocho	las ocho de la mañana	*8 a.m.*
9 h	las nueve	las nueve de la mañana	*9 a.m.*
10 h	las diez	las diez de la mañana	*10 a.m.*
11 h	las once	las once de la mañana	*11 a.m.*
12 h	las doce	las doce del mediodía	*12 p.m.*
13 h	las trece	la una de la tarde	*1 p.m.*
14 h	las catorce	las dos de la tarde	*2 p.m.*
15 h	las quince	las tres de la tarde	*3 p.m.*
16 h	las dieciséis	las cuatro de la tarde	*4 p.m.*
17 h	las diecisiete	las cinco de la tarde	*5 p.m.*
18 h	las dieciocho	las seis de la tarde	*6 p.m.*
19 h	las diecinueve	las siete de la tarde	*7 p.m.*
20 h	las veinte	las ocho de la tarde	*8 p.m.*
21 h	las veintiuno	las nueve de la tarde	*9 p.m.*
22 h	las veintidós	las diez de la tarde	*10 p.m.*
23 h	las veintitrés	las once de la tarde	*11 p.m.*
00 h	medianoche	las doce del medianoche	*12 a.m.*

More examples:

8.15	las ocho quince
14.30	las catorce treinta
19.45	las diecinueve cuarenta y cinco

16 False friends

These are words which can mislead us since they seem the same in both languages, but are not:

	actual	*present-day, current, up-to-date*
	asistir (a)	*to be present at, to attend*
un	**autocar**	*coach*
un	**bigote**	*a moustache*
un	**caramelo**	*a sweet, a toffee*
un	**casco**	*a helmet*
una	**cava**	*a wine-cellar, a sparkling wine*
	comprensivo	*understanding, sympathetic*
un	**conductor**	*a driver*
	constipado	*full of the cold, having a cold*
un	**disco**	*a record*
una	**droguería**	*a chemist's*
	embarazada	*pregnant*
	emocionante	*exciting*
una	**fábrica**	*a factory*
el	**footing**	*jogging*
	genial	*brilliant, like a genius*
una	**goma**	*an eraser, a rubber*
	grave	*serious*
una	**moneda**	*coin*
	largo	*long*
	particular	*private*
un	**retrete**	*a toilet*
	sensible	*sensitive*
	simpático	*nice, likeable*

17 Expressions with **por**

The common expressions below all use **por**:

gracias por	*thank you for*
por aquí	*around here*
por completo	*completely*
por correo electrónico	*by e-mail*
por día	*per day*
por Dios	*for goodness' sake*
por ejemplo	*for example*
por eso	*for that reason*
por favor	*please*
por fax	*by fax*
por fin	*at last*

por hora	*per hour*
por la calle	*along the street*
por lo general	*generally, in general*
por la mañana	*in the morning*
por la tarde	*in the afternoon*
por la noche	*at night*
por supuesto	*of course*
por teléfono	*by phone*
por todas partes	*everywhere*

18   Expressions of quantity

The following expressions of quantity are useful to know:

	basta	*that's enough*
	cien gramos de	*a hundred grams of*
un	cuarto kilo	*a quarter of a kilo, 250 grams*
el	doble	*double, twice as much*
un	kilo de	*a kilo of*
un	litro de	*a litre of*
	lleno, vacío	*full, empty*
	más, menos	*more, less*
	medio kilo de	*half a kilo of*
	medio litro de	*half a litre of*
	nada, nada más	*nothing, nothing more*
	otro	*another*
un	pedazo, trozo	*a piece, slice*
un	poco	*a little*
	sólo	*only*
	suficiente	*enough*
	tanto … como	*as much … as*

19   Verbs of movement

The following is a list of useful verbs of movement:

acercarse a	*to draw near to, get close to*
andar	*to walk*
bajar, bajar de	*to go down, get out of (transport)*
coger (la calle …)	*to take (… street), catch (transport)*
correr	*to run*
cruzar	*to cross*
dar un paseo	*to go for a walk*
dar una vuelta (en bici)	*to go for a walk, stroll, spin (on bike)*
doblar (la esquina)	*to go round (the corner)*

Help Yourself to Essential Spanish Grammar

entrar en	*to go into*
ir/irse	*to go/to go off, to go away*
llegar a/de	*to arrive at/from*
llevar	*to take, carry*
marcharse	*to go off*
moverse	*to move*
pasar (por)	*to pass, go (along, through, by)*
salir a/de	*to leave, go out to/from*
subir, subir a	*to go up, to get onto (transport)*
torcer	*to turn*
traer	*to bring*
venir	*to come*
viajar	*to travel*
volar	*to fly*

20 Exclamations

The following is a list of common exclamations:

¡ojalá!	*I wish it were true!/I wish it were so!*
¡qué amable!	*how kind!*
¡qué asco!	*how horrible!*
¡qué bien!	*that's great!*
¡qué calor!	*how hot it is!*
¡qué disgusto!	*what a shock/unpleasant thing to happen!*
¡qué frío!	*how cold it is!*
¡qué horror!	*how dreadful!*
¡qué ilusión!	*how exciting!*
¡qué lástima!	*what a shame!*
¡qué lo pase(s) bien!	*hope you have a good time!*
¡qué pena!	*what a shame!*
¡qué rollo!	*what a pain!*
¡qué sorpresa!	*what a surprise!*
¡qué susto!	*what a fright!*
¡y qué!	*so what!*

Help Yourself to Essential Spanish Grammar

21   Beginning and ending letters

a   To someone you don't know personally, a formal letter of enquiry or complaint:

BEGINNINGS	ENDINGS
Muy señor mío	Le saluda atentamente
Muy señora mía	Reciba un atento saludo de
Muy señores nuestros	Les saluda atentamente

b   To people whom you know, but with whom you have a formal relationship and to whom you use *usted*:

BEGINNINGS	ENDINGS
Estimado señor (López)	Reciba un cordial saludo de
Estimada señora (Martín)	
Estimada señorita (Galdós)	

c   To friends and people you know well, to whom you use the informal *tú*:

BEGINNINGS	ENDINGS
Querido (Paco)	un abrazo de
Querida (María)	saludos
Queridos (Maite y Raúl)	recuerdos a todos
Queridos amigos	besos

English – Spanish glossary

sing. *singular*
plur *plural*
inform. *informal*
form. *formal*
poss. adj. *possessive adjective*
prep. *preposition*

A

a un/uno/una
a (*per*) por
afterwards después
ago hace
any (*not… any*) ningún,
  ninguno/a/os/as
around (*here*) por (aquí)
as … as tan … como
at (*time of day*) a

B

bad malo/a/os/as
best (el, la, los, las) mejor(es)
better mejor/es
big grande/s
by por

C

to call llamar
century siglo
cheap barato/a/os/as
to communicate with
  comunicarse con

D

to dance bailar
day un día
to decide to decidirse a
delicious delicioso/a/os/as
to do hacer

E

each, every cada
every todo/a/os/as

evening la tarde
to explain explicar

F

first primer, primero/a/os/as
flat un piso
for para, por

G

garden un jardín
to get to know conocer
good bueno/a/os/as
great grande/s

H

to have tener
her (*after a prep.*) ella
him (*indirect object pronoun*)
  le
him (*after a prep.*) él
his su/sus
to hope to esperar
hundred cien, ciento

L

last (*month, year etc.*)
  pasado/a/os/as
later más tarde
less than menos que
to listen to escuchar
a little un poco
to lock cerrar con llave
to look mirar
to love encantar

M

many muchos/as
me mí
midnight medianoche
mild suave/s
mine mío/a/os/as

money   el dinero
month   un mes
more than   más que
morning   la mañana
my   mi/mis

N

new   nuevo/a/os/as
nice (*pretty*)   bonito/a/os/as
nice (*person*)   simpático/a/
os/as

O

often   muchas veces
old   antiguo/a/os/as
once   una vez
one   un, una
oneself   mismo/a
in order to   para
to ought to   deber
our (*poss. adj.*)   nuestro/a/
os/as

P

to pay attention   prestar atención
per   por, a
poor   pobre/s
to put (into)   poner (en)

R

to return (something)   devolver

S

salty   salado/a
same   mismo/a/os/as
to see   ver
several   varios/as
small   pequeño/a
to smile   sonreír
spicy   picante

T

tasty   rico/a/os/as
taxi   un taxi
ten   diez

that   ese (*m*), esa (*f*), eso
that (*over there*)   aquel (*m*),
aquella (*f*), aquello
that one   ése, ésa
that one (*over there*)   aquél,
aquélla
their   su/sus
theirs   suyo/a/os/as
them   ellos, ellas
then   luego
these   estos, estas
these ones   éstos, éstas
third   tercer, tercero/a/os/as
this   este, esta, esto
this one   éste, ésta
those (*over there*)   aquellos,
aquellas
those ones   ésos, ésas
those ones (*over there*)
aquéllos, aquéllas
to   a
to touch   tocar
TV   la tele
twice   dos veces
typical   típico/a

U

us   nosotros/as

W

we   nosotros/as
week   una semana
with   con
worse   peor
worst   (el, la, los, las) peor(es)
to write   escribir

Y

year   un año
yesterday   ayer
you (*sing. inform.*)   tú, ti
you (*form.*)   usted
you (*plur. inform.*)   vosotros
you (*plur. form.*)   ustedes
your (*sing. inform.*)   tu, tus
your (*sing. form.*)   su, sus
your (*plural, inform.*)
vuestro/a/os/as
your (*plural, form.*)   su, sus

Spanish – English glossary

A

a   to, at
abajo   below, underneath
un abanico   a fan
una abducción   an abduction
abducido (*adj.*)   abducted
un abeto   pine-tree, Christmas
   tree
abiertamente   openly
abierto (*adj.*)   open
un abrazo   a hug
un abrigo   overcoat
abril   April
abrir   to open
una abuela   grandmother
abuelos   grandparents
aburrido (*adj.*)   boring
aburrirse   to get bored, to be
   bored
abusado (*adj.*)   abused
acabar   to finish
acabar de (+*infin.*)   to have
   just ...
un accidente   accident
una acción   action
un aceite   oil
una aceituna   olive
aceptable (*adj.*)   acceptable
una acera   pavement
acercarse   to draw near
acompañar   to accompany
aconsejar   to advise
un acontecimiento   an event,
   happening
acordarse (*ue*) de   to
   remember about
acostarse (*ue*)   to go to bed
activo (*adj.*)   active
un actor   actor
actos: salón de –   assembly
   hall
una actuación   performance
actuar   to act, behave
acuarela: pintar a la –   to
   paint in water-colour
acuático (*adj.*)   aquatic
de acuerdo   agreed! O.K!
una acusación   accusation

adecuado (*adj.*)   adequate,
   proper, correct
además   moreover
adiós   goodbye
una administración
   administration
administrativo (*adj.*)
   administrative
admirar   to admire
un, una adolescente   teenager
¿adónde?   where ... to?
adoptar   to adopt
adulto (*adj.*)   adult, grown-up
el aerobic   aerobics
un aeropuerto   airport
un aerosol   aerosol
afectar   to affect
afeitarse   to shave
afirmar   to affirm, confirm
las afueras   outskirts
una agenda   diary
agosto   August
la agresión   aggression
el agua (*f.*)   water
aguantar   to bear, to stand
ahora   now
el aire   air
aislado (*adj.*)   isolated, alone
el ajedrez   chess
el ajo   garlic
ajustado (*adj.*)   tight
un albergue (juvenil)   (youth)
   hostel
un alcalde   mayor
al alcance (de)   within reach
   (of)
un alcatraz   goose
el alcohol   alcohol
alcohólico   alcoholic
alegrarse   to be pleased
alegre (*adj.*)   happy, cheerful
alegremente   happily,
   cheerfully
alemán (*adj.*)   German
Alemania   Germany
una alfombra   a rug, a carpet
la algebra   algebra
algo   something
el algodón   cotton

alguien   someone
alguno (*adj.*)   some
allá   over there
allí   there
un almacén   store
almacenes: grandes –
   department stores
un almuerzo   lunch
el alojamiento   accommodation
alojarse   to stay
alquilar   to hire
el alquiler   hire, hiring
alrededor (*de*)   around
alto (*adj.*)   tall
la alumna   (female) pupil
el alumno   (male) pupil
amable (*adj.*)   kind
amarillo (*adj.*)   yellow
un ambiente   atmosphere
una ambulancia   ambulance
amenazar   to threaten
americano (*adj.*)   American
una amiga   (female) friend
un amigo   (male) friend
un analgésico   pain-killer
analizar   to analyze
anciano (*adj.*)   old, former
la anchura   width
andar   to walk, to go
animado (*adj.*)   lively,
   animated
un animal   animal
animar   to encourage, to
   liven up
anoche   last night
un, una antagonista   antagonist,
   opponent
anteayer   the day before
   yesterday
antes (de)   before
antiguo (*adj.*)   old
un antiplano   mountain
una antología   anthology
un año   year
años: tener … –   to be …
   years old
apagado (*adj.*)   put out,
   turned off
apagar   to put out, turn off
un aparato   an appliance
aparcado (*adj.*)   parked
un aparcamiento   car-park
aparcar   to park

aparecer   to appear
una aparencia   appearance
apetecer   to feel like
un apóstol   apostle
apoyar   to lean on, support
apreciar   to appreciate
aprender   to learn
aprovechar   to take
   advantage of, make use of
apuntar   to note down
a que …   I bet that …
aquel (*adj.*)   that
aquí   here
un árbol   tree
una área   area
la arena   sand
armado (*adj.*)   armed
un armario   cupboard
arreglado (*adj.*)   arranged,
   organised
arreglar   to arrange, to
   organise
arriba   up
el arte   art
un artículo   article, item
artificial (*adj.*)   artificial
una asamblea   assembly
un ascensor   lift
el asco   disgust
asegurar   to assure
un aseo   toilet
un asiento   seat
una asignatura   subject
la asistencia   help, assistance
una aspirina   aspirin
un asunto   matter, subject, topic
así   thus, in this way
¡atención!   take care!
atender   to attend to, to pay
   attention to
atentamente   sincerely
atento (*adj.*)   attentive,
   watchful
aterrizar   to land
la atmósfera   atmosphere
atmosférico (*adj.*)
   atmospheric
una atracción   attraction
atraído (*adj.*)   attracted
atrás   behind
atrasado (*adj.*)   slow, late
atropellar   to knock down
el atún   tuna

una audición   hearing, audition
una aula   classroom
aumentar   to increase
un aumento   increase
aun   even
aún   still, yet
aunque   although, even though
ausente (*adj.*)   absent
auténtico (*adj.*)   authentic, genuine
un autobús   bus
un autocar   coach
un autógrafo   autograph
automático (*adj.*)   automatic
un automóvil   car
una autopista   motorway
un autor   author
una autoridad   authority
una avenida   avenue
una aventura   adventure
un avión   aeroplane
avisar   to warn
un aviso   warning, notice
ayer   yesterday
ayudar   to help
un ayuntamiento   Town-Hall
una azafata   air-hostess
azul (*adj.*)   blue

B

bailar   to dance
un baile   dance
bajar (*de*)   to go down, get out (of)
bajito (*adj.*)   a bit on the short side
bajo (*adj.*)   short (height), low
bajo   below
un balcón   balcony
las Baleares   Balearic Islands
un banco   bank
barato (*adj.*)   cheap
un barco   boat
una barra   loaf
barrer   to sweep
un barrio   an area, quarter
bastante   enough
la basura   rubbish
un bañador   swimsuit
bañarse   to bathe, have a bath
un baño   bath
un bebé   baby

beber   to drink
una bebida   drink
la belleza   beauty
bello (*adj.*)   beautiful
un beneficio   benefit, profit, gain
un beso   kiss
un bicho   insect, creature
una bici(cleta)   bicycle
bien   well
una bienvenida   welcome
un billete   ticket, (bank)note
biológicamente   biologically
biológico (*adj.*)   biological
bisiesto: año –   leap year
blanco (*adj.*)   white
una blusa   blouse
un bocadillo   sandwich
una boda   wedding
una bolera   bowling alley
un boli/bolígrafo   ball-point pen
una bolsa   bag
la Bolsa   the Stock-exchange
un bolsillo   pocket
un bolso   bag, purse
una bomba   bomb
bomba: pasarlo –   to have a great time
la bondad   goodness
bonito (*adj.*)   nice, pretty
un bosque   wood
una bota   boot
botánico (*adj.*)   botanic
un bote   can, tin, pot, jar
una botella   bottle
a la brasa   (charcoal)grilled
brillante (*adj.*)   brilliant, shining
británico (*adj.*)   British
una broma   joke
un brujo   wizard, magician
buenísimo (*adj.*)   very good
bueno (*adj.*)   good
una bufanda   scarf
un burro   donkey
buscar   to look for
una butaca   armchair

C

la caballería   chivalry, cavalry
caber   to fit into
una cabeza   head

una cabina   cabin, booth
al cabo   at the end
una cabra   goat
un cacharro   piece of junk, container
cada (*adj.*)   each, every
un cadáver   corpse
caer; dejar –   to fall; to drop
caerse   to fall over
una cafetería   café
un café   coffee
una caja   box, till
la Caja de Ahorros   Savings Bank
un cajón   drawer
un calcetín   sock
calcular   to calculate
la calefacción   heating
un calentador   heater
calentar   to heat
la calidad   quality
caliente (*adj.*)   hot
¡calma!   quiet!
el calor   heat
los calzoncillos   underpants
callarse   to be quiet
una calle   street
una cama   bed
una cámara   camera
una camarera   waitress
un camarero   waiter
cambiar   to change
un cambio   change
un camino   path, way
camino: ponerse en –   to set out
un camión   lorry
una camisa   shirt
un campamento   camp
una campaña   campaign
un camping   campsite
una campiña   countryside, open country
un campo   field, countryside
un campo de fútbol   a football field
el Canadá   Canada
canadiense (*adj.*)   Canadian
un canal   canal, channel
las Canarias   Canary Islands
la canción   song
cansado (*adj.*)   tired
cansarse   to get tired

un, una cantante   singer
cantar   to sing
una cantina   canteen
una capacidad   capacity
capitalista (*adj.*)   capitalist
un capitán   captain
un capricho   whim, craze, notion
una cara   face
un cardo   thistle
el cariño   affection
la carne   meat
caro (*adj.*)   dear, expensive
una carretera   road
un carrito   shopping trolley, cart
una carta   letter
una cartera   schoolbag
un cartero   postman
una casa   house
en casa   at home
casarse (con)   to get married (to)
un caserío   country house, farm
casi   almost
una casilla   box, small square
una casita   little house
castellano (*adj.*)   Castillian
un castillo   castle
una casucha   horrible little house
catalán (*adj.*)   Catalán
catorce   fourteen
una causa   cause, reason
el caviar   caviar
celeste (*adj.*)   heavenly, sky-blue
una cena   dinner, evening meal
cenar   to dine, have dinner
un cenicero   ash-tray
central (*adj.*)   central
una central   plant, (power) station
una centro   centre
la cerámica   pottery
cerca (de)   near (to)
cercano (*adj.*)   near
un cereal   cereal
una cerilla   match
cerrado (*adj.*)   closed
cerrar   to close
una cerveza   beer
una cesta   basket
cibernético (*adj.*)   cybernetic
el ciclismo   cycling

Help Yourself to Essential Spanish Grammar

el cielo   sky, heaven
cien   hundred
las ciencias   sciences
científico (*adj.*)   scientific
ciento   hundred
cierto (*adj.*)   certain
un cigarrillo   cigarette
un cigarro   cigar
una cima   top
cinco   five
cincuenta   fifty
un cine   cinema
una cinta   tape
una cita   appointment, date
una ciudad   town, city
una ciudadana   (female) citizen
un ciudadano   (male) citizen
claramente   clearly
claro (*adj.*)   clear, light
una clase   class
un, una cliente   client, customer
un clima   climate
una clínica   clinic
un club juvenil   youth club
un cobre   copper
una cocina   kitchen
cocinar   to cook
un cocinero   cook, chef
un coche   car
una coexistencia   coexistence
coger   to catch
una cola   tail, queue
un colchón   mattress
un colegio   school
una colina   hill
colocar   to place, put
una colonia   colony, cologne
un color   colour
los columpios   swings
un comedor   dining-room
comenzar (*ie*)   to begin
comer   to eat
comercial (*adj.*)   commercial
un comercio   business, commerce
un cometa   comet
cometer   commit
una comida   food, meal, lunch
una comisaría   police-station
un comité   committee
como   how, as, since
una cómoda   chest-of-drawers
una comodidad   commodity

cómodo (*adj.*)   comfortable
un compacto: disco –   compact disc
una compañera   (female) companion, work mate
un compañero   (male) companion, work mate
una compañía   company
una comparación   comparison
compartir   to share
compasivo (*adj.*)   compassionate
compatible (*adj.*)   compatible
un complejo   complex
completamente   completely
completar   to complete
componer   to compose
comportarse   to behave oneself
una compra   purchase
comprar   to buy
comprarse   to buy for oneself
comprensivo (*adj.*)   sympathetic, understanding
la comunicación   communication
comunicarse   to communicate
una comunidad   community
con   with
un concejo   council
concentrarse   to concentrate on
una conciencia   conscience
un concierto   concert
un concurso   competition
una condición   condition
conducir   to drive, lead
un conductor   (male) driver
una conductora   (female) driver
conectarse   to connect
un conejo   rabbit
una conferencia   conference, phone-call
la confianza   confidence, faith
confiar (en)   to trust (in), rely (on)
confundir   to confuse, to mistake
conmigo   with me
conocer   to (get to) know
consciente (*adj.*)   conscientious

conseguir   to achieve, succeed, get
un consejo   advice
conservar   to conserve, preserve
un conservatorio   music school
consistir (en)   to consist (of)
construir   to build, construct
consumidor (*adj.*)   consumer
consumir   consume, use
contacto: ponerse en –   contact
la contaminación   pollution
contaminado (*adj.*)   polluted
contento (*adj.*)   happy
contestar   to answer
contigo   with you
contrario (*adj.*)   opposite
un contrato   contract
contribuir   to contribute
una conversación   conversation
convertirse   to convert, turn into
una copa   glass
una copia   copy
copiar   copy
un corazón   heart
una corbata   tie
correctamente   correctly
correcto (*adj.*)   correct, right
el correo electrónico   e-mail
Correos   Post Office
un, una corresponsal   pen-pan
una corrida   bull-fight
la corrupción   corruption
cortar   cut
cortarse   to cut oneself
una cortina   curtain
corto (*adj.*)   short
una cosa   thing
coser   sew
una costa   coast
costar   cost
un coste   cost, price
una costumbre   custom
creer   believe
una crema   cream
un crimen   crime
una crisis   crisis
una crítica   criticism
cruzar   cross
un cuaderno   exercise-book

un cuadro   picture
cual   which
cualquier   whichever
cuando   when
cuanto (*adj.*)   how much, how many
cuarenta   forty
cuarto (*adj.*)   fourth
un cuarto   quarter
un cuarto de baño   bathroom
cuatro   four
cubierto (*adj.*)   covered
un cubierto   place-setting
cubrir   cover
una cucaracha   beetle
un cuchillo   knife
una cuenta   bill, account
un cuento   story, tale
el cuero   leather
un cuerpo   body
cuestionar   to question
una cueva   cave
¡cuidado!   careful!
cuidarse   to take care of oneself
la culpa   blame
cultivado (*adj.*)   cultivated
una cultura   culture
una cumbre   top
un cumpleaños   birthday
cumplir   to accomplish, reach
un cuñado   brother-in-law
un cursillo   short course
un curso   course
una curva   curve
cuyo (*adj.*)   whose

CH

un chaleco   waistcoat
un chandal   track-suit
una chaqueta   jacket
charlar   to chat
una chica   girl
un chico   boy
chico (*adj.*)   small
chiflar   to love
chino (*adj.*)   Chinese
chirriar   chirp, squeak, screech
chocar (con)   bump (into)
un churro   doughnut

D

un, una dálmata   Dalmatian (dog)
dar   to give
darse cuenta (de que)   to realise (that)
de   of, from
debajo (de)   underneath, below
deber   to ought to, to owe
los deberes   homework
débil (*adj.*)   weak
decidir   to decide
decidirse (a)   to decide to
décimo (*adj.*)   tenth
decir   to say, to tell
decorativo (*adj.*)   decorative
un dedo   finger
dejar   to leave, let
delante (de)   in front (of)
delgado (*adj.*)   slim, thin
delicioso (*adj.*)   delicious
demasiado (*adj.*)   too
demostrar   to show, demonstrate
denso (*adj.*)   dense
un, una dentista   dentist
dentro (de)   inside, within
una denuncia   report, complaint
depende   it depends
un deporte   sport
deportivo (*adj.*)   sporty, sporting
deprimido (*adj.*)   depressed
la derecha   right
desagradable (*adj.*)   disagreeable
desaparecer   to disappear
un desaparecido   missing person
un desastre   disaster
desastroso (*adj.*)   disastrous
desayunar   to have breakfast
un desayuno   breakfast
descansar   to rest, relax
un descanso   rest, pause
descargar   to unload, download
descortés (*adj.*)   rude, discourteous
describir   to describe
una descripción   description
descrito (*adj.*)   described

descubierto (*adj.*)   discovered
descubrir   to discover
descuidado (*adj.*)   uncared for, unkempt
desde   from
un desfile   procession
desgraciadamente   unfortunately
un desierto   desert
desmayarse   to faint
desmontar   to dismantle, take down
despacio   slowly
despedirse (*i*) (de)   to say goodbye (to)
un despertador   alarm-clock
despertarse (*ie*)   to wake up
despistado (*adj.*)   absent-minded, vague
un despiste   an absent-minded person
despoblado (*adj.*)   depopulated
despoblar   to depopulate
después (de)   after, afterwards
destrozar   to destroy, smash
destruir   to ruin, destroy
un desván   attic
un detalle   detail
detener   to detain, hold back
detenido (*adj.*)   detained
devolver (*ue*)   to return (something)
un día   day
un diamante   diamond
diario (*adj.*)   daily
dibujar   to draw
un dibujo; – animado   drawing; cartoon
un diccionario   dictionary
dicho (*adj.*)   said, afore-mentioned
dieciocho   eighteen
dieciséis   sixteen
un diente   tooth
diez   ten
una diferencia   difference
diferente (*adj.*)   different
diferir   to differ
difícil (*adj.*)   difficult
difícilmente   with difficulty

Help Yourself to Essential Spanish Grammar

una dificultad   difficulty
un dilema   dilemma
un dineral   fortune, a lot of
   money
el dinero   money
   Dios   God
   diplomáticamente
   diplomatically
   diplomático (*adj.*)
   diplomatic
un director   director, (male)
   head-teacher
una directora   director, (female)
   head-teacher
un disco   record
una discoteca   disco
una discusión   argument,
   discussion
   discutir   to argue, to discuss
un diseñador   (male) designer
una diseñadora   (female)
   designer
un disfraz   disguise, mask
   disfrutar   to enjoy
   disgustado (*adj.*)   upset,
   annoyed
un disgusto   upset, annoyance
una distancia   distance
   divertido (*adj.*)   amusing,
   entertaining, fun
   divertirse (*i*)   to enjoy
   oneself
   divorciado (*adj.*)   divorced
un dobladillo   hem
   doblar   to double, fold over,
   go round
   doce   twelve
un documento   document
   doler (*ue*)   to hurt
un dolor   pain, ache
   doméstico (*adj.*)   domestic
   dominar   to dominate
el domingo   Sunday
   donde   where
   Doña   Mrs. (*polite address*)
   dorado (*adj.*)   golden
   dormir (*ue*)   to sleep
un dormitorio   bedroom
   dos   two
   doscientos   two hundred
una ducha   shower
   ducharse   to take a shower
un dueño   owner

   dulce (*adj.*)   sweet
   durante   during
   duro (*adj.*)   hard
un duro   a five-peseta coin

E

   e   and
la ecología   ecology
   ecológicamente   ecologically
   ecológico (*adj.*)   ecological
   echar   to throw, put in, pour
   out
   echar una carta   to post a
   letter
un edificio   building
   Edimburgo   Edinburgh
una educación   education
un ejemplar   model, specimen,
   copy
un ejemplo   example
un ejercicio   exercise
   el   the
   él   he
la electricidad   electricity
   eléctrico (*adj.*)   electrical
un electrodoméstico   household
   appliance
   electrónico (*adj.*)   electronic
un elefante   elephant
   elegante (*adj.*)   elegant
   elegir   to choose
   ella   she
   ellas   they (female)
   ellos   they (male)
una emergencia   emergency
   emocionado (*adj.*)   deeply
   moved, stirred
   emocionante (*adj.*)   exciting
una empanada   pie, pastie
   empapelado (*adj.*)   papered
   empezar (*ie*)   to begin
una empleada   (female) employee
un empleado   (male) employee
un empleo   job, employment
un empresario   business man
   en   in, at
   enamoradísimo (*adj.*)   very
   much in love
   enamorado (*adj.*)   in love
   enamorarse   to fall in love
   encantado (*adj.*)   delighted

encantar   to love, really like
encender (*ie*)   to switch on, light
encendido (*adj.*)   switched on, lit up
encima (*de*)   on top (of)
encontrar (*ue*)   to find
un encuentro   meeting
una encuesta   survey
una enchilada   stuffed tortilla
la energía   energy
enfadado (*adj.*)   annoyed, angry
enfadarse   to get annoyed, angry
una enfermedad   illness
una enfermera   (female nurse)
un enfermero   (male nurse)
enfermo (*adj.*)   ill
enfrente (*de*)   opposite (to)
enorme (*adj.*)   enormous
una ensalada   salad
enseñar   to teach, show
ensuciar   to get (something) dirty
entender (*ie*)   to understand
enterarse (*de*)   to find out, to get to know
entonces   then, at that time
un entorno   setting, environment
una entrada   entrance, ticket
entrar (*en*)   to enter (into)
entre   between
entregar   to deliver, hand over
un entrenamiento   training, coaching
entrenarse   to train
una entrevista   interview
entusiasmado (*adj.*)   enthusiastic
entusiasmarse (con, por)   to get excited (about)
un entusiasmo (por)   enthusiasm (for)
un envase   container, packaging
enviar   to send
envolver   to wrap up
envuelto (*adj.*)   wrapped up
un equilibrio   balance
el equipaje   luggage
un equipo   team, equipment

equivocarse   to make a mistake, be wrong
un error   mistake, error
las escaleras   stairs
escalofriante   spine-chilling
un escándalo   scandal
escandinavo   Scandanavian
un escaparate   shop-window
una esclava   slave
escocés (*adj.*)   Scottish
Escocia   Scotland
escoger   to choose
escolar (*adj.*)   school
Escorpión   Scorpio
escribir   to write
escrito (*adj.*)   written
escuchar   to listen to
un escudero   squire, page
ese (*adj.*)   that
esforzarse   to make an effort to
un esfuerzo   effort
eso   that
un espacio   space
los espaguetis   spaghetti
España   Spain
español (*adj.*)   Spanish
un esparadrapo   sticking plaster
una especialidad   speciality
especializado (*adj.*)   specialised
esperar   to wait for, hope
un espíritu   spirit
una esquina   corner
el esquí   ski
una estación   station
los Estados Unidos   United States
un estante   book-case
estar   to be
una estatua   statue
este (*adj.*)   this
el este   east
éste   this one
esterilizar   to sterilize
esterlinas: libras –   pounds sterling
un estetoscopio   stethoscope
estimulante (*adj.*)   stimulating
esto   this
estrecho (*adj.*)   narrow, tight
una estrella   star

estricto (*adj*.)   strict
un, una estudiante   student
estudiar   to study
un estudio   study, studio
estupendo (*adj*.)   great,
marvellous
estúpidamente   stupidly
estúpido (*adj*.)   stupid
una etapa   stage
una etiqueta   label, ticket
la Europa   Europa
europeo (*adj*.)   European
evitar   to avoid
exactamente   exactly
exagerar   to exaggerate
un examen   examination
excelente (*adj*.)   excellent
excesivamente   excessively
una excursión   excursion, trip
una excusa   excuse
la existencia   existence
una experiencia   experience
experimentado (*adj*.)
experienced
experimentar   to experiment,
experience
un experto   expert
explicar   to explain
explorar   to explore
una exposición   exhibition
extender (ie)   to extend, stretch
al extranjero   abroad
extranjero (*adj*.)   foreign
extraño   strange, odd
extraterrestre (*adj*.)   extra-
terrestrial

F

una fábrica   factory
fabricar   to make, make up
fácilmente   easily
una falda   skirt
una falta   lack, want, need
falta; hacer –   to need
faltar   to be lacking, to be
missing
la fama   fame
una familia   family
familiar (*adj*.)   family
famoso (*adj*.)   famous
fanático (*adj*.)   fanatical

una farmacia   chemist's
un faro   lighthouse, headlight
fastidia: ¡qué – !   what a
nuisance!
fastidiar   to annoy, to irritate
un favor   favour
favorable (*adj*.)   favourable
favorito (*adj*.)   favourite
el febrero   February
la fecha   date
¡felicitaciones!
congratulations!
feliz (*adj*.)   happy
¡fenomenal!   wonderful!
feo (*adj*.)   ugly
una fiebre   fever
una fiesta   festival, party,
holiday
una figura   figure, face
¡fíjate!   just imagine! fancy
that!
una fila   row, line, queue
una finca   farm
la física   Physics
físicamente   physically
físico (*adj*.)   physical
el flamenco   gypsy music/
dancing
una flauta   flute
una flor   flower
una fonda   boarding house,
cheap inn
al fondo   at the bottom
forma; estar en –   to be in
good shape, on good form
formar   to form
una foto   photo
una fotografía   photo
fotográfico (*adj*.)
photographic
una fractura   fracture
francamente   frankly
francés (*adj*.)   French
Francia   France
franco (*adj*.)   frank, open
un fregadero   sink
fregar   to wash dishes
un freno   brake
fresco (*adj*.)   fresh, cool
freír   to fry
frío; hacer –   cold, to be
cold
frito (*adj*.)   fried

frustrado (*adj.*)   frustrated
un frutal   fruit-tree
un fuego   fire
una fuente   fountain
fuera (de)   outside (of)
fuerte (*adj.*)   strong
una fuerza   strength, force
fumar   to smoke
una función   a function, performance
funcionar   to function, work
furioso (*adj.*)   furious
el fútbol   football
un, una futbolista   footballer
un futuro   future

G

las gafas   glasses
Gales   Wales
galés (*adj.*)   Welsh
gallego (*adj.*)   Galician
una gama   range
un gamberro   ragamuffin, street urchin
ganar   to win, earn
ganas; tener – de   to feel like
una ganga   bargain
un garaje   garage
la gaseosa   lemonade
la gasolina   petrol
gastar   to waste, spend
un gastrónomo   gourmet
un gato   cat
el gaz   gas
la gemela   (female) twin
el gemelo   (male) twin
generoso (*adj.*)   generous
la gente   people
la geografía   geography
un gerente   manager
gigante (*adj.*)   huge, enormous
un gigante   giant
la gimnasia   gymnastics
un gimnasio   gymnasium
una gira   tour, trip
glorioso (*adj.*)   glorious
un gobierno   government
un golpe   blow, bump
una goma   rubber, eraser
gordo (*adj.*)   fat

una grabación   recording
gracias   thanks
un grado   grade, step, stage
grande (*adj.*)   big
la grasa   fat, grease
gratis   free
Grecia   Greece
griego (*adj.*)   Greek
un grifo   tap
gris (*adj.*)   grey
un grupo   group
el guacamole   avocado dish
un guante   glove
guapo (*adj.*)   handsome, good-looking
guardar   to keep
una guardarropa   wardrobe
una guardería   nursery
un guardia   policeman
una guerra   war
un, una guía   guide
una guitarra   guitar
gustar   to like, to be pleasing to
gusto: mucho –   pleased to meet you
el gusto   taste, flavour

H

haber   to have (*as auxiliary verb*)
una habitación   room
un, una habitante   inhabitant
hablador (*adj.*)   talkative
hablar   to talk
¡ni hablar!   no way!
hace (… días)   (…days) ago
hacer   to do, make
hacia   towards
el hambre (*f*)   hunger
una hamburguesa   hamburger
harto (*adj.*)   fed-up
hasta   until
hay   there is, there are
hecho (*adj.*) ; bien –   done: well-done
una heladería   ice-cream parlour, stand
un helado   ice-cream
un helicóptero   helicopter
herido (*adj.*)   wounded

herir   to wound, injure
una hermana   sister
una hermanastra   step-sister
un hermanastro   step-brother
un hermano   brother
hermanos   brothers and
   sisters
hermoso (*adj.*)   pretty
un héroe   hero
el hielo   ice
la hierba; mala –   grass; weed
higiénico (*adj.*): papel –
   hygenic: toilet paper
una hija   daughter
un hijo   son
un hipermercado   hypermarket
un hipnosis   hypnosis
un hipnotizador   hynotist
una historia   story, history
histórico (*adj.*)   historic
un hogar   home, hearth
una hoja   sheet of paper, leaf
hola   hello
holandés (*adj.*)   Dutch
holgado (*adj.*)   baggy
un hombre   man
un hombro   shoulder
homosexual (*adj.*)
   homosexual
una hora   hour
un horario   timetable
una hormiga   ant
un horóscopo   horoscope
horrible (*adj.*)   horrible
horriblemente   horribly
un horroroso (*adj.*)   horrendous
una hospedería   hostal, inn
una hostal   hostal
un hotel   hotel
hoy   today
un hueso   bone
un huevo   egg
humano (*adj.*)   human

I

ideal (*adj.*)   ideal, perfect
un idioma   language
un idiota   idiot
un ídolo   idol
la ignorancia   ignorance
igual (*adj.*)   equal, the same

una ilusión; ¡qué –!   excitement;
   how exciting!
una imagen   image, picture
imaginario (*adj.*)   imaginary
imaginarse   to imagine,
   fancy, suppose
impedir   to prevent, hinder
implicar   to involve,
   implicate
la importancia   importance
importante (*adj.*)   important
imposible (*adj.*)   impossible
imprescindible (*adj.*)
   essential, indispensable
una impresión   impression
impresionante (*adj.*)
   impressive
impresionar   to make an
   impression on
imprevisto (*adj.*)
   unforeseen, unexpected
un incendio   fire
una incidencia   incidence,
   impact, effect
incluso   including
incompatible (*adj.*)
   incompatible
un índice   index, rate
indiferente (*adj.*)   indifferent
indio (*adj.*)   Indian
individual (*adj.*)   individual,
   single
el infierno   hell
influir   to influence
la información   information
informarse (sobre)   to find
   out (about)
la informática   computer
   studies
una infusión   infusion, herbal tea
Inglaterra   England
inglés (*adj.*)   English
ingrato (*adj.*)   ungrateful,
   unrewarding
un ingrediente   ingredient
ingreso   admission, entry
iniciar   to start, initiate
inmediatamente
   immediately
inocente (*adj.*)   innocent
inofensivo (*adj.*)   inoffensive
inscribirse (en)   to enrol (in),
   to join

insistir (en)   to insist (on)
una insolación   sun-stroke
insospechado (*adj.*)
  unsuspected
inspirar   to inspire, to
  breathe in
una instalación   facility,
  equipment
un instituto   school
una instrucción   instruction
un instrumento   instrument
intelectual   intellectual
una inteligencia   intelligence
inteligente (*adj.*)   intelligent
una intención   intention
intensivo (*adj.*)   intensive
intentar   to try to, attempt to
un intercambio   exchange
el interés   interest
interesante (*adj.*)   interesting
interesar   to interest
interesarse (en)   to be
  interested (in)
interminable (*adj.*)
  unending, interminable
internacional (*adj.*)
  international
una interrupción   interruption
una inundación   flood
inútil (*adj.*)   useless
una invasión   invasion
inventar   to invent
un invernadero   green-house,
  conservatory
una investigación   investigation,
  research
un investigador   researcher
el invierno   winter
una invitación   invitation
invitar   to invite
una inyección   injection
Irlanda   Ireland
irlandés (*adj.*)   Irish
la ironía   irony
irse   to go off, to go away
una isla   island
italiano (*adj.*)   Italian
la izquierda   left

J

jamás   never

el jamón   ham
el Japón   Japan
japonés (*adj.*)   Japanese
un jardín   garden
una jarra   jug, pitcher
  (earthenware)
jarro   jug, pitcher
una jefa   (female) chief, boss
un jefe   (male) chief, boss
un jerez   sherry
una jeringa   syringe
joven (*adj.*)   young
un, una joven   a young person
una jovencita   young lady
un jovencito   young man
un juego   game
el jueves   Thursday
jugar   to play
un juguete   toy
una juguetería   toy-shop
un juicio   judgement, reason
el julio   July
el junio   June
junto (*adj.*) (a)   beside, next
  (to)
junto (*adj.*) (con)   together
  with
justo (*adj.*)   just, fair, right
juvenil (*adj.*); albergue –
  youthful; Youth Hostel
la juventud   youth
juzgar   to judge

K

un kilo   kilo
un kilómetro   kilometre

L

un laboratorio   laboratory
al lado (de)   beside, next (to)
un lado   side
ladrar   to bark
un lago   lake
una lágrima   tear
una lámpara   lamp
la lana   wool
un lápiz   pencil
largo (*adj.*)   long
una lasaña   lasagne

una lástima; ¡qué lástima! pity,
   shame; what a pity!
   lata: dar la – a to be a
   nuisance
una lata tin, can
 un lavabo washbasin
 un lavado de coches carwash
una lavadora washing machine
   lavar to wash
   lavarse to wash oneself
 la lectura reading
 la leche milk
   leer to read
   lejos (de) far (from)
   lentamente slowly
   lento (*adj.*) slow
   levantarse to get up
una leyenda legend
una libra pound
   libre (*adj.*) free
 un libro book
 un líder leader
   ligero light
   lila (*adj.*) lilac
una limonada lemonade
   limpiar to clean
   limpiarse: – los dientes to
   clean one's teeth
   limpio (*adj.*) clean
   listo (*adj.*) clever, ready
una litera bunk
   loco (*adj.*) mad
   Londres London
 un loro parrot
una lotería lottery
   luchar to fight
   luego then
 un lugar place
 de lujo luxury
 la luna moon
 el lunes Monday
una luz light

LL

una llamada a telephone call
   llamado (*adj.*) called
   llamar to call, telephone
   llamarse to be called
   llano (*adj.*) level, flat,
   smooth, even
una llave key

una llegada arrival
   llegar to arrive
   llenar to fill
   lleno (*adj.*) full
   llevar to take, carry, wear
   llover to rain
 la lluvia rain

M

una madera wood
una madre mother
   madrileño (*adj.*) from
   Madrid
   majo (*adj.*) nice, lovely
   mal badly
una maldición curse
una maleta suitcase
   malhumorado (*adj.*) bad-
   tempered
   malo (*adj.*) bad
   mandar to send
una manera manner, way
una manga sleeve
una mano hand
una manta blanket
   mantener to maintain, keep
una manzana apple
   mañana tomorrow
una mañana morning
 un mapa map
una máquina machine
una máquina fotográfica camera
una maravilla marvel
   maravilloso (*adj.*)
   marvellous
   marcha; ponerse en – to
   start, get going
   marcharse to go off, set off
 un marido husband
   marino; (*adj.*) azul – navy;
   navy blue
los mariscos seafood
   marrón (*adj.*) brown
 el Marruecos Morocco
 el martes Tuesday
   mas but
   más more
una masa dough, mass, volume
una mascota mascot
   masculino (*adj.*) masculine
 la masificación over-crowding
   matar to kill

una material   material
matricularse   to enroll
mayor (*adj.*)   main, major,
    larger, older
una mayória   majority
me   to me
un mecánico   mechanic
a mediados (de)   in the middle
    of
a medianoche   at midnight
las medias   tights, stockings
un médico   doctor
una medida   measure
medio (*adj.*)   half
a mediodía   at midday
mediterráneo (*adj.*)
    Mediterranean
Méjico   Mexico
mejor (*adj.*)   better
mejorarse   to get better, to
    improve
una memoria   memory
menor (*adj.*)   smaller, lesser,
    younger
Menorquina (*adj.*)   from
    Menorca
menos   less, fewer
una mente   mind
mentir   to tell a lie
una mentira   lie, falsehood
un mercadillo   flea-market
un mercado   market
merecer   to deserve
merendar (ie)   to have a
    snack, picnic
una merluza   hake
un mes   month
una mesa   table
una mesilla   small table
meterse (en)   to get into, to
    put oneself
un método   method
un metro   metre
mezclar   to mix
mi   my
mí   to me
un microondas   microwave
el miedo; tener –   fear, to be
    afraid
un miembro   member
mientras   while
el miércoles   Wednesday
mil   thousand

el milenio   millennium
un milímetro   millimetre
un millón   million
un millonario   millionaire
un minibús   minibus
un ministro   minister
un minuto   minute
mío (*adj.*)   mine
mirar   to look at
la miseria   misery
una misión   mission
un misionero   misionary
mismo (*adj.*)   same, oneself
un misterio   mystery
una mitad   half
una moda   fashion
un modelo   model
modernizado (*adj.*)
    modernised
moderno (*adj.*)   modern
un molino   mill
un momento   moment
un monedero   purse
monetario   monetary
mono (*adj.*)   nice, sweet
una montaña   mountain
montar   to put up (a tent),
    assemble
un montón   heap, lot of
una moqueta   fitted carpet
morir   to die
mostrar   to show
la movida   action, a lot going
    on
un movimiento   movement
muchísimo (*adj.*)   very much
mucho (*adj.*)   much, a lot
una muerte   death
muerto (*adj.*)   dead
una mujer   woman, wife
mundial (*adj.*)   world
un mundo   world
municipal (*adj.*)   muncipal,
    of the town
un museo   museum
muy   very
una muñeca   doll
una música   music

N

nacer   to be born

una nacionalidad   nationality
nada   nothing
nadar   to swim
nadie   no-one
naranja (*adj.*)   orange
  (colour)
una naranja   orange
un naranjo   orange-tree
la natación   swimming
nativo (*adj.*)   native
la naturaleza   nature
náutico (*adj.*)   nautical,
  seafaring
navegar   to sail, navigate
la Navidad   Christmas
una neblina   mist
necesario (*adj.*)   necessary
necesitar   to need
negro (*adj.*)   black
una nevera   refrigerator
ni … ni   neither … nor
una niebla   fog
la nieve   snow
ninguno (*adj.*)   none, not any
una niña   girl
un niño   boy
una noche   night
un nombre   name
una norma   norm, rule, pattern
normalmente   normally
el norte   north
nosotros   we
notarse   to note, notice
notas; sacar buenas –
  marks; to get good marks
una noticia   item of news
una novela   novel
noveno (*adj.*)   ninth
una novia   girlfriend
un novio   boyfriend
un núcleo   nucleus
nuestro (*adj.*)   our
nueve   nine
nuevo (*adj.*)   new
un número   number
nunca   never

O

o   or
un objeto   object, item
un obrero   workman

obtener   to obtain, get
occidental   western
octavo (*adj.*)   eighth
el octubre   October
ocurrir   to happen, occur
ochenta   eighty
ocho   eight
ochocientos   eight hundred
odiar   to hate
oficial (*adj.*)   official
una oficina   office
ofrecer   to offer
oír   to hear
¡ojalá!   I wish! I wish it was
  it was like that!
un ojo   eye
olvidado (*adj.*)   forgotten
olvidarse (de)   to forget
  (about)
opinar   to think, believe,
  have the opinion that
una opinión   opinion
una oportunidad   opportunity,
  time
oportunidades   sales
optimista (*adj.*)   optimist
ordenado (*adj.*)   tidy,
  ordered
un ordenador   computer
una organización   organisation
organizarse   to get oneself
  organised
oscuro (*adj.*)   dark
el otoño   autumn
otro (*adj.*)   other, another
una oveja   sheep
un OVNI   UFO
el oxígeno   oxygen
¡oye!   hey! listen!

P

paces; hacer las –   to make
  one's peace with
la paciencia   patience
paciente (*adj.*)   patient
un padrastro   step-father
un padre   father
pagar   to pay
una página   page
un país   country
un paisaje   countryside

una palabra   word
un palacio   palace
la pana   cord, corduroy
un pantalón   trousers
el papel   paper
un paquete   packet
un par (de)   pair (of)
   para   for
una parada: – de taxis   stop;
   taxi-rank
un parador   government-run
   hotel
   parar   to stop, halt, check
   pararse   to stop, come to a
   halt
   parecer   to seem
una pared   wall
una pareja   pair
un parque   park
una parte   part
   particular (*adj.*)   private,
   personal
un partido   match
el paro   unemployment
el pasado   past
   pasado (*adj.*)   past, last
   pasado mañana   the day
   after tomorrow
un pasajero   passenger
   pasar   to pass, spend, happen
un pasatiempo   pastime
un paseo: dar un –   walk,
   avenue; to go for a walk
un pasillo   corridor
una pasión   passion
la pasta   pasta, money
un pastel   cake
una pastilla   tablet, bar
una patata   potato
   patinar   to skate
un patio   patio
la paz   peace
   pedir   to ask for, request
   pegar   to hit, smack, stick
una pela   one peseta
   pelearse   to fight, squabble
una película   film
   peligroso (*adj.*)   dangerous
el pelo   hair
una peluquería   hairdresser's
la pena; ¡qué –!   grief, anxiety;
   what a shame!
   pensar (*ie*)   to think

   peor (*adj.*)   worst
   pequeño (*adj.*)   small
   perder (*ie*)   to lose
   perdido (*adj.*)   lost
   perdonar   to forgive, pardon
   perdonc   sorry
   perezoso (*adj.*)   lazy
   perfectamente   perfectly
   perfecto (*adj.*)   perfect
un periódico   newspaper
un periodo   period of time
   perjudicar   to damage, harm,
   impair
un permiso   permission
   permitir   to allow, permit
   permitirse   to allow oneself
   pero   but
una perra   bitch
un perrito; – caliente   hot dog
un perro   dog
una persona   person
   personal (*adj.*)   personal
el personal   staff
   personalmente   personally
la perspicacia   insight,
   shrewdness
   persuadir   to persuade
   persuasivo (*adj.*)   persuasive
una pesadilla   nightmare
   pesado (*adj.*)   boring,
   annoying, heavy
   pesar   to weigh
un pescado   fish (dead)
una peseta   peseta
   pesimista (*adj.*)   pessimist
un peso   weight, Mexican unit
   of currency
   pesquero (*adj.*)   fishing
una pez   fish (alive)
   picante (*adj.*)   spicy, hot
un pie   foot
una piedra   stone
un pijama   pyjamas
una pila   battery
un pimiento   (sweet) pepper
   pintar   to paint
una pintura   painting
una piña   pineapple
el piragüismo   canoeing
una piscina   swimming-pool
un piso   flat
una pista   track, clue
   planchar   to iron

un planeta planet
planificar to plan
una planta plant, floor (of building)
plantar to plant
de plástico plastic
un plato plate, dish
una playa beach
una plaza square
pleno (*adj.*) full, complete
una población population, town, village
pobre (*adj.*) poor
una pocilga pigsty
poco (*adj.*) little, small, slight, scanty
poder to be able to
podrido (*adj.*) rotten
la policía police
un policía policeman
un polideportivo sports centre
un polo pole
político (*adj.*) political
un pollo chicken
poner to put (on) set, lay
ponerse to put on (clothes)
ponerse (a) to begin to, start to
ponerse en las manos (de) to put oneself in the hands (of)
popular (*adj.*) popular
por along, by through, for
por qué why
porque because
portugués (*adj.*) Portuguese
una posibilidad possibility
posible (*adj.*) possible
una posición position
positivo (*adj.*) positive
posponer to postpone, put off
una postal postcard
un póster poster
practicar to practice
práctico (*adj.*) practical
precioso (*adj.*) lovely, precious
precipitar to throw, hurl, hasten
precisamente precisely, exactly
preferido (*adj.*) preferred, favourite

preferir (ie) to prefer
una pregunta question
preguntar to ask
una prenda garment
preocupado (*adj.*) worried, anxious
preocuparse (por) to worry (about)
preparado (*adj.*) prepared
preparar to prepare
prepararse to get oneself ready
los preparativos preparations
presentarse to introduce onself, to apply for
un presidente president
prestar to lend
una prima (female) cousin
la primavera spring
primero (*adj.*) first
un primo (male) cousin
principal (*adj.*) main, principal
un principio beginning
la prisa; tener – hurry: to be in a hurry
privado (*adj.*) private
un probador changing cubicle
probar (ue) to prove, show, try, taste
probarse (ue) to try on
un problema problem
producir to produce
un producto product
profesional (*adj.*) professional
un profesor (male) teacher
una profesora (female) teacher
un programa programme
prohibido (*adj.*) forbidden
prohibir to forbid
un prójimo fellow human being
prometer to promise
un pronóstico weather forecast
pronto soon
la propaganda propaganda, publicity
propio (*adj.*) own
proteger to protect
un prototipo prototype
una provincia province
provocar to provoke, stir up, invite

próximo (*adj.*)   next
un proyector   projector
prudentemente   prudently,
   with care
una publicidad   advertisement,
   publicity
publicitario (*adj.*)
   advertising
público (*adj.*)   public
el público   public
un pueblo   small town, village
se puede   one can
una puerta   door, gate
pues   then
un puesto   stall
un pulpo   octopus
un punto   point

Q

que   that, which
qué   what
la quechua   Amerindian
   language
quedar   to stay, remain, be
   left
quedarse   to stay
los quehaceres   household
   chores
una queja   complaint
quejarse   to complain
una quemadura   burn
quemarse   to burn oneself
querer (*ie*)   to want to, wish
   to, love
querido (*adj.*)   dear
un queso   cheese
quien   who, whom
la química   Chemistry
químico (*adj.*)   chemical
quince   fifteen
quinientos   five hundred
quinto (*adj.*)   fifth
un quiosco   kiosk
quisiera   would like to
quitar   take away, remove
quitarse   to take off

R

la rabia; ¡qué rabia!   anger,
   rage; how annoying!

una radio   radio
una radiografía   X-ray
rápidamente   quickly
rápido   quickly
una raqueta   racquet
raramente   rarely
raro (*adj.*)   rare, odd, strange
un rascacielos   sky-scraper
rasgar   to tear, rip, slash
Rastro   Madrid flea-market
un rato   while, time
un ratito   short time
un ratón   mouse
una raya   ray, line, stripe
de rayas   striped
una razón   reason
razón; tener –   to be right
real (*adj.*)   royal
la realidad   reality
realista (*adj.*)   realistic
reanimar   reawaken, revive
rebelde (*adj.*)   rebel
un recado   message
la recepción   reception
un, una recepcionista   receptionist
una receta   recipe
recibir   to receive
reciclar   to recycle
una recital   recital, perfomance
una reclamación   claim,
   complaint, protest
reclamaciones; libro de
   complaints book
recoger   to tidy, pick up, put
   away
una recogida   collection
una recomendación
   recommendation
recomendar   to recommend
reconocer   to recognise
un recreo   break, pause
recto (*adj.*)   straight, direct
un recuerdo   souvenir, memory
recuerdos (de)   best wishes
   (from)
una red   network
reemplazar (con) (por)   to
   replace (with) (by)
referirse (a)   to refer to
reflejar   to reflect
un refresco   cool drink
un refugio   refuge, shelter
regalar   to give as a present

un regalo   present
regar   to water
una región   region
una regla   ruler
regular (*adj.*)   normal, fine,
   all right, so-so
un reino   kingdom
reír   to laugh
reírse (de)   to laugh (at)
una relación   relationship
relajado (*adj.*)   relaxed,
   easy-going
relajarse   to relax
un relato   story, tale, account,
   report
religioso (*adj.*)   religious
un reloj   watch
rellenar   to fill, fill out
relleno (*adj.*)   filled
un rendimiento   performance,
   efficiency
renombrado (*adj.*)   renowned
reñir   to scold
reparar   to repair
de repente   suddenly
repetir (i)   to repeat
un reportaje   report, article,
   news item
resbalarse   to slip
rescatar   to rescue
reservar   to reserve
una residencia   residence
resolver (ue)   to resolve
el respeto   respect,
   consideration
responsable (*adj.*)
   responsible
una respuesta   reply, answer
un restaurante   restaurant
el resto   rest, remains
un resultado   result
resultar   to be, turn out to
   be, result
una reunión   meeting,
   get-together
reunirse   to meet up
al revés   the other way round
una revista   magazine
un rey   king
rico (*adj.*)   rich, delicious
un riesgo   risk
un rincón   corner
un río   river

riquísimo (*adj.*)   very rich,
   really delicious
un ritmo   rhythm
rodear   to surround
rogar (ue)   to ask, request
rojo (*adj.*)   red
un rollo; ¡qué –!   roll of film;
   what a pain!
romper   to break
la ropa   clothes
la ropa exterior   outer garments
la ropa interior   underwear
rosa (*adj.*)   pink
una rosa   rose
el rosbif   roast beef
un rostro   face
roto (*adj.*)   broken
ruidosamente   noisily
ruidoso   noisy
Rusia   Russia
ruso (*adj.*)   Russian
una rutina   routine

S

el sábado   Saturday
una sábana   sheet
saber   to know
sacar   to take out, get (out)
un saco   bag
una sala   room
salado (*adj.*)   salty
salir   to go out, leave
un salón   living-room
un salón de actos   assembly hall
una salsa   sauce
la salud   health
saludar   to greet
un salvavidas   life-guard
una samba   Brazilian dance
una sandalia   sandal
una sangría   fruit punch
sano (*adj.*)   healthy
un satélite   satellite
seco (*adj.*)   dry
en secreto   in secret
la sed ; tener –   thirst; to be
   thirsty
la seda   silk
en seguida   straight away, right
   now
seguir   to follow, carry on

según   according to
una segunda   second (of time)
segundo (*adj.*)   second
la seguridad   security, safety
los seguros   insurance
seis   six
seiscientos   six hundred
un sello   stamp
los semáforos   traffic lights
una semana   week
sencillo (*adj.*)   simple, single
un sendero   path, way
sentarse (*ie*)   to sit down
un sentimiento   feeling
sentir (*ie*)   to feel, sense, be sorry
sentirse (*ie*)   to feel
un señor   gentleman, Mr.
una señora   lady, Mrs., Ms.
los señores   lady and gentleman, Mr. and Mrs.
una señorita   young lady, Miss
separado (*adj.*)   separated
separar   to separate
el septiembre   September
séptimo (*adj.*)   seventh
ser   to be
un ser   being
una serie   series
una serpiente   snake
un servicio   service
los servicios   toilets
servir   to serve, do a favour
servirse   to help oneself
sesenta   sixty
setenta   seventy
sevillano (*adj.*)   from Seville
sexto (*adj.*)   sixth
si   if
sí   yes
una sidra   cider
siempre   always
lo siento   I'm sorry
una sierra   mountain range
siete   seven
un siglo   century
una silla   chair
un sillón   armchair
silvestre (*adj.*)   wild
un símbolo   symbol
simpático (*adj.*)   nice
sin   without
sinceramente   sincerely

sincero (*adj.*)   sincere
sino   but
el sirimiri   fine drizzle or mist
un sistema   system
un sitio   place
situado (*adj.*)   situated
sobrar   to be left over, remain
sobre   on, upon, over, about (time)
sobreestimado (*adj.*)   overestimated
sobreexcitado (*adj.*)   overexcited
sobresaliente (*adj.*)   excellent
sobrevivir   to survive
un sofá   sofa
la soja   soya
el sola   sun
a solas   alone, by oneself
soleado (*adj.*)   sunny
soler   to be accustomed to, to usually …
solicitar   to request, seek
una solicitud   request, application, care
solo (*adj.*)   alone, single, sole
sólo   only, merely, just
soltero (*adj.*)   single, unmarried
solucionar   to solve
un sombrero   hat
someterse   to submit to, give in to
sonreír   to smile
soñar   to dream
una sopa   soup
sorprenderse   to be surprised
un sótano   basement
su (*adj.*)   his, her, your, their
suave (*adj.*)   soft, gentle
subir (a)   to go up, get (into)
un suceso   event, incident
sucio (*adj.*)   dirty
una sudadera   sweatshirt
un suelo   ground
un sueño   dream
la suerte; tener –   luck; to be lucky
sufrir   to suffer, undergo
una sugerencia   suggestion

sugerir   to suggest
Suiza   Switzerland
superar   to surpass, excel, overcome
un supermercado   supermarket
un, una suplente   supply (teacher), locum
suponer   to suppose
un, una surfista   surfer
suyo (*adj.*)   his, hers, yours, theirs

T

el tabaco   tabacco
un tablero   board, plank, panel
un tacón   heel
el tacto   tact, touch
un talento   talent
un tamaño   size
también   also
tampoco   neither
tan ... como   as ... as
tanto (*adj.*)   so much
tardar   to take (a long) time, delay
una tarde   afternoon
una tarea   task, job
una tarjeta   card
una taza   cup
te   you, to you
un té   tea
un teatro   theatre
un tebeo   comic
una técnica   technique, method
la tecnología   technology
un teleférico   ski lift, cable railway
un teléfono   telephone
un telegrama   telegram
la televisión   television
un televisor   television set
un tema   theme
temblar   to tremble
temer   to fear, be afraid of
una temperatura   temperature
temprano   early
un tenedor   fork
tener   to have
el tenis   tennis
tercero   third
terminar   to finish, end

un termómetro   thermometer
una terraza   terrace
un territorio   territory, area, land
un testigo   witness
una tía   aunt
el tiempo   time, weather
una tienda   shop
una tierra   land, earth
las tijeras   scissors
tímido (*adj.*)   shy
un tinte   dye
tinto (*adj.*)   dyed, red (of wine)
un tinto   red wine
típico (*adj.*)   typical
un tipo   type, kind, sort
tiquismiquis (*adj.*)   fussy
un tío   uncle
los tíos   uncle and aunt
tirar   to pull, draw
una tirita   sticking plaster
un tisú   tissue
toca: me – a mí   it's my turn
un tocador   dressing table
tocar   to touch
todavía   still
todo (*adj.*)   all, every
tomar   to take, get, have (food and drink)
tomar el sol   to sunbathe
torcer (ue)   to turn, twist
una tormenta   storm
un toro   bull
una torre   tower
una tortilla   omelette
la tortura   torture
una tostada   (slice of) toast
trabajador (*adj.*)   hard-working
tradicional (*adj.*)   traditional
traer   to bring, get, carry, fetch
el tráfico   traffic
tragar   to swallow
un traje   suit
tramposo (*adj.*)   cheating, swindling
tranquilamente   calmly
tranquilizar   to tranquillise, make calm
tranquilo (*adj.*)   quiet, calm
transformarse   to transform oneself, change

transnacional (*adj.*)
  transnational, world-wide
un transporte   transport, means
  of transport
un tranvía   tram
un trapo   cloth, rag
  trasladar   to move, transfer
un traslado   move, removal
un tratamiento   treatment
  tratar (de)   to try (to), treat
un trato   dealing, manner,
  treatment
  travieso (*adj.*)   mischievous
  treinta   thirty
  tremendo (*adj.*)   tremendous
  tres   three
  trescientos   three hundred
un triángulo   triangle
una tribu   tribe
un trimestre   term
  triste (*adj.*)   sad, gloomy
  tropical (*adj.*)   tropical
  tu (*adj.*)   your
  tú   you
un tubo   tube
  el turismo   tourism
  turismo: hacer –   to go sight
  seeing
un, una turista   tourist
  turístico (*adj.*)   tourist
  el turrón   nougat
  tuyo (*adj.*)   your

U

  u   or
  último (*adj.*)   last
  un   a, one
  una   a, one
  único (*adj.*)   only, unique
una unidad   unit
  unido (*adj.*)   united
un uniforme   uniform
una universidad   university
  urbano (*adj.*)   urban, town
  urgentemente   urgently
  usar   to use
  usarse   to be used, to be in
  use
  usted   you (polite, singular)
  ustedes   you (polite, plural)
  útil (*adj.*)   useful

  utilizado (*adj.*)   used
  utilizar   to use

V

las vacaciones   holidays
  vale   O.K., fine
  valer   to be worth
en vano   in vain
  vano (*adj.*)   vain, superficial
los vaqueros   jeans
  varios (*adj.*)   several, some,
  different
  vasco (*adj.*)   Basque
un vecino   neighbour
  vegetariano (*adj.*)
  vegetarian
un vehículo   vehicle
  veinte   twenty
  veintidós   twenty-two
  veintiocho   twenty-eight
  veintiuno   twenty-one
la vela   sailing
una venda   bandage
un vendaje   dressing,
  bandaging
  vender   to sell
  venderse   to be sold
  venezolano (*adj.*)
  Venezuelan
  venir   to come
una ventana   window
  ver   to see
un, una veraneante   holiday-maker
  el verano   summer
la verdad   truth
  verdadero (*adj.*)   true
  verde (*adj.*)   green
una vergüenza   shame
  verificar   to check, verify
un Vespino   scooter
  vestirse (en)   to get dressed
  (in)
un vestuario   cloakroom,
  changing room
tal vez   perhaps
una vez   time, occasion
de vez en cuando   from time to
  time
  viajar   to travel
un viaje   journey
un viajero   traveller

vibrante (*adj.*)   vibrant,
  bright
una víctima   victim
una vida   life
un vídeo   video
un videoclip   videoclip
un videoclub   video rental store
un vidrio   glass
viejo (*adj.*)   old
un viento   wind
el viernes   Friday
vigilar   to watch over,
  supervise
un vino   wine
la violencia   violence
violento (*adj.*)   violent
la visibilidad   visibility
visitar   to visit
una vista   visit
una viuda   widow
un viudo   widower
vivir   to live
voluntario (*adj.*)   voluntary
volver (ue)   to return, come
  back

vosotras   you (informal,
  feminine, plural)
vosotros   you (informal,
  masculine, plural)
un vuelo   flight
una vuelta   return
vuestro (*adj.*)   your

Y

y   and
ya   now, already
el yoga   yoga
un yogur   yoghurt

Z

un zapato   shoe
un zar   Tsar, Czar
una zona   zone, area
un zoológico   zoo
un zumo   juice

Help Yourself to Essential Spanish Grammar

Grammar index

Key to exercises
Detachable answer section for class use

Key to exercises

Chapter 1 What do you know? (page 1)

A *¡Qué desastre!*
1 ¡Hay papeles en **el** patio!
2 ¡Hay bolsas de patatas fritas en **las** cocinas!
3 ¡Hay coca-cola y limonada en **las** mesas!
4 ¡Hay mucha basura en **los** pasillos!
5 ¡Hay mesas en **la** entrada!
6 ¡Hay un montón de sillas en **el** gimnasio!
7 ¡Hay ropa de deporte y raquetas en **los** laboratorios!
8 ¡Hay un proyector en **el** campo de fútbol!
9 ¡Hay un elefante en **la** oficina de la directora!

B *Mi piso y el Palacio Real*
1 hay tres **cocinas**
2 hay cincuenta y dos **dormitorios**
3 hay miles de **pasillos**
4 hay cuarenta **aseos**
5 hay treinta **garajes**
6 hay cinco **comedores**
7 hay veintidós **cuartos de baño**

Chapter 1 What have you learnt? (page 4)

A *El Hotel Alfonso XIII*
Mis **habitaciones** preferidas son los **salones** en la planta baja. El más bonito tiene tres **ventanas** grandes. Hay **alfombras** azules encima de la moqueta, y en las **paredes** hay muchos **cuadros** antiguos. Tiene muchas **butacas** y muchos **sofás**. Como es enorme, tiene dos **televisores**, uno en el salón y otro cerca de las **puertas** principales. Está empapelado de azul claro con **rayas** blancas. En los **jardines** hay **flores** y **plantas**, con muchos **árboles** y **frutales**. Hay también tres **patios** bonitos, con **fuentes** y **terrazas** donde se puede tomar el sol.

B *Mi instituto – lo bueno y lo malo*
1 **Los** edificios son muy antiguos.
2 **Las** instalaciones deportivas son nuevas.
3 **Las** aulas son viejas y pequeñas.
4 En **la** sala de profesores, se puede fumar: esto no es aceptable.
5 **El** gimnasio es grande y moderno.
6 **La** piscina es muy bonita.
7 **La** cantina es demasiado pequeña.

8 **El** campo de fútbol está lejos.
9 En general, **los** profes son simpáticos.
10 **Las** clases prácticas son interesantes.

Lo malo: 1, 3, 4, 7, 8.
Lo bueno: 2, 5, 6, 9, 10.

Chapter 2   What do you know? (page 5)

A *La Reunión*
  1 Tú
  2 Usted
  3 Ustedes
  4 Vosotros
  5 Usted
  6 Tú

B *La corresponsal*
  Hola, ¿qué tal? Me llamo Rosario y vivo en Venezuela con mi familia. En total,
  somos cinco: mis padres, mis hermanos y yo. En realidad, yo **soy** española, porque
  nací en Madrid en España. Pero Eduardo y Felipe **son** venezolanos. Mi padre **es**
  cartero – ¿qué hacen tus padres? Mi profe dice que vosotros vivís en Barcelona: ¿**sois**
  catalanes? Yo **soy** bastante alta, y delgada, y me encanta viajar. Y tú, ¿cómo **eres**?
  ¡Un día quiero visitar tu país!

C *En la cola*
  1 Este año, aprendo **el** catalán también.
  2 No, no hablo español muy bien.
  3 ¿El hombre grande? Es el director – **el** Señor Ruiz.
  4 ¡Tengo hambre! ¿Qué hora es? ¿Es **la** una ya?
  5 ¿Hay algo para vegetarianos? No me gusta **la** carne.
  6 ¿Eres vegetariana? ¡A qué te dan ensalada!

Chapter 2   What have you learnt? (page 8)

A *El Instituto Mundial*
  El Instituto Mundial **es** un ejemplo maravilloso de una coexistencia alegre. Los
  estudiantes hablan español en las aulas, pero **son** rusos, griegos, chinos, irlandeses –
  ¡una auténtica ensalada de nacionalidades! En el recreo, hablé con un chico, Ruani:
  – ¿Y tú, Ruani, de qué nacionalidad **eres**?
  – ¿Yo? ¡**soy** internacional!
  – Y cuántos **sois** en vuestra clase?
  – Bueno, **somos** unos quince en total, pero todos de nacionalidades diferentes.
  – ¿Y a veces, esto no **es** un poco difícil?
  – Claro hay dificultades en comunicarse, de vez en cuando, pero ¡nosotros **somos**
    muy pacientes!

B *Milagros*

SR. RUIZ Eres de Perú, ¿verdad? ¿Qué idiomas hablas?

MILAGROS Hablo español, claro.

SR. RUIZ ¿Aprendes **el** inglés?

MILAGROS Sí. Y aprendo **el** quechua también.

SR. RUIZ ¿El idioma de **los** indios?

MILAGROS Sí. Mis amigos quechuas viven en el 'antiplano', es decir en **la** sierra. Vamos allí durante **las** vacaciones, a Quillabamba.

SR. RUIZ Pero hablar quechua es muy difícil, ¿no?

MILAGROS ¡Sí! Pero **las** chicas del pueblo son simpáticas. Nos reímos mucho.

SR. RUIZ ¿Te gusta **la** vida allí?

MILAGROS Sí, es muy diferente; **el** ritmo de vida es más lento y relajado.

SR. RUIZ Bueno, ya es **la** una y media. **El** señor Martín nos llama. ¿Quieres comer?

MILAGROS Sí. Pero primero, me lavo **las** manos. Vuelvo en dos minutos.

Chapter 3   What do you know? (page 9)

A *Lugares de interés*

1 ¿Para ir **al** museo del Prado?

2 ¿Para ir **a la** Plaza de Cibeles?

3 ¿Para ir **a las** tiendas en el Diagonal?

4 ¿Para ir **al** Rastro?

5 ¿Para ir **a las** Ramblas?

B *La llamada*

JOSE LUIS ¡Claire! ¿Dónde **estás**?

CLAIRE En la Plaza Mayor. No **estoy** muy bien: me duelen los pies

JOSE LUIS ¿Y tu amiga Sasha? ¿**está** contigo?

CLAIRE No. Yo **estoy** un poco preocupada …

JOSE LUIS Tú y Claire – ¿no **estáis** con Rob y James?

CLAIRE ¡No sé dónde **están** los chicos!

JOSE LUIS ¡Qué desastre!

C *Si nos vemos …*

1 ¿Si nos vemos detrás del **Teatro Real**?

2 ¿Claire? ¿Nos encontramos delante de los **almacenes grandes**?

3 Oye Sasha – ¿te espero en la entrada de la **estación**?

4 ¿Rob? Nos encontramos enfrente de **Correos** – ¿vale?

5 ¿Me esperas en el parque cerca de las **residencias**?

Chapter 3   What have you learnt? (page 12)

A *En la calle*

1 El mercado está **detrás de la** Oficina de Turismo.
2 ¿El Banco de España? Está **al lado de** Correos.
3 Vamos a ver. La discoteca está **enfrente de la** cafetería.
4 ¿Cerca? ¡No, qué va! La discoteca está **lejos de los** servicios.
5 La farmacia está **delante del** mercado.
6 No, no. No está lejos. El parque está **cerca del** banco.

B *Las vacaciones – ¡qué horror!*

ANA ¡Es que **estoy** aburrida!
YOLI Sí, es verdad que las vacaciones **son** muy aburridas.
ANA ¡A qué no haces nada, pero **estás** cansada todo el día!
YOLI Sí, tienes razón. ¿Y tu hermana Isabel – qué tal **está**?
ANA Sabes que **es** viuda, ¿no? Mis padres **están** preocupados porque Isabel no
quiere salir de casa, no quiere ponerse en contacto …
YOLI Pobrecita. A lo mejor no **está** lista para hablar del accidente.
ANA Sí… Y mi otra hermana y su marido **están** separados, así que …
YOLI **Es** muy triste, todo eso.
ANA ¡Y mira las plantas! Incluso las plantas **están** muertas.
YOLI Falta agua. El parque no **es** nada bonito en verano. ¡Odio las vacaciones!

Revision test 1–3 (page 13–14)

A *El piso de alquiler*

En el salón-comedor hay dos **sofás**, tres **sillones**, un **televisor**, unas **cortinas** azules,
dos **estantes** y dos **alfombras**. Luego hay una **mesa** con seis **sillas**. En el dormitorio
principal, hay dos **camas** individuales, dos **armarios**, y dos **tocadores**. Ah, hay dos
mesillas de noche también. En el dormitorio de los niños hay dos **literas**, y dos
cómodas.

B *¿Qué sabes?*

1 **la** luna	a) condiciones atmosféricas: **la** temperatura, **la** lluvia, **el** viento …
2 **el** cometa	b) masa gaseosa que rodea **el** mundo.
3 **el** planeta	c) astro satélite de **la** Tierra.
4 **el** clima	d) cuerpo celeste que sólo brilla por **la** luz que refleja del sol.
5 **la** atmósfera	e) astro central en **el** sistema planetario que produce calor.
6 **el** sol	f) astro con **el** núcleo poco denso y **la** cola larga.

C *¿Hay alguien en casa?*

MAMA   Manolo – ¿dónde **estás**?

MANOLO   **Estoy** en mi dormitorio.

MAMA   ¿Y tu papá?

MANOLO   Ni idea – ¿no **está** en el sótano?

MAMA   ¡Miguel y Juanjo! ¿Dónde **estáis**?

MANOLO   **Estamos** en el desván, jugando con el ordenador.

MAMA   ¿Las chicas **están** con vosotros?

JUANJO   No – Clara **está** en casa de su amiga, y Ana – no sé.

MAMA   Pues, yo no voy a preparar la cena sóla – ¡si me necesitáis, **estoy** en el jardín con un Martini!

D *¡Tramposa!*

TERE   Es que **estoy** muy cansada – ¿puedo ir a la cama?

PAPA   Pero, son las siete de la tarde – ¿qué te pasa?

TERE   No me siento muy bien, papá – **estoy** enferma.

PAPA   ¿Sí? Voy a buscar el termómetro … ¡Dios mío – cuarenta y cuatro grados! No puedes **estar** viva con una fiebre tan alta. ¡Qué lista **eres**! ¡Has puesto el termómetro en tu taza de café!

TERE   Es que los deberes **son** aburridos – ¿no puedo ver la televisión un poco?

PAPA   ¡Ni hablar!

E *La carta*

1 El vídeo está **dentro del** armario, **detrás de la** puerta en el salón.

2 Las cerillas están **en el** cajón, **debajo del** fregadero, en la cocina.

3 Si tenéis frío, hay dos mantas más **al lado de la** cama, **encima de la** silla verde.

4 La nevera está en el armario alto **entre la** lavadora y el microondas.

5 El lunes, ¿puedes bajar la basura **a la** calle? Vienen por la mañana a recogerla.

6 Si quieres pan temprano, hay un supermercado pequeño **al final de la** calle.

F *El primer día*

1 ¿Dónde está **la** oficina del director?   Al final **del** pasillo.

2 ¿Dónde están **los** vestuarios?   A la derecha **de la** entrada.

3 ¿**Los** servicios están por aquí?   No, al lado **de los** vestuarios.

4 ¿**El** gimnasio está cerca?   Enfrente **de las** duchas.

5 ¿Dónde están **las** cocinas?   Detrás **del** salón de actos.

6 ¿**Las** aulas de español y francés?   Cerca **del** laboratorio.

Chapter 4 What do you know? (page 15)

A *El intercambio*

PROFESOR Díme, Zeneida – ¿**tienes** hermanos?

ZENEIDA Sí, **tengo** dos hermanastras, un hermanastro y un hermano gemelo, Iñaki.

PROFESOR ¿Iñaki y tú sois gemelos? ¿Cuántos años **tenéis**?

ZENEIDA Tenemos quince años. Y mi hermanastro Felipe **tiene** once años.

PROFESOR ¿Y tus hermanastras?

ZENEIDA Pepa y Gema son gemelas también – **tienen** seis años.

PROFESOR ¡Vaya! ¡Y tenéis animales en casa también?

ZENEIDA Sí – pues Iñaki y yo **tenemos** dos perros, Pepa y Gema tienen tres conejos, y Felipe tiene una serpiente y un loro.

PROFESOR ¡Dios mío! Eso no es una familia – ¡es un zoológico!

B *La Calle Sagunto*

Aquí en el número **veintiuno** vive mi hermano. Un poco más lejos, vive mi tía en el número **cincuenta y cinco**. ¿Ves las cortinas azules? – allí. En el número **cien** vive mi cuñado y enfrente en el **ciento dos**, mis primos. Es una calle muy larga – en el número **quinientos quince** viven otros primos.

C *Los pisos*

El señor Aguirre vive **en el segundo piso**.

La señorita Cánovas vive **en el quinto piso**.

Los señores Clemente viven **en el sexto piso**.

La señora Elizalde vive **en el tercer piso**.

El doctor Guerra vive **en el primer piso**.

Los señores Martínez viven **en el cuarto piso**.

Chapter 4 What have you learnt? (page 18)

A *Las Quejas*

LOLA ¿Cuántos niños **tiene** usted?

ANA Mi marido y yo **tenemos** siete hijos en total: tres hijos y cuatro hijas.

LOLA ¡Uf! Ustedes **tienen** mucho trabajo en casa, con tantos niños.

ANA ¡Eso sí que es verdad! Como mi marido trabaja fuera hasta las ocho, yo **tengo que** hacer todo – la ropa, fregar y, preparar la comida.

LOLA Pues yo **tengo** dos hijos. Y siempre quieren dinero.

ANA ¡Los míos también! Mi hijo me dice – ¡Mamá, voy a la discoteca! ¿No **tienes** mil pesetas? –

LOLA ¿El no **tiene** dinero?

ANA ¡Qué va! Y yo le digo – Yo, hijo, no **tengo** ni un duro. ¡Si tú quieres dinero, **tienes que** trabajar!

LOLA Son todos iguales. ¡Los niños de hoy no **tienen** nada **que** hacer!

ANA Bueno, **tengo que** irme – mi hija Alicia está en casa con los pequeños. ¡Adiós!

B *Las preguntas*
1 Es que sólo tengo **una** goma.
2 ¿Un lápiz? Lo siento, pero no tengo más que **uno**.
3 ¿Qué página es? Página **ciento una**.
4 ¡Esto no es la **primera** vez que te dejo mi regla!
5 El problema es que sólo tengo **un** lápiz rojo.
6 ¡Oye, no copies los deberes! ¡Te he dicho **cien** veces que no!
7 ¿Otro boli? ¡No! ¡Éste es el **tercer** boli que has perdido!
8 ¿Una hoja? Bueno, toma – tengo **ciento un** hojas…

Chapter 5   What do you know? (page 19)

A *Mi familia*
1 Tengo cinco hermanos. Todos son **diferentes**.
2 ¡Mi hermana **mayor** está **loca**!
3 Mi hermana menor, que es **tímida**, se llama Clara.
4 Mi hermano Juan tiene 16 años. Es muy **divertido** y las chicas dicen que es **guapo**.
5 Mi hermanito David tiene 8 años. ¡Es **perezoso** pero es muy **listo**!
6 Mi hermana gemela se llama Ana y es más **habladora** que yo.
7 Mis padres son muy **simpáticos**.
8 Al otro lado de la ciudad viven mis abuelos: son **ancianos** ya, pero mi abuelo es una persona muy **animada** y mi abuela es muy **trabajadora**.

B *La Ropa*

1 el bañador **rojo**	7 el pantalón corto **naranja** para el fútbol
2 los guantes **marrones**	8 la jersey **rosa** con mangas **largas**
3 la bufanda **azul**	9 las zapatillas **negras**
4 el chaleco **verde**	10 la chaqueta **marrón** de pana
5 los pantalones **grises**	11 las botas **rojas** de goma
6 los calzoncillos **blancos**	12 el chandal **amarillo** para la gimnasia

Cajón 1. Ropa interior y bañadores: el bañador rojo, los calzoncillos blancos.
Cajón 2. Ropa exterior: los guantes marrones, la bufanda azul.
Cajón 3. Zapatos etc: las zapatillas negras, las botas rojas de goma.
Cajón 4. Ropa deportiva: el pantalón corto naranja para el fútbol, el chandal amarillo para la gimnasia.
Cajón 5. El resto: el chaleco verde, los pantalones grises, el jersey rosa con mangas largas, la chaqueta marrón de pana.

Chapter 5   What have you learnt? (page 22)

A *Los míos*

Paola quiere ser una diseñadora **famosa** – es mi hermana y vive en un piso en París con unas amigas **divertidas**. Su mejor amiga es **española** y muy **trabajadora**.

Tiene muchos compañeros **franceses** – por lo general, son **guapos** y **ricos**. Paola es **pobre** – tiene que trabajar mucho. ¡Qué lástima!

David es mi hermano – pero es terrible. Es muy **travieso** en clase. En su cartera tiene libros **sucios** y fruta **podrida**. ¡Qué asco!

Marisa, mi hermana, es muy **bonita**, **delgada** y **elegante**. Tiene los ojos **verdes**. ¡Qué suerte!

Quiero mucho a mis padres – son **generosos**. Cada año vamos de vacaciones a un país **diferente**. Este año nos vamos a Argentina.

B *¡No es justo!*

1 ¡No es justo – tengo que trabajar **todos** los días!
2 **Cada** sábado por la mañana tengo que trabajar también.
3 En mi oficina tengo dos compañeros **perezosos** que nunca trabajan los sábados.
4 Estas **últimas** semanas, tenemos **muchos** clientes, y hay mucho que preparar.
5 Soy una empleada **consciente** – no puedo dejar todo sin hacer.
6 Preparo los dibujos **difíciles** primero.
7 Voy a trabajar hasta medianoche – ¡no es la **primera** vez, pero va a ser la última!

Chapter 6   What do you know? (page 23)

A *Quique y Rosa*

QUIQUE ¡Toni! ¡quiero ver **tu** revista!

TONI No puedes – no es **mi** revista. Es de Tomás.

ROSA ¿Por qúe tienes **su** revista?

TONI Porque él tiene **mis** tebeos.

QUIQUE No son **tus** tebeos, Toni. ¡Son **nuestros** tebeos!

TONI Quique y Rosa, ¡éstos son **vuestros** juguetes! ¡Dejadme en paz!

ROSA ¡Mamá! ¡Toni no nos deja **sus** tebeos!

TONI ¡Sois imposibles!

B *¡Ay, qué pena!*

TONI ¡Qué **malas** noticias!

MERCHE ¿Qué pasa?

TONI ¿Conoces a la **nueva** chica en tu clase?

MERCHE ¿Belén? La que vive en la torre **grande** donde hubo un incendio la semana **pasada**?

TONI Sí – ¡pues hubo otro incendio en la **misma** torre anoche! El piso de Belén está completamente destrozado.

MERCHE ¡Ay, qué pena! La **pobre** familia! ¿Dónde van a vivir?

TONI Hay **varias** posibilidades.

MERCHE A lo mejor, pueden alquilar un piso **moderno** aquí.

TONI O tal vez volver a su **antiguo** pueblo y vivir con los abuelos.

Chapter 6   What have you learnt? (page 26)

A *Franco*

RAUL Era un **gran** hombre, Franco.

MIGUEL ¿De verdad?

RAUL Siempre lleno de **buenas** ideas.

MIGUEL ¿Sí?

RAUL Siempre tenía tiempo para la gente **pobre**.

MIGUEL No me digas.

RAUL Este **nuevo** gobierno – es imposible.

MIGUEL ¿Por qué?

RAUL Porque no aprecian las **antiguas** maneras de hacer las cosas.

MIGUEL ¿Sí?

RAUL Es la **misma** cosa todos los días – corrupción, escándalos …

MIGUEL ¿Y no había escándalos **grandes** en la época de Franco?

RAUL ¡Qué va!

MIGUEL Pues yo tengo **varios** periódicos de los años de Franco, y no todo era tan bonito como lo dice usted.

B *Querida Corazón …*

¿Me puede ayudar? ¡Me llamo Ana, y estoy harta! Tengo que compartir **mi** dormitorio con **mis** dos hermanas. **Mi** hermana menor, Alicia, no hace **su** cama y Rafaela, la mayor, no hace la **suya** tampoco. Alicia no recoge nunca **sus** cosas. Es que el cuarto es muy pequeño. Mi hermano tiene suerte: **su** dormitorio es grande y para él sólo; está muy ordenado, pero Mamá dice que **el nuestro** es una pocilga. ¿Qué puedo hacer?

Querida Ana,

¿Por qué no habláis con **vuestros** padres? Tal vez podéis cambiar de habitación. Y muchos jóvenes tienen problemas con **sus** hermanos: ¡me acuerdo de discusiones interminables con los **míos**! ¡Buena suerte! Corazón.

Revision test 4–6 (page 27–28)

A *¿Por qué …?*

1 Porque tengo calor.
2 Porque no tengo sed.
3 Porque no tenemos hambre.
4 Porque tengo miedo.
5 Porque tengo frío.
6 Porque tenemos sueño.

B *Números*

1 Hay **veintiocho** días en febrero.
2 Las historias de 'Las **mil y una** noches'.
3 Hay **quinientos** milímetros en medio metro.
4 El año bisiesto tiene **trescientos sesenta y seis** días.
5 El tablero de ajedrez tiene **sesenta y cuatro** casillas.
6 Hay **tres mil seiscientos** segundos en una hora.

C *El puzzle*

1 Lunes es el **primer** día de la semana.
2 El **tercer** día de la semana es miércoles.
3 La **primera** estación del año es la primavera.
4 Mayo es el **quinto** mes del año.
5 El **sexto** mes es junio.
6 Abril es el **cuarto** mes.
7 El verano es la **segunda** estación del año.
8 El **séptimo** día de la semana es domingo.
9 ¿Octubre? Es el **décimo** mes.
10 La **tercera** estación, otoño, es la que más me gusta.

D *East Lothian*

Las **largas** playas de arena y los **dorados** campos de cereales son las **primeras** impresiones que tendrá de East Lothian, una región **renombrada** por sus **soleados** veranos. Las **históricas** comunidades de Gifford o Haddington, **situadas** en la **bonita** campiña al pie de las **impresionantes** colinas de Lammermuir, merecen ser exploradas. Entre las **muchas** atracciones de la costa se encuentra Bass Rock, con su **famosa** colonia de alcatraces. Se puede visitar también el **hermoso** pueblo de Dunbar, cerca del John Muir Country Park, un bosque **precioso** con senderos que llegan a una costa que se conserva en su estado **natural**: todo a **poca** distancia de la capital de Escocia.

E *La lista*

ANITA ¡Mira! ¡Tenemos compañeros nuevos! Raoul es **francés**.

TRINI Y Nikos es **griego**. Hay un chico que se llama Jas – ¡qué nombre más raro!

ANITA No sé como se pronuncia. Jas es **americano**.

TRINI Y Ana es **portuguesa**. A lo mejor habla español, o lo entiende.

ANITA Luego, está Martine – es **canadiense**. Me gustaría visitar el Canadá un día.

TRINI La última es Tanja, que es **alemana**.

ANITA Pues yo no sé nada de Alemania. ¡Va a ser un año muy interesante!

F *¡Atención!*

1 Felipe, **mis** zapatillas nuevas – ¿dónde están? ¡No los encuentro!

2 ¡Merche, **tu** cartera está en **nuestro** dormitorio. ¿Por qué? ¡Y la raqueta encima de la cama no es **mía** tampoco!

3 Gabi y Unai – **vuestras** zapatillas nuevas están delante de la tele. ¡No es su sitio!

4 Marta – Antonia ha llamado por teléfono: ¿puedes ir a verla a **su** casa? ¡Y estoy disgustado con Unai y Gabri – **sus** chaquetas están en las escaleras y el montón de libros en la cocina es **suyo** también! ¡Hasta luego!

Chapter 7 What do you know? (page 29)

A *¿Adónde van?*

¿**Adónde va** usted de vacaciones? Según un estudio, depende de la nacionalidad de la persona. Los británicos **van** a la costa mediterránea, pero si nosotros los españoles **vamos** al extranjero, preferimos explorar las grandes ciudades de Europa. La familia francesa típica no **va** al extranjero – prefiere quedarse en Francia. Los escandinavos **van** a Suiza o a Europa Occidental.

B *Preguntas y más preguntas*

1 ¿Cuándo hay que … c volver al autocar?

2 ¿Qué se puede … e comprar – hay churros con chocolate?

3 ¿Cuánto cuesta … a una Coca-cola?

4 ¿Dónde están … f los servicios?

5 ¿Quién quiere ir … d a la tienda conmigo?

6 ¿Cuánto tiempo b pasamos aquí? ¿Una hora?

C *En la estación de servicio*

CELIA Oye, Ana – ¿no vienes a la tienda **conmigo**?

ANA ¿**Contigo**? No sé. ¿No sabes dónde está Marta? No quiero ir **sin ella**.

CELIA Mira, está allí con Paco. A lo mejor Marta va **con él** a la cafetería.

ANA Entonces voy **con ellos** también. ¿Te traigo algo de comer?

CELIA No, gracias – nada **para mí**. Me compro un poco de chocolate en la tienda.

ANA Pero ¿de quién es esta chaqueta en el asiento? ¿Es de Paco?

CELIA Vamos a mirar la etiqueta dentro – sí, es **de él**.

ANA ¡Qué despistado es! Se la llevo. Hasta pronto, Celia.

Chapter 7 What have you learnt? (page 32)

A *Las vacaciones de verano*

ANA   Paco, ¿adónde **vas** de vacaciones?

PACO No lo sé. Mi familia **va** a Francia, pero yo no.

ANA   ¿Por qué no **vas** tú?

PACO Mis dos primos **van** también – ¡pero son niños horrorosos!
¿Y tú?

ANA   Mi hermano mayor, Enrique, y yo **vamos** a Inglaterra.

PACO ¿**Vais** vosotros a Londres?

ANA   Sí, y luego a Edimburgo. Normalmente, yo **voy** a casa de mis tíos en Oxford,
pero este año, no.

PACO ¿Por qué no?

ANA   Porque mis tíos **van** a los Estados Unidos por tres semanas.

PACO ¡Pues tienes suerte, Ana! Me encantaría visitar Gran Bretaña.

B *En el aeropuerto*

1 ¿De **quién** es esta maleta?
2 ¿**Adónde** vas de vacaciones?
3 ¿**Cuántos** años tienes?
4 ¿**Cuándo** es tu cumpleaños?
5 ¿**Cómo** vas a volver a España? ¿En avión?
6 ¿**Cuánto** tiempo vas a quedarte en Gran Bretaña?
7 ¿**Por qué** vas a Inglaterra? ¿Tienes familia allí?
8 ¿**Qué** tienes en esa bolsa?

C *¡Qué habladora!*

¿Es para **mí** el regalo? ¡Qué amable! Tu tío está allí en el quiosco – ¿ves? Sí, tu
amigo está con **él** también. ¿Qué tal tu madre? Hablé con **ella** ayer. Va a pasar dos
semanas tranquilas sin **vosotros** dos. ¡Rápido, o el autobús va a salir sin **nosotros**!

Chapter 8 What do you know? (page 33)

A *Un día ideal*

– *Juan, eres un jóven Pisces. ¿A los Pisces les gustan las vacaciones acuáticas?*
– A mí, sí. ¿Mi día ideal? ¡**Paso** toda la mañana en la playa! Si hace buen tiempo,
nado en el mar y **tomo** el sol. Luego, por la tarde, depende. Si tengo mucha
energía, **hago** algún deporte acuático con mis amigos: esquí o vela.

– *Señora Carilla, usted es Escorpión. ¿Su día ideal consiste en algo más tranquilo?*
– Sí. Por la mañana, **leo** la última novela de los 'best-sellers' en mi jardín. Luego,
sobre las dos, **como** en la terraza de un restaurante tranquilo cerca de mi casa. Por
la tarde, muchas veces **visito** un museo o una exposición interesante en el centro. Y
por la noche **salgo** al teatro o al cine si ponen algo bueno que me interesa.

B *¡Qué rabia!*

JUAN   ¿Cuándo vas a los Estados Unidos, Santi?

SANTI   Bueno, me voy **el** seis de agosto y vuelvo en quince días.

JUAN   ¿Así que no vas a estar aquí **el** fin de semana?

SANTI   No. ¿Por qué?

JUAN   Bueno, ¿sabes que **los** sábados de agosto invitamos a varios expertos al club náutico? ¡Viene Marcos Martín!

JUAN   ¿El famoso surfista? ¿Viene **el** sábado?

SANTI   Sí, para mostrarnos sus técnicas del windsurf.

JUAN   ¡Qué rabia! Estoy fuera a mediados **de** agosto – ¡y viene mi héroe aquí!

SANTI   ¿Por qué no te vas **en** septiembre?

JUAN   No sé …

Chapter 8   What have you learnt? (page 36)

A *La Universidad de Santander*

IÑIGO   Señores Soriano, ¿por qué **pasan** ustedes las vacaciones aquí?

SR.   Nosotros – mi mujer y mi niña Mar – **vivimos** cerca de Madrid …

SRA.   … y una semana aquí en la costa del norte **parece** ideal.

IÑIGO   Y tú, Mar, ¿qué **haces** en tu cursillo?

MAR   **Aprendo** a hacer vela. A veces **salgo** en un barco yo sola – ¡es muy emocionante! – pero normalmente **practico** con mi pareja.

IÑIGO   Y ustedes, ¿qué **hacen**?

SR.   ¡Yo **cocino**! En casa, **hago** el desayuno, pero es todo.

IÑIGO   Señora, ¿le parece que su marido **necesita** aprender a cocinar?

SRA.   ¡Sí, por supuesto! Por la tarde, mi marido **trae** a la residencia los platos que ha preparado. Son deliciosos … Mi hija y yo **comemos** todo lo que él **prepara**.

IÑIGO   ¿Y su mujer **aprende** algo útil y práctico tambien, Señor Soriano?

SR.   ¡No! ¡Mi mujer **pinta** a la acuarela y **visita** exposiciones!

IÑIGO   ¿Y el año que viene?

SR.   No lo **sé** todavía. Lo bueno es que ahora yo **conozco** a mucha gente y tengo amigos nuevos. ¡A ver lo que **dice** mi mujer!

B *Los anuncios*

1   ¿Le interesa aprender el piragüismo? Clases con Toni empiezan **el** lunes 12 **de** julio.

2   **Los** domingos por la tarde **en** agosto – recitales de piano, aula 5, 20.00h.

3   **A** primeros **de** agosto – posibilidad de visitas a las cuevas de Altamira. Infórmese en la recepción.

4   Llegada del grupo musical Los Garay del Perú **el** treinta de julio. Recepción para todos a las 21.00, sala 3.

5   ¡Atención! **el** fin de semana 17–18 julio se sirve la cena a las 21.30.

6   **En** septiembre, no habrá clases de yoga con la Señora Puig.

7   Todos los cursillos terminan **a** finales **de** septiembre este año.

Chapter 9   What do you know? (page 37)

A *Jugamos al tenis*

PACO   Pues lo siento amigos, pero yo no **juego** bien al tenis.

FERNANDA Sylvia sí **juega**. ¡Es buenísima!

PACO   Sí, es verdad. Y Xavier es fenomenal. ¿Por qué no **juegas** tú, Xavier?

XAVIER   Lo siento – no estoy libre el sábado.

FERNANDA ¿Elena y Gabi? ¿**jugáis** al tenis vosotros dos?

ELENA   Bueno, sí – pero no **jugamos** muy bien.

FERNANDA Faltan cinco días – ¡hay que practicar cada tarde! ¿De acuerdo?

B *Receta para ganar la Copa*

1 Treinta minutos de ejercios cada **día**

2 más dos horas en la piscina cada **semana** …

3 más un fin de semana de entrenamiento intensivo cada **mes** …

4 ¡y ganamos la Copa cada **año**!

C *El profe de deportes*

Enseño **todo el** día – ¡y luego preparo clases **toda la** tarde! Normalmente, paso **todos los** sábados en el campo de deporte viendo los partidos, y paso **todas las** vacaciones preparando materiales para el nuevo trimestre. Antes de volver en septiembre, tengo pesadillas **toda la** noche. Durante el trimestre, paso **todos los** fines de semana pensando en el lunes. No sé por qué soy profesor – ¡qué vida!

Chapter 9   What have you learnt? (page 40)

A *Inma y Internet*

PABLO Inma, ¿**tienes** tu proprio ordenador?

INMA   ¡Ojalá! No, **suelo** usar el ordenador de mi madre.

PABLO ¿Tú **puedes** conectarte cuando quieras?

INMA   No, siempre **pido** permiso a mi madre antes. Si ella lo necesita para trabajar, entonces **vuelvo** a pedirle más tarde.

PABLO ¿Qué tipo de cosas **prefieres** tú hacer con tus amigas en la red?

INMA   Normalmente mi amiga Carla y yo **empezamos** con los canales de chat. Me gusta conectarme con chicas ingleses. A veces yo no **entiendo** lo que **dicen**, ¡y **pierdo** mucho tiempo buscando en el diccionario!

B *¿Eres perezoso o no?*

1 Haces los deberes
  a **todos los días**
  b de vez en cuando
  c muy pocas veces

2 Recoges tu cuarto
  a cada día
  b **una vez a la semana**
  c una vez al mes

3 Practicas el deporte
  a dos veces a la semana
  b cada quince días
  c **una o dos veces al año**

4 Vas a la piscina
  a **cada semana**
  b una vez a la semana
  c una o dos veces al mes

5 Juegas en un equipo
  a cada sábado
  b cada seis meses
  c **pocas veces**

6 Haces aerobic
  a cada noche
  b **dos veces al mes**
  c raras veces

Results of the Test

Mayoría de a: ¡qué bien! – eres muy activo/a.

Mayoría de b: debes esforzarte un poco más.

Mayoría de c: ¡qué perezoso/a eres!

Revision test 7–9 (page 41–42)

A *La agenda*

lunes 22	Carmen **va** al conservatorio (exámen de música).
martes 23	Yo **voy** al médico a las 11.00.
miércoles 24	Martín y José **van** al partido de fútbol (16.30).
jueves 25	Enrique y yo **vamos** al teatro (21.00).
viernes 26	¡Atención, Felipe! Tú y Rosario **vais** al dentista a las 11.00.
sábado 27	José **va** al campamento (10.00 en el colegio).

B *El Camino de Santiago*

1 ¿Con **quién** vas? ¡Si vas con un amigo o una amiga, hay que ser compatible!

2 ¿**Cómo** vas a viajar? ¿A pie? ¿En bicicleta?

3 ¿**Dónde** vas a quedarte de noche? El camping es más barato, pero hay que llevar más cosas.

4 ¿**Cuánto** dinero vas a necesitar? Es importante llevar algo para emergencias.

5 ¿**Qué** tipo de zapatos vas a llevar? Necesitas algo cómodo y fuerte – y dos pares.

6 ¿**Cuándo** piensas llegar a Santiago? Mejor evitar el 25 de julio – Día del Apóstol – porque habrá mucha gente en la capital.

C *En el camping*

1 Vamos a ver. Esta tienda es **para mí**.

2 ¡Oye – tú, Charo! La lámpara de bolsillo es **para ti**.

3 ¿Dónde está Nacho? Bueno, las cerillas son **para él**.

4 ¿Y María? El plato, el cuchillo y el tenedor son **para ella**.

5 Ximena y Nuria, los dos sacos de dormir son **para vosotras**.

6 ¡Quiero comprar una barra grande de chocolate! ¡Es **para nosotros**!

7 ¿Quién viene al supermercado **conmigo**?

D *El futbolista*

Música y cine

Ronaldo **disfruta** con un buen CD o una buena película. En música **prefiere** la samba y en el cine lo tiene bien claro: las películas de acción. Él siempre **ve** las películas en el vídeo de su casa:

– 'Si **voy** al cine, **llego** tarde, porque la gente me **pide** autógrafos. Es el precio de la fama' – dice Ronaldo.

Comidas

¿Qué tipo de comida le gusta más? Depende.

– Me encanta la comida brasileña, y ¡más todavía si es mi madre quien **cocina**! Si yo **salgo** a cenar fuera de casa, siempre **como** hamburguesas o pizzas.

Amor

Ronaldo está enamorado de la futbolista y modelo Susana Werner. Lo difícil es que él **juega** en Barcelona y ella **vive** en Brasil. Muchos kilómetros les **separan** pero los dos **pasan** las vacaciones juntos en América o en Europa.

– Estoy enamoradísimo y **quiero** formar una familia – **afirma** Ronaldo.

E *El Telegrama*

1 Rosa necesita tratamiento **en agosto**.
2 Llega aquí **el cinco de agosto**.
3 Tiene cita con el médico **el lunes**.
4 Necesita descanso total **los fines de semana**.
5 Vuelve a Oreña **a finales de agosto**.

F *El correo electrónico*

Querida Begoña,

Quieres saber algo de lo que hago en mi tiempo libre. Bueno, juego al squash **tres veces a la semana** y practico la natación **todos los días**. Voy al gimnasio **cada dos días** para entrenarme. Me encanta el ciclismo y **una vez al mes** voy a la montaña con un grupo de amigos. Soy una persona muy activa: ¡sólo duermo cinco horas **al día**! Como sabes, me encanta la informática. ¿Y tú? ¿**Cuántas veces** navegas por Internet **a la semana**? Leo mi correo electrónico **cada noche** antes de irme a la cama, así que ¡escríbeme pronto!

Chapter 10   What do you know? (page 43)

A *La rutina*

1 **Me despierto** a las siete. ¡Qué disgusto!
2 **Me ducho**. ¡Qué frío!
3 **Me visto en** mi uniforme escolar. ¡Qué asco!
4 **Me voy** a las ocho menos cuarto. ¡Qué temprano!
5 En clase **me aburro**. ¡Qué rollo!
6 **Me acuesto** muy tarde. ¡Qué bien!

B *El fin de semana*

1c El sábado no hago mucho por la mañana.
2d No desayuno, pero tomo algo ligero a la una.
3a Me acuesto muy tarde, a medianoche.
4e El domingo no me levanto hasta las once de la mañana.
5f Salgo con mis amigos a mediodía.
6b No vuelvo a casa hasta las seis o siete de la tarde.

C *La pobre Alicia*

1 ¡Alicia! ¡Haz tu cama **antes de** bajar para desayunar!
2 ¡No te olvides de lavarte los dientes **después de** desayunar!
3 Y **antes de** irte al insti, prepárate un bocadillo para el recreo.
4 **Después de** volver a casa, ¡haz tus deberes en tu cuarto y no delante de la tele!
5 Y **antes de** las seis ve a la casa de tu tía para recoger a tu hermano. Tu tía sale a las seis en punto, ¡así que no llegues tarde!
6 **Después de** recoger a tu hermano, dale algo de comer aquí en casa: fruta o yogur.

Chapter 10 What have you learnt? (page 46)

A *El horario*

IÑIGO   ¿Qué asignaturas tenemos mañana **por** la mañana?
ANTÓN   **A** las nueve tenemos música.
IÑIGO   ¿No tenemos música **a** la una **de** la tarde?
ANTÓN   No – el lunes no. Y luego **a** las diez hay dos horas de ciencias.
IÑIGO   ¿Hay asamblea **a** mediodía o **por** la tarde?
ANTÓN   No hay mañana. Hay geografía **a** la una. ¿Has hecho tus deberes?
IÑIGO   ¡Se me olvidó! Tendré que hacerlos. Y son las diez **de** la noche ya.
        ¡A qué me acuesto **a** medianoche!

B *¿Optimista o pesimista?*

Si tú eres optimista …
1 **te levantas** temprano casi todos los días.
2 **te duchas** o **te bañas** cantando.
3 **te vistes** bien y estás contento/a con tu cuerpo.
4 **te diviertes** mucho – todo te parece interesante.

La persona pesimista …
5 **se preocupa** mucho de su aparencia física.
6 no **se organiza** bien – es despistado/a.
7 **se aburre** fácilmente.
8 **se acuesta** muy tarde.

C *Al Polo Sur*

1 **Al despertarse**, se pone en contacto con Madrid.
2 **Después de levantarse**, prepara una comida.
3 **Antes de vestirse** en un mono de nieve, se pone una crema.
4 **Antes de marcharse** temprano, escucha el pronóstico.
5 **Después de llegar** al próximo campamento, monta la tienda.

Chapter 11　What do you know? (page 47)

A *La encuesta*

1　A 95% les **gusta** la coca-cola.
2　A 92% les **gustan** los helados italianos.
3　A 87% les **gustan** las hamburguesas.
4　A 85% les **gusta** la lasaña.
5　A 80% les **gusta** el queso holandés.
6　A 76% les **gustan** las perritos calientes.
7　A 70% les **gustan** los espaguetis.
8　A 15% les **gusta** el rosbif.

B *¿Qué les gusta hacer?*

JON　　　　Oye, Conchita, ¿qué tipo de música **te** interesa?
CONCHITA　Pues, a mí **me** encanta la música 'hip-hop'. ¡Pero a mis padres, no **les** gusta nada!
JON　　　　¿Y tu hermano? ¿**Le** parece buenos los grupos británicos?
CONCHITA　Sí. A nosotros **nos** interesa mucho la música inglesa y americana.
JON　　　　¿Qué hacéis el fin de semana? ¿**Os** gusta salir?
CONCHITA　Mucho. ¿**Te** gustaría venir con nosotros al club juvenil el vienes?
JON　　　　¡Cómo no!

C *Lo mejor y lo peor*

Lo bueno es que le encanta España, y Conchita es muy amable con él. ¡Pero **lo malo** es que hablamos muy rápido, y le resulta difícil entender! Para él, **lo aburrido** es que va al instituto con Concha. ¡Dice que no entiende nada de nada! Pero **lo divertido** es que sale con Concha y sus amigos por la tarde, y lo pasa bomba.

Chapter 11　What have you learnt? (page 50)

A *Los jóvenes tiquismiquis*

INMA　A los jóvenes de cualquier nacionalidad, no **les** interesa la cultura.
ROSA　¡Es verdad! A la inglesa que tengo yo, sólo **le** gusta salir con amigos.
TERE　Pero cuando tú tenías catorce años, **te** gustaba salir también, ¿no?
INMA　¡Y además son muy tiquismiquis! A la niña japonesa no **le** apetece nada. ¡No quiere comer nada!
TERE　¡Pues yo tengo dos chicos escoceses en casa, y **les** gusta todo!
ROSA　Tienes suerte, hija. A mí, **me** encanta cuando los niños comen bien.
TERE　Pero cuando estáis en el extranjero vosotras, ¿**os** gusta siempre la comida?
INMA　Sí, tienes razón. Muchas veces sólo probamos lo que **nos** gusta en casa.
ROSA　Bueno, vamos al castillo: ¡a ver si **les** interesa a mis dos chicas!

B *Mis gustos*
1 **Me gusta mucho** la coca-cola.
2 **Me gustan mucho** las hamburguesas.
3 **Me gusta mucho** la fruta.
4 **Me gusta mucho** el chocolate.
5 **Me gustan mucho** los mariscos.
6 **No me gusta mucho** el zumo de piña.
7 **No me gusta mucho** el pescado.
8 **No me gustan mucho** las aceitunas.
9 **No me gusta mucho** la leche.
10 **No me gustan** los bocadillos de jamón.

C *En mi opinión*
Me gusta mucho España en general. **Lo** bueno es que la gente es muy simpática, pero **lo que** me fastidia es que los españoles hablan tan rápidamente. El paisaje es muy bonito y **lo** mejor es que todavía hay ciudades y regiones enteras sin turistas. Pero **lo que** no me gusta nada, es la contaminación del paisaje por todas partes – la conciencia ecológica no existe en muchos sitios. Esto es **lo** peor para mí.

Chapter 12   What do you know? (page 51)

A *¡No me gusta mi nueva casa!*
Querida Corazón,
No me gusta mi nueva casa, **ni** el cambio de mi rutina. Vivo ahora en las afueras de Madrid, pero no me gusta **nada**. Mis antiguos amigos viven en el centro, y no quieren venir aquí **nunca**, donde es aburrido y **no** hay mucha movida. El fin de semana, no veo a **nadie**. No hay **ni** cine **ni** discoteca. ¡Ayúdame!
Carmen.

B *Mis recomendaciones*
1 Hay que hacer un esfuerzo para conocer **a** otras personas – ¡anímate!
2 Haz un cursillo de noche: pide información en el ayuntamiento.
3 Invita **a** una compañera de clase a tu casa; así vas a hacerte amigas.
4 Visita el hospital o la clínica cerca, para ver si necesitan voluntarios.
5 Pregunta **a** tu tutor, para ver si hay clubs después del día escolar.
6 Si te sientes muy sola y muy triste, llama a la organización Juventud.

C *Lo siento …*
1 Lo siento, no queda **ninguno**.
2 Es que no hay **ninguna** en el almacén.
3 No quedan **ningunas**. Lo siento mucho.
4 Lo siento, no queda **ningún** paquete.
5 Vendí los últimos ayer. No tenemos **ningunos**.

Help Yourself to Essential Spanish Grammar

Chapter 12   What have you learnt? (page 54)

A *¡Qué desastre de familia!*
1 Mi mujer **no** hace mucho.
2 Nuestro hijo mayor **jamás** prepara la comida.
3 Mi hija mayor **no** hace **nunca** su cama.
4 **Nadie** lava los platos.
5 La madre de mi marido **ni** pone **ni** quita la mesa.
6 Mi hija menor **no** ayuda **a nadie** en casa.

B *La chica despistada*
PAPÁ   ¿Estás preparada? ¿Tienes un boli?
BELÉN **No, no tengo ninguno.**
PAPÁ   Toma. ¿Y tus zapatillas?
BELÉN **No tengo ningunas.**
PAPÁ   ¡Cómo qué no! ¡Están en tu cuarto! ¿Y la llave de la casa?
BELÉN **No tengo ninguna.**
PAPÁ   Te presto la mía – toma. ¿Has hecho los deberes?
BELÉN **No tengo ningunos.**
PAPÁ   ¡Qué raro! Pero, ¿no tienes una bolsa para tus cosas?
BELÉN **No tengo ninguna.**
PAPÁ   ¡Dios mío! Toma esta bolsa de plástico. Corre – ¡allí viene el autobús!
BELÉN **¡No tengo dinero!**

C *Marifé y Zeneida*
1 A mí **tampoco**.
2 Yo **también**.
3 A mí **tampoco**.
4 A mí **también**.
5 Yo **también**.
6 A mí **tampoco**.

Revision test 10–12 (page 55–56)

A *La carta de Ahmed*
Quieres saber algo de mi familia, ¿verdad? ¡Pues nosotros no **nos llevamos** bien por la mañana! Yo **me levanto** a las siete en punto, y mis padres **se despiertan** también – pero como sólo tenemos un cuarto de baño, mi madre **se mete** primero mientras que yo **me lavo** los dientes en el lavabo del aseo y papá prepara el desayuno. A veces, papá **se afeita** en la cocina, ¡pero mi madre **se pone** furiosa si lo hace! Yo **me río** mucho cuando mis padres **se enfadan** porque nunca dura mucho tiempo, y luego hacen las paces. ¿Y tú? ¿**Te llevas** bien por la mañana con tu familia o **os peleáis** también? ¡Escríbeme pronto!

B *¡Qué vida de perro!*
1 Me levanto a las seis y media **de la mañana**.
2 **Luego**, me ducho y me visto. ¡Siempre tengo prisa!
3 **Un poco más tarde** me tomo un café con leche y una tostada.
4 **Después** me preparo un bocadillo para el almuerzo.
5 Preparo la cena y despierto a mi marido **a las ocho** – él cuida a los niños.
6 Diez minutos **más tarde** cojo el autobús a la oficina.
7 Vuelvo a casa, muy cansada **a las siete de la tarde**.
8 Traigo tanto trabajo a casa, que me acuesto **a medianoche**. ¡Qué vida de perro!

C *La azafata*
1 Después de **levantarme** de mi asiento, voy a ver a los pasajeros.
2 Antes de **relajarse** un poco, el capitán verifica su posición.
3 Al **ver** los carritos, los viajeros se preparan para comer.
4 Después de **recoger** todo, descansamos un poco.
5 Al **aterrizar**, nos despedimos de nuestros clientes.
6 Antes de **volver** al terminal, pongo la cabina en orden.

D *Una encuesta*

JAIME	¿Qué **le gusta** comer al mediodía, Señorita?
SÉNORITA	**Me gustan** los perritos calientes, sobre todo.
JAIME	Señor y Señora, ¿qué **les gusta** tomar para la comida principal?
SR. Y SRA.	**Nos gusta** mucho el pescado. Más que la carne.
JAIME	Y tú, chiquitito – ¿qué te gusta comer?
CHICO	**¡Me gustan** los helados de chocolate!
SRA.	A mi hijo **le gustan** mucho los dulces – churros, donuts, y pasteles.
JAIME	¡Es normal!
JAIME	¡Hola, jóvenes! ¡Un momento! ¿Qué **os gusta** comer al mediodía?
JÓVENES	Somos de padres italianos, así que **nos gustan** las pastas y las pizzas.
JAIME	¿Y tus amigos españoles? ¿Qué prefieren?
JÓVENES	**Les gusta** más algo típico español – una tortilla, o una paella.
JAIME	Gracias – ¡qué aproveche!

E *Punto de encuentro*
¡Hola! Soy Silvia y me gustaría conocer **a gente** de todo el mundo. Me encanta también el cine: me gusta ir a ver **las películas** de acción, y los dibujos animados de Disney. También quiero mucho **a mi serpiente** – tengo **una cobra**, que se llama Coki. Si queréis **una amiga divertida**, escribid a Silvia, c/ San Clemente 132, Alhucemas o por correo electrónico a Fer0634@.ols.com.es. (¡Pregunta **a tus padres** primero!)

Chapter 13   What do you know? (page 57)

A *Vamos al parque*

1 Juanito, quédate aquí a mi lado. Camina **lentamente**.
2 ¡Anda por la acera y no por la carretera! Te comportas **estúpidamente**.
3 Vale, Paquito. Puedes ir hasta la entrada. Pero espera allí **tranquilamente**.
4 Juanito, ¡sal de allí! Pon la silla de la cafetería **bien**.
5 ¡A qué sí, entiendes! ¡Me entiendes **perfectamente**!
6 ¡Cuidado con esa taza! Se rompe **fácilmente**.
7 No, no vamos a tomar algo en la cafetería. Vamos al parque para merendar. Se abre **normalmente** a las diez.

B *¿Por dónde?*

1 **Ustedes**.
2 **Usted**.
3 **Vosotros**.
4 **Usted**.
5 **Tú**.
6 **Usted**.
7 **Ustedes**.
8 **Vosotros**.

Chapter 13   What have you learnt? (page 60)

A *En la guardería de niños*

1 Alicia, ¡**saca** el boli de tu boca! ¡Lo vas a tragar!
2 Chicos, ¡**poned** las sillas bien, por favor!
3 ¡Eh!, ¡**salid** de debajo de la mesa! No puedo ver lo que hacéis.
4 Paquito, ¡**dibuja** en la hoja de papel, y no en la mesa!
6 ¡**Tened** cuidado, chicas! Esta torre va a caer.
7 ¿Qué te pasa, Miguel? ¡**Ven** aquí!

B *El arte de vender*

1 Escuchen a los clientes **atentamente**.
2 Sirvan a los clientes **rápidamente**.
3 Hablen de nuestros productos **responsablemente**.
4 Hablen al cliente de los beneficios del producto **persuasivamente**.
5 Expliquen las condiciones del contrato **lenta** y **claramente**.
6 Si surge algún problema, intenten solucionarlo **diplomáticamente**.
7 Si al fin y al cabo, el cliente no quiere comprar el producto, despídanse de él **educadamente**.

C *Al conductor del minibús ...*
Al salir del aparcamiento, **tome** la carretera principal y **siga** todo recto hasta los semáforos. Allí **tuerza** a la izquierda y **suba** la calle. Cuando llegue al hipermercado, **coja** la segunda calle a la izquierda. **Tenga** cuidado porque hay una curva peligrosa inmediatamente después. **Busque** el edificio Miraflores a la derecha. **Aparque** el minibús debajo de los árboles, delante del edificio. Si tiene problemas, **llame** al número 82.45.71.09.

Chapter 14   What do you know? (page 61)

A *La moda*
¿Qué se lleva **este** año? Pues, **estas** faldas largas están muy de moda. Hay que llevarlas con uno de **estos** jerseys largos y ajustados. ¿Le gusta **esta** chaqueta de seda? Le va muy bien. ¿Quiere probarla con **este** pantalón holgado? **Estos** colores van muy bien juntos. Los probadores están allí, al fondo.

B *¿No tiene otro?*
Ésta: this one
... ésa: that one
... aquél: that one over there
... éstos: these ones
Ésos: those ones
Aquéllos: those ones over there

C *Aviso importante*
Todos nuestros platos **se hacen** con los mejores productos de España. **Se prepara** la comida con ingredientes frescos y cultivados biológicamente donde sea posible. ¡Aquí **se come** sólo lo mejor! No **se venden** bebidas alcohólicas, pero **se puede** traer su propia botella de vino, y beberla aquí.

Chapter 14   What have you learnt? (page 64)

A *La hija y su madre*
No me gusta nada **esta** falda gris. ¡Es demasiado larga! ¡Y **ese** jersey es horrible! Quiero algo de lana o de algodón. ¡Odio **aquellos** zapatos! Todo el mundo lleva tacones altos este año. ¿Y **esas** medias? ¡Ni hablar! Quiero **aquella** sudadera negra y **estos** vaqueros azules Levi's. ¡Me va muy bien **esa** camisa blanca a cuadros azules y **aquel** par de botas negras de cuero en el escapatate! ¡ Y ya está!

B *El puesto de regalos*

PEPE ¿Le interesan los platos de cerámica? **Éstos** son muy bonitos.

TÚ ¿Cuánto valen **ésos**?

PEPE **Ése** cuesta dos mil y **aquél** tres mil quinientas.

TÚ Son un poco caros. ¿Cuánto cuesta la taza azul?

PEPE **Ésta** vale mil quinientas.

TÚ Me gustan también las muñecas: **aquéllas**.

PEPE Cuestan mil pesetas. ¿Usted ve **éstas** las pequeñas? Sólo ochocientas pesetas.

TÚ Perfecto. Me llevo dos. Y un cenicero. Sí, **ése**. Gracias.

C *Anuncios*

1 ¡Hága**se** millonario! ¡Compre su billete de lotería aquí!

2 ¡Jóvenes! ¡Imagina**os** súper inteligentes, sacando buenas notas en vuestros exámenes! Clases particulares con profesor experimentado.

3 ¿Eres tímido/a? ¿Careces de confianza en ti mismo/a? Inscríbe**te** en nuestro próximo cursillo "Todo a tu alcance".

4 ¡Atención, chicos/as de 15–18 años! ¿Queréis ganar un poco de dinero extra? ¡Presenta**os** el día 20 en la recepción del Hotel Finlandia.

5 ¡Señoras! ¿Se sienten cansadas y aburridas? ¡Transfórmen**se** en nuestro salón de belleza, El Rostro Bello!

Chapter 15   What do you know? (page 65)

A *¡Gangas estupendas!*

SEÑOR El póster es **más** barato que el plato de cerámica.

SEÑORA Sí, pero la cerámica es mejor. Es **más** típica de Méjico.

SEÑOR ¿No te gustan las flautas? Son **menos** caras que la cerámica y también son muy típicas.

SEÑORA Sí, pero los platos son **menos** útiles que la cerámica. Las flautas son ideales para niños, pero para adultos no.

SEÑOR ¿Qué te parecen los abanicos? Son los **más** baratos de todo.

SEÑORA No son **tan** típicos como las cosas hechas aquí en Méjico.

SEÑOR Las muñecas son bonitas. Y **más** baratas que los pósteres.

SEÑORA ¿O un cenicero? Son **tan** baratos como las muñecas pero más útiles.

SEÑOR ¡Idiota! ¡Nuestros vecinos no fuman!

B *¡Ni hablar!*

1c ¡Yo quiero ir a la playa!
¡Nadar en el mar es aburrido!

2e Me apetece ir al cine.
¡Ver películas es muy pesado, mamá!

3g Quiero jugar al fútbol.
Practicar deporte es para bebés como tú Miguelito. ¡Yo no quiero!

4b ¡Vamos a las tiendas!
¿Comprar recuerdos otra vez? ¡No, gracias!

5d ¡Quiero ir a la discoteca!
¡No – no voy a pasar toda la tarde bailando!
6a Quisiera ir de excursión.
¿Haciendo turismo en un grupo? ¡No!
7f Podemos descansar en nuestras camas.
¡Dormir es lo más aburrido de todo!

Chapter 15   What have you learnt? (page 68)

A *¡Qué desastre de padre!*

¿Dónde están los niños? Yoli está **charlando** con el camarero de la cafetería, Luis está **subiendo** a un árbol enorme, Miguelito está **durmiendo** en la hierba, Juanita está en la arena **comiendo** no sé qué, Merche está **jugando** sola en los columpios, Rafa está **pidiendo** un helado del dueño de la heladería … ¿Y mi marido? ¡Está **leyendo** el periódico tranquilamente en un banco! ¡Qué desastre!

B *América del Sur*

1 El río Amazonas es **el más largo**.
2 La montaña Aconcagua es **la más alta**.
3 El lago Titicaca es **el más grande**.
4 El desierto de Atacama es **el más seco**.
5 El país de Chile es **el más estrecho**.
6 Los habitantes del Paraguay son **los más pobres**.
7 La ciudad de Méjico es **la más contaminada**.

C *Las especialidades mexicanas*

LUIS   El guacamole es **más delicioso que** la sopa.

YOLI   Sí, pero las chimichangas son **más típicas**.

MAMÁ   Miguelito no puede comerlas. Son **más picantes que** las enchiladas.

PAPA   Sí. Me parece que las empanadas son **más suaves** para él.

MERCHE ¿Los burritos son **tan buenos como** las empanadas, Yoli?

YOLI   Sí, son **más ricos**. Y la salsa es **la más deliciosa** de todas las salsas.

MAMÁ   Para mí, los pimientos fritos. Son **menos salados que** los otros platos.

PAPÁ   Pues, yo voy a pedir el plato **más barato**. ¡Como somos ocho, me va a costar un dineral!

Revision test 13–15 (page 69–70)

A *¿Buen amigo o no?*

1 Tu novio/a te acompaña a una fiesta. Lleva algo que no te gusta.
   a Le dices **francamente** lo que opinas.
   b Le explicas **diplomáticamente** que la fiesta no es tan formal (o informal) y que
     sería mejor tal vez llevar otra cosa.
   c Le piropeas **alegremente**.

2 Alguien te dice que tu novio/a sale con otro/a.
   a Cuestionas a tu novio/a **abiertamente**.
   b Hablas **rápidamente** a alguien quien os conoce **bien** a los dos.
   c No lo crees. Tu novio/a siempre se comporta **sincera** y **correctamente**.

B *Peluquería con vídeos*

¡**Abra** los ojos! ¡**Aprenda** peluquería! Es más sencillo de lo que parece. **Invite** a un grupo de amigas y **miren** juntas el nuevo Curso de vídeos de GEP. Ésta es la mejor manera: mirando, sin horarios en casa. **Conviértase** en una auténtica profesional de la peluquería. **Decídase** y **matricúlese** en el nuevo curso, o **solicite** ahora información de cualquiera de nuestros cursos. **Póngase** en nuestros manos, ahora es el momento de aprender.

C *La pobre Charo*

TUTOR ¡**Estos** deberes no son muy buenos, Charo!

CHARO Es que no tuve mucho tiempo **esta** semana. Tuve que …

TUTOR ¡Excusas, excusas! **Ese** ejercicio está sin hacer todavía y **esas** páginas son un desastre, llenas de errores.

CHARO Hice todo **eso** en casa, porque estaba ausente cuando se hizo en clase.

TUTOR Hay que hacer el ejercicio número once otra vez, y **ése** también. Siéntate en una mesa. Sí, **aquella**.

D *La comida española*

¿Cuáles son las diferencias entre la comida española y la británica? Primero, **se nota** que **se usa** menos aceite y más grasa animal, aunque esto está cambiando. No **se compra** tanto ajo allí como aquí, pero **se utiliza** en los platos mediterráneos que son muy populares. En el Reino Unido **se beben** muchos tés e infusiones de hierbas. Incluso en las estaciones de servicios en las autopistas **se sirve** una gama enorme. **Se ven** también en los supermercados mucho tipos de leche: de cabra, de oveja, de soja. Aquí en España, estas cosas sólo **se compran** en tiendas especializadas.

E *Los niños pesados del avión*

REME Yo soy más alta que **tú**, Carlos.

CARLOS ¡Qué va! Eres más baja que **yo**.

NURIA ¡Yo soy más alta que **vosotros** dos!

FELIPE Y Carlos no es muy fuerte. Yo soy más fuerte que **él**.

REME ¡Y qué, Felipe! No eres tan inteligente como **nosotros**.

AZAFATA ¡Sentaos y callaos! Si no, voy a hablar a vuestros padres.

NURIA Me da igual. ¡Es usted más estricta que **ellos**!

F *En el vuelo*

Hay mucha movida. La azafata **está leyendo** un cuento a un grupo de niños rebeldes, y la mayoría le **está escuchando**. Un padre detrás de mi asiento **está riñiendo** a su hijo menor que quiere ir para ver lo que **está pasando**. Las otras azafatas **están yendo** y **viniendo** de la cocina, y **están haciendo** mucho ruido. ¡Y nos quedan cinco horas todavía!

Chapter 16   What do you know? (page 71)

A *El viaje desastroso*

El viernes, yo **salí** de casa a las ocho y **llegué** al aeropuerto dos horas más tarde. Allí, **encontré** a Iñigo y **pasamos** una hora en el bar. Pero – ¡fíjate! – **perdimos** el avión. Por fin, **cogimos** un vuelo a las cinco. En la Oficina de Turismo **reservé** un hotel en el centro para la noche: ¡qué ruidoso! Yo no **dormí** mucho. Por la mañana, Iñigo y yo **desayunamos** chocolate con churros en un café enfrente y **escribimos** un montón de postales. Yo **compré** una guía de Bilbao pero a lo contrario de lo que dice, ¡Bilbao no es ni turístico ni bonito!

B *La Primera Semana*

Llegamos el viernes de **la semana pasada**. El fin de semana descansamos, pero **el lunes por la mañana** alquilé un Seat Ibiza y fuimos hasta San Vicente. Un día, tomamos el sol en la playa y **hace tres días** subimos a Potes en los Picos de Europa. Cogimos el teleférico a la cumbre Fuente Dé. Luego llovió **durante dos días**, así que no fuimos a la playa el jueves ni el viernes. Me encantó la visita **anteayer** a las cuevas. Luego **ayer** fuimos a las tiendas en Santander. Fuimos a una discoteca **anoche** – ¡y me duelen los pies algo terrible hoy! Os escribo pronto – un abrazo, Iñigo.

Chapter 16   What have you learnt? (page 74)

A *¿Sevilla? ¡Es una maravilla!*

JOSÉ   ¿Cómo **encontraste** trabajo en Sevilla, Raúl?

RAÚL   Bueno, **llegamos** Juanjo y yo en mayo. Juanjo **buscó** trabajo en los bares, y yo **conseguí** un puesto en un café, como camarero.

JUANJO Y por la noche, **salimos** los dos a los clubs y discotecas.

RAÚL   Yo **toqué** la guitarra y Juanjo **bailó** flamenco para los turistas.

JUANJO Para nosotros, que estupendo. **Conocimos** a mucha gente.

RAÚL   Y los turistas nos **regalaron** muchas cosas – vino, dinero.

JUANJO Me **cayeron** muy bien los ingleses – ¡**Sacaron** muchas fotos!

IÑIGO   ¡Qué bien! A lo mejor, nos vamos nosotros.

B *Un poco de historia*

Sevilla ha cambiado mucho en los últimos años. **Durante muchos años** era una ciudad famosa pero un poco descuidada – pero **hace diez años** ocurrió algo que cambió la ciudad para siempre: empezaron a planificar la EXPO 1992. **Ayer** Sevilla era antigua y turística – hoy es moderna e internacional. **Durante seis siglos** durmió Sevilla, envuelta en las memorias de su pasado glorioso – pero **el año pasado** se despertó y empezó a convertirse en un símbolo vibrante de un futuro brillante.

C *¡Madrid es mejor!*

M Bueno, Sevilla es bonita, **pero** no es tan importante como Madrid.

S ¿Qué? Madrid es administrativo – ¡**pero** no tiene nada de cultura!

M ¿Y Sevilla? Tiene flamenco y toros, **pero** es todo. ¡Cosa de provincias!

S ¡Sevilla no es provincial, **sino** internacional! Madrid es sucio y feo.

M Oye – no es fea Madrid, **sino** precioso. Hay contaminación, sí – ¡**pero** igual que en Sevilla!

Chapter 17 What do you know? (page 75)

A *Las Baleares*

1e En verano en Menorca, hace más viento que en las otras islas.

2d En Mallorca, en verano hace mucho sol.

3a En la isla menorquina, a veces hay neblina.

4c En Formentera hace muchísimo calor.

5b En todas las islas en verano hay riesgo de tormenta.

B *Catriona y Carlos*

RAMÓN Catriona y Carlos, ¿**desde hace** cuánto tiempo viven aquí en Menorca?

CARLOS Catriona vino aquí **hace** quince años – de Escocia, pero yo soy nativo.

RAMÓN ¿Y **hay** mucha gente como ustedes, en la isla?

CATRIONA Bueno, en aquella época, no. Pero ahora **hay** más.

RAMÓN Usted habla muy bien el español. ¿Aprende **desde hace** mucho tiempo?

CATRIONA ¡Tuve que aprender! – ¡**hace** quince años, casi nadie hablaba inglés aquí!

C *El romance*

Yo **vine** aquí a Menorca en en 1980, cuando **tuve** dieciséis años. No **traje** más que una maleta y veinte libras esterlinas en total. Claro, no **pude** sobrevivir sin dinero, así que **puse** un anuncio en el periódico. Me llamó una madre: ella **quiso** una señorita inglesa para enseñar inglés a su hijo, Carlos. Nos enamoramos y me casé con él en el año 1985.

Chapter 17 What have you learnt? (page 78)

A *Galicia*

¡Qué tiempo más malo! Cuando llegué, hacía mucho sol y calor, pero por la tarde, **hizo** mucho viento. Por la noche **hubo** una tormenta tremenda y llovió mucho. Luego **hubo** neblina por toda la costa – se llama orbayu aquí – y no pudimos bañarnos, porque **hizo** fresquito. Parece que **hizo** malo el verano pasado – ¡y que ya en agosto **hizo** bastante frío para ponerse un jersey!

B *En el camping*

MARI PAZ No hay ni pan, ni agua. ¡Paco! ¿No **trajiste** tú agua ayer?

PACO Sí, **fui** a los lavabos y **llené** el cacharro con agua del grifo.

MARI PAZ Pues, no queda. Mila, ¿no **hiciste** tú la compra esta mañana?

MILA No **vino** el camión con el pan. Me **dijo** el dueño que es fiesta.

MARI PAZ ¡Ay, no me di cuenta! Tal vez haya un supermercado en Orense.

DAVID ¿Tenemos dinero? Ayer Mila y yo no **pudimos** sacar dinero porque dejamos las tarjetas aquí en la recepción.

PACO Y Mari Paz y yo **estuvimos** toda la tarde sin comer, ¡porque no **trajisteis** vosotros bastante pizza para todos!

MARI PAZ Yo **tuve** hambre ayer, ¡pero hoy va a ser peor todavía!

C *¡Estoy harto!*

1 **Hace** una semana **que** estamos aquí.
2 No vemos el sol **desde hace** cinco días.
3 No comemos bien **desde hace** dos días y yo tengo hambre.
4 **Hace** cinco años **que** conozco a Mari Paz.
5 Pero **desde hace** tres días Mari Paz está de muy mal humor. ¡Estoy harto!

Chapter 18 What do you know? (page 79)

A *Las quejas del Señor Gonzalo*

1 **Leyó** en la guía que el hotel era excelente.
2 **Eligió** el hotel porque lo recomendó un amigo.
3 En la cafetería, **pidió** un té con leche – pero la leche era caliente.
4 **Se vistió** elegantemente, pero sin corbata – y no le dejaron entrar en el restaurante.
5 El vídeo no funcionó – pero **siguió** las instrucciones correctamente.
6 No **durmió** bien – el colchón era muy duro.

B *Lo siento mucho, pero …*

1 Lo siento que usted se encuentre **mal** esta mañana.
2 Pero le asegura que nuestro hotel no es **malo**.
3 Nuestros clientes dicen que este hotel es **mejor** que los otros.
4 El servicio aquí siempre es muy **bueno**.
5 Hay quien opina que es el **mejor** de la provincia.
6 ¡Lo que es cierto, es que no es el **peor**!

C *El libro de reclamaciones*

Nos decidimos hacer un viaje por esta regíon de España porque es bonita **e** interesante. No queríamos un hotel **u** hostal barato y feo – y leímos que este hotel era muy antiguo **e** histórico. Siento decírselo, pero en su cafetería hay bichos – no sé si son cucarachas **u** hormigas – y el jardín está lleno de cardos **y** hierbas malas. ¿El mejor de la región? ¡Qué va! ¿Me trae el libro de reclamaciones, por favor?

Chapter 18   What have you learnt? (page 82)

A *El fin de semana*

¡Es que fue un desastre! Belén, Tere, Carlos y yo no **conseguimos** una mesa hasta las diez de la noche. Tere estaba enfadada con Carlos y no **sonrió** ni una vez. ¡La música era tan fuerte, que nos **impidió** de hablar mucho! Así que, de conversación estimulante, nada. Los otros **pidieron** pimientos rellenos, y yo merluza, pero el cocinero nuevo **frió** todo en tanto aceite que no nos gustó nada. Y luego el camarero **sirvió** un vino tinto de la casa tan desgradable que no lo pudimos beber. Belén **se sintió** tan mala, que volvimos todos al hotel. Allí, había una fiesta de boda – y como Carlos y Tere estaban en la planta baja, durmieron muy poco. Belén me **riñó** toda la noche porque yo no **pedí** el libro de reclamaciones en el restaurante.

B *Recordando lo ocurrido*

BELÉN De verdad, la comida no era muy **buena**.
MARIO ¡Y el vino era **peor** que la comida!
BELÉN El hotel no me gustó nada. Era **el peor** de mi vida.
MARIO ¡Qué va! El hotel no era **malo** – tenía cuatro estrellas.
BELÉN ¿Y Carlos, tu **mejor** amigo? Estaba de muy mal humor.
MARIO Tu amiga Tere fue **peor** – ¡no sonrió en toda la tarde!
BELÉN ¡De verdad, no fueron **las mejores** vacaciones del verano!

C *El alojamiento en España*

1 Lo más caro es quedarse en paradores **u** hoteles de lujo.
2 Hay muchos campings de buena calidad **y** precio en la costa.
3 ¡Pero cuidado! Fondas **u** hostales muy baratos pueden ser sucios.
4 Los albergues juveniles son limpios **e** higiénicos.
5 En las sierras, hay refugios **y** hospederías sencillas.
6 Es mejor alojarse donde cumplen las normas municipales **u** oficiales.

Revision test 16–18 (page 83–84)

A *Vendo, Busco y Cambio*

1 ¿Os gusta El último de la Fila **u** os interesa material de Chris O'Donnell? Escribid urgentemente **y** mandad sello respuesta Marta, C/ Sta. Ana, SALOU.

2 Pósters, reportajes, entrevistas de cantantes, grupos **e** incluso actores. Tengo más de 700 videoclips. Escribe a Juan, C/ Font n°12 **o** a la revista.

3 ¡Hola! ¿Tenéis material de Take That **y** de East 17 que váis a tirar a la basura **o** se lo váis a dar a alguien? Yo os lo cambio por material de vuestras estrellas **e** ídolos: Keanu Reeves, Magneto, NKOTB. Escribid a Elsa, Aptdo. 251, MADRID.

B *El concurso*

Jueves. El viaje: yo **llegué** al aeropuerto con Ainhoa de Smash Hits a las once. ¡El avión no **salió** hasta las cuatro! **Leí** revistas y **charlé** con Ainhoa. Viaje interminable.

Viernes. Turismo: Nueva York era impresionante. Por la mañana, **subí** con Ainhoa a la cima del famoso Empire State Building – ¡qué vistas más maravillosas! Por la tarde, **hice** un poco de compra, **di** un paseo en Central Park, y luego Ainhoa y yo **comimos** en un restaurante en el barrio chino – era riquísima, la comida.

Sábado. La actuación: ¡qué ilusión! **Pasé** dos horas en el estudio, viendo las preparaciones para la grabación para su nuevo disco. Cuando **vi** a Janet, estaba yo muy emocionada – pero la más pequeña del clan de los Jackson era muy simpática. Ella **vino** a saludarme personalmente y hablarme un ratito. Luego **empezó** a cantar – ¡Qué maravilla!

C *¡No me toca a mí!*

UNAI ¡Oye, Pili! Te toca a ti fregar hoy. Yo fregué **ayer**.

PILI ¡Mamá – esto no es justo! Yo lavé los platos **anoche**.

UNAI Y **ayer por la mañana** cuando tú estabas en la cama, ¡yo planché!

PILI ¡Tus cosas que ensuciaste **el otro día** jugando al fútbol!

UNAI Planché tu ropa también – y **hace dos días** recogí toda la casa.

MAMÁ ¡No me toca a mí! Yo hago los quehaceres **desde hace quince años**.

D *¿Cómo nos afecta el tiempo?*

1d Cuando **hace** buen tiempo, todo el mundo se siente mejor.

2g Si no **hace** mucho sol en invierno, la falta de luz afecta y deprime a mucha gente.

3a Cuando **hace** mucho viento, los niños se comportan peor.

4f Cando **hay** tormentas eléctricas, mucha gente sufre de dolor de cabeza.

5b Si **hay** neblina, se aumenta el riesgo de accidentes.

6e Cuando **hay** hielo se sube la incidencia de fracturas.

7c Cuando **hace** frío la gente se vuelve menos enérgica.

E *¿Opinas tú igual?*

1 Las **mejores** máquinas electrónicas se hacen en Japón.
2 El agua británica es la **peor** de Europa.
3 Los franceses hacen los **mejores** vinos de Europa.
4 Alemania fabrica los electrodomésticos **mejores** del mundo.
5 Los italianos son los **peores** conductores de coche en el mundo.
6 En cuanto a la comodidad, los automóviles Lada son los **peores**.
7 Las chicas obtienen **mejores** resultados en los examenes de GCSE que los chicos.
8 El **mejor** caviar del mundo viene de Rusia.
9 El índice de crímenes domésticos en Inglaterra es **peor** que en Irlanda del Norte.
10 Escocia hace los **mejores** whiskys del mundo.

F *Garibaldi*

ANA 'Garibaldi Caribe' es vuestro sexto album. ¿Cómo **empezasteis**?

CHARLY La idea de 'Garibaldi' **fue** de Oscar Gómez y Luis De Llano.

VICTOR Ellos **quisieron** formar un grupo que cantara música mejicana modernizada, e **hicieron** una serie de audiciones en Méjico.

ANA ¿Oscar y Luis **escogieron** a los que ahora forman parte del grupo?

VICTOR No, sólo a cinco. Tres otros **se fueron** y ya han sido reemplazados.

CHARLY Paola, Ingrid y Adrián **entraron** después de la fiesta de Acapulco.

ANA ¿Y la música de 'Garibaldi Caribe' – de dónde **vino**?

VICTOR Nosotros **mezclamos** la música tropical con el tinte Garibaldi.

ANA El album **tuvo** mucho éxito en Méjico – ¿va a pasar lo mismo aquí?

CHARLY La gente española nos **cayó** muy simpática en nuestra gira. Nos **encantó** actuar en España hace tres años – ¡espero que sea igual!

Chapter 19   What do you know? (page 85)

A *Los preparativos*

MAMÁ Yo **he lavado** el coche, **he cambiado** las pesetas en libras esterlinas, **he dejado** las llaves con la vecina, y **he regado** las plantas.

PAPÁ Yo **he planchado** un montón de ropa, **he recogido** los dormitorios, **he salido** a la agencia de viajes, y **he reservado** los billetes.

NACHO Yo **he ido** a la caja de ahorros, **he sacado** un poco de dinero, **he comprado** caramelos para el viaje – ¡y los **he comido** casi todos ya!

B *El momento de la verdad*

MAMÁ	¿Quién tiene <u>el jabón</u>?	PAPÁ	¡Yo no **lo** tengo!
PAPÁ	Dónde están <u>las toallas</u>?	MAMÁ	¡**Las** dejé encima de la cama!
NACHO	No encuentro <u>el walkman</u>.	MAMÁ	¿No **lo** tienes tú?
PAPÁ	¿Y <u>los bañadores</u>?	NACHO	No **los** veo, papá.
MAMÁ	¿<u>La crema de sol</u> está allí?	PAPÁ	No **la** tengo yo.
NACHO	¿<u>Las revistas</u>, Mamá?	MAMÁ	**Las** he dejado en el coche.
PAPÁ	¿No has traído <u>el talco</u>?	MAMÁ	¿Por qué no **lo** trajiste tú?
MAMÁ	¿No veo <u>los pasaportes</u>!	PAPÁ	¡Calma! ¡**los** tengo yo!

Chapter 19   What have you learnt? (page 88)

A *En el aeropuerto*

1   Has llegado a España. En la recogida de equipaje, te das cuenta de que …
   a   Tú **has dejado** la máquina fotográfica en el avión.
   b   La línea aérea **ha perdido** una de tus maletas – porque tú no **has atado** bien la etiqueta de viaje.
   c   Tus maletas **han llegado** juntas en estado perfecto.

2   Tu hotel está todavía en construcción. Un día, vuelves y …
   a   **Han entrado** muchas moscas porque tú no **has cerrado** las persianas.
   b   Los obreros **han ensuciado** el cuarto de baño lavándose las manos.
   c   La criada **ha limpiado** perfectamente la habitación porque la **has impresionado** tú, intentando hablar español.

3   Al final de las vacaciones, vuelves al aeropuerto. Descubres que …
   a   Tu avión **ha salido** ya, porque tú **te has equivocado** de la hora.
   b   La agencia de viajes no **ha rellenado** correctamente tu billete de vuelta.
   c   Todo está en orden. Tú **te has divertido** mucho.

B *Los desastres de Nuria*

TÍO	¡Nuria! ¿Qué tal? Pero ¿dónde están las maletas? ¿No **las** tienes ya?
NURIA	¡No, no tengo el equipaje! Iberia **lo** ha perdido entre Londres y aquí.
TÍO	¡Qué rabia! Y tus padres, ¿dónde están? No **les** veo.
NURIA	Pero, ¿no recibiste los recados de parte de Papá? **Los** mandó ayer.
TÍO	No recibí nada. Sólo una postal que **me** mandó tu padre hace mucho.
NURIA	Mamá tuvo apendicitis. **La** visité en el hospital ayer. Va mejor.
TÍO	¡Dios mío! Bueno, puedes venir a mi casa, Nuria. **Te** llevo en coche.

Chapter 20   What do you know? (page 89)

A *El médico malhumorado*

1 ¿No se ha **puesto** usted los guantes para lavar los instrumentos?
2 ¿Las recetas? ¡No, no las he **escrito** todavía! Necesito mi boli. ¿Dónde está?
3 ¿El esparadrapo? No sé dónde está. No lo he **visto**.
4 ¡Oye, hay que recoger bien! He **descubierto** estas tijeras en el suelo.
5 ¡No tengo sitio para hacer nada! ¡Alguien ha **cubierto** mi mesa de papeles!
6 ¿Quién ha **abierto** mi correo? ¡Si dice 'privado', lo abro yo!

B *Los preparativos*

1 Los instrumentos **esterilizados** correctamente …
2 Las vendas **preparadas** …
3 La mesa **recogida** bien …
4 El estetoscopio **puesto** en su caja …
5 Las jeringas **envueltas** en su plástico …
6 La cama **cubierta** con una sábana limpia …

C *El trabajo de la recepcionista*

DOCTOR Me duele la cabeza, Marta. ¿Me da una aspirina **a mí** también?
MARTA Claro, doctor. Y le traigo **a usted** un buen café en seguida.
DOCTOR Gracias. Y a la enfermera. Tráigale algo **a ella**.
MARTA Viene el Dr. Gómez a las tres. Le he mandado **a él** las radiografías.
DOCTOR Marta, ¡es usted un sol! ¿Nos ha dejado **a nosotros** los documentos?
MARTA Sí. Y les he dejado **a ustedes** una lista de los pacientes de la tarde.

Chapter 20   What have you learnt? (page 92)

A *Hay que …*

Yolanda
1 **He puesto** el botiquín en el coche.
2 **No he dicho** adiós a mi suplente.
3 **No he devuelto** mis llaves a la recepción.
4 **He escrito** una receta para la Sra. Muñoz.

Ignacio
1 **He abierto** una lata de atún.
2 **No he frito** las patatas y la cebolla.
3 **He roto** huevos en un bol.
4 **No he hecho** la tortilla.

B *Sucesos*

1 Accidente en la N630: veinte heridos **trasladados** al hospital.
2 Tres personas **muertas** en un accidente de tráfico en Mieres.
3 Autobús francés **precipitado** al mar cerca de Estepona.
4 Mal estado de la carretera por lluvias **caídas** anoche.
5 Dos cadáveres **rescatados** de un Seat en la Sierra de Gredos.
6 Una niña **desaparecida** en un accidente de helicóptero.

C *En la clínica*

1 ¿El chico se ha roto el dedo? Hay que hacer**le** una radiografía.

2 Marta – el señor Garay y yo tenemos sed. ¿Puedes preparar**nos** un té?

3 ¿Las víctimas tienen quemaduras graves? Sería mejor no poner**les** nada.

4 Pero, ¿qué te pasa, chiquitita? ¡Tranquila! Voy a poner**te** una inyección.

5 Chicos – vosotros dos tenéis una insolación. Voy a dar**os** una crema.

6 ¡Ay! ¡Me he cortado el dedo con las tijeras! Debo poner**me** una tirita.

Chapter 21   What do you know? (page 93)

A *El accidente*

1c El testigo era un Señor Blasco y Beltrán.

2f Estaba tomando un refresco en la terraza del Hotel Miramar.

3a Hacía viento y estaba lloviendo un poco.

4e Un vespino rojo estaba pasando el hotel hacia las 11.15.

5g El joven del vespino quiso evitar un coche mal aparcado.

6b Un Seat estaba saliendo de una calle enfrente del hotel.

7h El conductor del Seat no vio el Vespino.

8d El Seat chocó con el Vespino y el joven se cayó al suelo.

B *¿En qué puedo servirle?*

1 No funciona mi cámara. ¿**Me la** puede reparar?

2 Mis padres quieren lavar el coche, pero ¿**se lo** puede hacer usted?

3 Nuestra habitación no está arreglada todavía. ¿**nos la** arregla pronto?

4 Quiero mandar un fax. ¿**Me lo** puede mandar usted?

5 Los zapatos de mi marido están muy sucios. ¿**Se los** puede limpiar?

6 ¿La habitación del Sr. Roldán no está lista? ¡Pero **se la** prometí para las tres!

Chapter 21   What have you learnt? (page 96)

A *Guipúzcoa antigua*

En los caseríos vascos antiguos, la vida de la familia **se hacía** en la cocina. Allí **estaba** el hogar o 'llar', donde mi madre **encendía** el fuego que **era** la única calefacción. De día, mi madre y yo **preparábamos** la comida. Por la noche, toda la familia **se reunía** allí también. Mi hermana mayor **cosía** la ropa y mi madre **enseñaba** a mis hermanos a leer. Cuando **nos íbamos** a la cama, mi padre **colocaba** algunas brasas en un calentador de cobre, y con eso **solía** calentar el interior de nuestras camas … Una vida tranquila, ¡pero dura!

B *El accidente*

CELIA   Yo **estaba viendo** la tele cuando oí el ruido de los frenos.

JORGE   Pero yo **estaba** fuera. Estaba barriendo la acera delante de la casa.

CELIA   Mientras **se acercaba** a la esquina, el conductor miró hacia atrás.

JORGE   La señora **estaba cruzando** la calle cuando le atropelló el coche.

CELIA   La visibilidad **era** buena cuando se produjo el accidente.

JORGE   Aunque **hacía** frío, no **había** hielo en la carretera.

CELIA   Una chica guapa le **estaba llamando** la atención – ¡qué estúpido!

C *Asistencia medical*

1   ¡Rápido – el botiquín! ¡Páse**me**lo!

2   La señora necesita oxígeno. Sí, dé**se**lo en seguida.

3   ¿Agua, señora? Lo siento, no **se** la puedo dar.

4   Ese vendaje – ¿**nos** lo abre, por favor?

5   La camilla – búsca**me**la. Está en la ambulancia.

6   ¿Esa venda? – dé**se**la a mis compañeros allí.

7   ¿Un analgésico? Dé**se**lo por inyección.

Revision test 19–21 (page 97–98)

A *Hay que ...*

ABUELA   Se debe devolver el vídeo al videoclub.

TÚ   **Andreu lo ha devuelto.**

ABUELA   Es imprescindible escribir al hotel con la fecha de nuestra llegada.

TÚ   **Sr. y Sra. Velázquez han escrito.**

ABUELA   Hay que hacer la maleta grande.

TÚ   **¿No la ha hecho usted?**

ABUELA   Ah sí, es verdad. Pero debo cerrarla con llave.

TÚ   **La hemos cerrado.**

ABUELA   Necesito poner mis gafas de sol en una de las maletas.

TÚ   **Las he puesto en la maleta pequeña.**

ABUELA   Entonces, ¿por qué estamos esperando aquí? ¡Vamos al coche!

B *¿Te gusta la ropa?*

1   Te tocan cincuenta mil pesetas en la lotería:

   a   **Las** gastas en seguida en tu tienda de ropa favorita.

   b   llamas a tu amigo/a, y **le** invitas a ayudarte a gastar la mitad.

   c   no gastas el dinero – **lo** ahorras todo.

2   Cuando vas a una tienda de ropa con un/a amigo/a:

   a   Eliges muchas prendas, y te **las** pruebas todas.

   b   Eliges una prenda que te gustaría llevar, y te **la** pruebas.

   c   **Lo** pasas mal en las tiendas de ropa. Esperas a tu amigo/a fuera.

3 Tu amigo/a recibe dos entradas gratis para un desfile de modas:
  a tu amigo/a **te** invita a acompañarle, porque sabe que te va a gustar.
  b lo pensáis, pero a ti y a tu amigo/a no **os** interesa mucho. No vais.
  c tu amigo no **te** dice nada. Sabe que es inútil.

4 Te invitan a un baile de disfraces:
  a sacas todas las cosas de tu guardarropa, y pasas todo el día probándote**las**
  b llamas a tu amigo/a y **lo** discutís por teléfono.
  c lees la invitación, y **la** echas a la basura.

C *En el Servicio Súper Rápido*
  1 Puede repar**ármela** para el lunes?
  2 ¿Usted puede cos**érmelo**?
  3 ¿Puede limpi**ársela** usted?
  4 ¿El mecánico puede mir**ármelos** hoy?
  5 ¿Puede cort**árnoslas** aquí?
  6 Voy a **dejarles** mi reloj.

D *¿Qué pasó exactamente?*
  GABI   Yo **salía/estaba saliendo** de la tienda, cuando **oí** el chirriar del coche gris.
  TERE   El coche **iba** muy rápido – demasiado rápido para las condiciones.
  GABI   Pero la joven de la moto **tuvo** la culpa también. **Hablaba/estaba hablando** con su pasajero cuando **se pusieron** rojos los semáforos.
  TERE   Es verdad. Los dos jóvenes no **prestaban** atención.
  GABI   Parece que el conductor del coche no **vio** la moto cruzando la calle.
  NACHO ¡Qué ruido más horrible cuando el coche **chocó** con la moto!
  GABI   ¿Has visto con qué fuerza **se cayó** el joven de delante?
  TERE   Sí. Y el coche **se resbaló** y **se paró** contra aquel árbol grande.
  NACHO Por el hielo, supongo. **Había** hielo en la carretera.
  TERE   Y lluvia también encima. **Llovía** hace poco, ¿te acuerdas?

E *Los regalos de Navidad*
  1 ¿Mis abuelos? **Les** voy a regalar este jarro.
  2 Las entradas para el teatro, **se las** doy a mis padres.
  3 ¡Tranquilos, chicos! O el hueso para el perro, ¡**os lo** regalo a vosotros!
  4 ¿Qué **le** voy a dar a mi hermano? ¡Nada!
  5 La botella de perfume, **se la** regalo a mi hermana.
  6 El vale-regalo del Corte Inglés – **se lo** doy a mi tía.
  7 ¿Y tú, Felipe? ¿Qué te gustaría? Ah, ¡el regalo 'misterio', **te lo** doy a ti!
  8 ¿La caja de turrón? **Me la** guardo para mí!

Chapter 22   What do you know? (page 99)

A *¡Cómo ha cambiado la zona!*
construido
hecho
contaminado
dado
desmontado
quitado
montado
cambiado

B *La exposición*
1 casita: **casa**
2 jardincito: **jardín**
3 rinconcillo: **rincón**
4 hotelucho: **hotel**
5 balconazo: **balcón**
6 chiquito: **chico**
7 garajote: **garaje**
8 grandona: **grande**

Chapter 22   What have you learnt? (page 102)

A *El desastre ecológico*

Nosotros, los habitantes de esta zona tan preciosa **habíamos perjudicado** el
equilibrio ecológico de nuestro lago, sin saberlo. Durante los años setenta y ochenta,
los veraneantes **habían ensuciado** las playas artificiales, la comunidad pesquera
había despoblado el lago de los peces nativos, y yo mismo **había contribuido** a este
desastre ecológico, como niño, cogiendo flores silvestres. Hablé con el alcalde,
Ramón Hernández Ferrol y le pregunté:
– ¿Qué medidas **había tomado** usted para proteger la naturaleza de este lugar?
– Pues, al principio, ningunas. Nosotros de aquí no **nos habíamos dado** cuenta de su
  importancia ecológica. En aquella época, nadie **había hecho** ningún estudio.
– Parece que un investigador científico de Guadalajara **había escrito** un artículo
  sobre la posibilidad de un desastre ecológico – ¿no lo **habían estudiado** ustedes?
– Lo **habíamos leído** nosotros que nos interesábamos en la naturaleza, sí. Pero el
  Concejo Municipal, desgraciadamente, no …

B *El padre consciente*
1 Yo **acabo de cerrar** el agua: José **acababa de abrir** el grifo antes de salir.
2 Sara y José **acaban de llevar** las bolsas y botellas de plástico para reciclar.
3 Yo **acababa de comprar** botellas de vidrio – José se queja porque pesan mucho.
4 Mi mujer **acaba de apagar** las luces en los cuartos que los niños **acababan de
   encender** hace poco. Es que cuesta mucho la electricidad.
5 **Acabamos de bajar** la temperatura de la calefacción, para no gastar energía.
6 Hoy **acabo de escribir** al periódico para apoyar su campaña de ahorrar energía.

C *¿A favor o no?*
1 ¡Psst! Miguel, mira la jovencita allí!: **favorable**.
2 Ese liderillo mc fastidia, ¿sabes?: **desfavorable**.
3 ¡Qué grandota es esa miembro del comité! ¡A la derecha! ¿No ves?: **desfavorable**.
4 El chico que habla ahora – ¡qué talentazo tiene!: **favorable**.
5 ¿Has visto el chico detrás de mí? ¡Qué guapetón es!: **favorable**.

Chapter 23 What do you know? (page 103)

A *El Tamagotchi*

Dentro de muy poco, **llegará** a vuestras tiendas un nuevo tipo de juguete – el tamagotchi. El prototipo **estará** listo dentro de muy pocos meses, y **venderán** hasta veinte millones de ejemplares sólo dentro del Japón, en nuestro opinión. En la propaganda publicitaria, el tamagotchi mismo explicará: 'Yo soy una mascota virtual. **Podré** vivir muchos años, como los animales domésticos. **Seré** como tu amigo o amiga. Tú **tendrás** que cuidarme y mostrarme cariño – si no, **moriré**'.

B *El hombre del siglo veintiuno*

Yo no soy – y nunca seré – un hombre del siglo veintiuno. Veo su imagen típica por todas partes. El **tener** buena salud es su pasión, y **hacer** ejercicio su hobby favorito. Miembro del lobby anti-tabaco, no aguanta el **fumar** en lugares públicos y según él, comprar cigarrillos o cigarros es **tirar** sus pocas pelas a la basura.

Tampoco le gusta **beber** – ni las bebidas fuertes como el whisky, ni los refrescos inofensivos como la limonada. Y no permite tampoco el pasatiempo favorito de millones de españoles: el **pasar** la tarde del sábado delante de la tele viendo el fútbol. En cuanto a **ser** gastrónomo ¡ni hablar! El **comer** es para vivir, y no al revés. Su misión es la misma que los fanáticos religiosos: **convertirnos** en seres sanos, delgados y (por último) tan tristes como él.

Chapter 23 What have you learnt? (page 106)

A *El mundo futuro*

El comercio

a Internet **ofrecerá** nuevas oportunidades para comprar y vender.

b Las compañías internacionales **dominarán** el comercio mundial.

c Con la crisis en el mercado de dinero, las unidades monetarias europeas no **valdrán** nada.

El trabajo

a La tecnología **hará** posible el pleno empleo.

b **Podremos** trabajar mucho más desde nuestras casas.

c Sólo los ricos **tendrán** trabajo – los demás **vivirán** en la miseria.

El transporte

a Los expertos **inventarán** una nueva forma de energía barata y limpia.

b El transporte privado no **será** rentable: **costará** mucho más que hoy.

c No **habrá** un sistema de transporte público. Y con la falta de seguridad ciudadana, ni tú ni yo **querremos** ir a ningún sitio.

B *Una vista al mundo del trabajo*
1 Miki **suele levantarse** cuando el despertador electrónico lo juzga necesario.
2 El robot-cocinero **suele preparar** el desayuno.
3 Miki no **suele lavar** los platos – el lavavajillas lo hace.
4 **Suele descargar** su correo electrónico primero.
5 Trabajadores como él **suelen pasar** toda la mañana delante del ordenador.
6 A la una, los aparatos-robot **vuelen** a hacer la comida.
7 Miki no **vuelve a trabajar** por la tarde: nadie trabaja más de veinte horas a la semana. Él y sus amigos **suelen** salir o **ir** al cine.

Chapter 24   What do you know? (page 107)

A *¿Qué sabéis?*
1 ¿Mamá, **conoces** el nuevo profesor de ecología?
2 Es un señor muy interesante. **Sabe** mucho de la ecología.
3 ¿**Sabíais** que España está muy atrasada, ecológicamente?
4 Yo no **sé** mucho de todo esto, pero quiero aprender.
5 ¿**Conocemos** alguna organización en que me pueda inscribir?

B *Si fuera yo Ministro …*
1 Tú, mamá, **utilizarías** productos biológicos en envases más ecológicos.
2 Dentro de casa, nosotros **ahorraríamos** mucha energía.
3 Usted, señor, no **compraría** uno de estos cochazos que gastan tanta gasolina.
4 ¡Vosotros dos, mamá y papá, **consumiríais** menos papel!
5 Mis hermanas **deberían** evitar los aerosoles – hay un montón en el cuarto de baño.
6 ¡Yo, por lo menos, **actuaría** de una manera responsable!

C *¡No seas irresponsable!*
Papá, cuando vayas al supermercado, no **hagas** la compra de una manera irresponsable. No **compres** productos con muchas químicas, no **elijas** cosas en envases de plástico, y no **pidas** bolsas de plástico – llévate la cesta grande de mamá. En el coche, no **conduzcas** rápidamente, porque eso usa mucha gasolina. Si vas a lavar el coche, no **busques** un lavado de coches automático – usan demasiada agua. Y por favor, no **traigas** a tu amigo, el Señor Gutiérrez, a casa para comer – ¡me fastidia este hombre, con sus ideas capitalistas!

Chapter 24   What have you learnt? (page 110)

A *Me imagino que ...*

1 **Trabajaría** desde casa, pero **iría** a una oficina central un día a la semana.
2 **Me pondría** en contacto todos los días con mi jefe o jefa.
3 Me **mandarían** información por medio de correo electrónico.
4 **Haría** mi trabajo más rápido y mejor.
5 Lo mejor es que **estaría** en casa para los niños.
6 Lo peor **sería** que **tendría** que organizar el día de otra manera.
7 **Podría** haber muchas interrupciones: los niños, los vecinos ...
8 Hay días cuando no **saldrías**. A veces **te sentirías** un poco aislada.
¿Les interesa la posibilidad? Hablen con su gerente.

B *Para una Navidad anti-consumidora*

A ustedes, los padres ...

1 No **regalen** un animal doméstico a su niño: 'adopten' un animal de un zoo.
2 No **elijan** un árbol natural: sería mejor comprar un abeto artificial.
3 No **den** mucha importancia a los regalos: ayuden a sus niños a pensar en la bondad de la gente, y no en el dinero que hayan gastado.
4 No **vayan** a los centros comerciales con sus hijos en los diez días antes de Navidad – ellos necesitan un descanso del bombo publicitario*.

A vosotros, los niños ...

1 No **deis** mucho trabajo a vuestros padres – ¡les sobra!
2 No **seáis** ingratos si no recibís los regalos que queríais.
3 No **calculéis** el coste de los regalos y no **hayáis** comparaciones.
4 No **os olvidéis** de decir 'gracias', o llamar por teléfono, a todos los que os hayan regalado algo.

Revision test 22–24 (page 111–112)

A *Ketima*

1 Un miembro masculino de la familia **había cometido** un crimen.
2 Para evitar una maldición, los padres **habían entregado** su hija Ketima al brujo.
3 Ketima **había tenido** que trabajar dieciocho horas por día, cuidando la casa.
4 El brujo la **había hecho** una de sus esclavas – condenada a un infierno diario.
5 Abusada, Ketima **había dado** a luz a un hijo, cuando tenía sólo doce años.
6 Después de cuatro años, la pobre Ketima **se había puesto** mala.
7 El brujo, que le **había roto** el espíritu, la llevó al desierto cercano.
8 Allí, a solas, sufriendo horriblemente, **había muerto** Ketima.

B *¿Qué opinas?*

– ¿No le gusta el piso?

¡Es un pisucho!

– ¿Pero tiene jardín, no?

¡Es un jardincillo!

– ¿No le gusta la playa?

¡Es chiquita!

– ¿Y el vigilante de la playa?

¡Qué simpaticón es!

C *Tu horóscopo*

Estudios   Tu rendimiento escolar **mejorará** con respecto al año pasado. En periodo de exámenes **tendrá** todo a tu favor, y **podrás** concentrarte en el estudio, aunque durante el resto del año **pasarás** por momentos de despiste.

Amor   **Resolverás** un importante dilema – si abres los ojos **verás** que alguien piensa en ti más de lo normal. Intenta ir paso a paso y te **saldrán** bien las cosas. Si no tienes pareja, este año **encontrarás** tu media naranja.

Dinero   En la primera mitad del año, te **lloverá** dinero de los sitios más insospechadas. Cuidado – tus amigos te **pedirán** dinero y si no se les das, te **harán** sufrir. Tú no **sabrás** que hacer: pero familiares te ayudarán.

D *Las relaciones con los demás*

¿Para las buenas relaciones, qué es lo más importante?

– **Escuchar** es más importante que hablar.

¿No es importante **el comunicarse** también?

– Sí. Pero **el hablar**, como medio de comunicación, está sobreestimado.
   Explicar tu punto de vista implica no **prestar atención** al otro.

¿Qué otras maneras hay de comunicarse?

– ¡Hay muchas! **Sonreír**, **mirar** compasivo, **tocar** el hombro o la mano – todas estas cosas demuestran tu cariño y tu solicitud.

¿**El saber** cómo mantener buenas relaciones es muy complejo, entonces?

– Sí. **Conocer** a otra persona es una aventura sin fin.

E *Los políticos y los intereses 'verdes'*

1   **Quisiera** saber lo que van ustedes a hacer para el medio ambiente.

2   ¿Qué **haría** usted para apoyar el movimiento 'verde'?

3   ¿Cómo **podríamos** nosotros, los jóvenes, ayudar?

4   ¿Qué medidas **recomendaría** usted para limpiar nuestras ciudades?

5   ¿Qué **diría** usted a la crítica que su partido apoya a los empresarios?

6   ¿Cómo **contestarían** los ministros a la acusación de ser indiferente?

F *No debes …*

No compres a locas – haz una lista, y sólo compra las cosas en tu lista.
No salgas con amigos todos los fines de semana. ¡Ver la tele no cuesta nada!
No vayáis, tú y tus amigos, a las boutiques – ¡ellos te animarán a comprar!
No seas súper generosa y **no prestes** dinero a todo el mundo.
No estés todo el día en el centro comercial – busca otras cosas que hacer.
No te permitas más de una hora en un almacén grande.
No hagas la compra en el supermercado cuando tienes hambre.

Chapter 25   Practice (page 116)

A *En la carretera*

1 Insisto en que <u>estés</u> (**Estar**) otra vez en casa antes de las doce.
2 Para decir la verdad, Mariluz, prefiero que no <u>vayas</u> (**Ir**) con él en el coche.
3 Os ruego que no <u>bebáis</u> (**Beber**) alcohol – beber y conducir son incompatibles.
4 No quiero que <u>haya</u> (**Haber**) algún accidente.
5 Tampoco quiero que <u>seáis</u> (**Ser**) detenidos por la policía.
6 ¡Y prefiero que no <u>déis</u> (**Dar**) positivo en la prueba del alcohol!
7 Os aconsejo que <u>tengáis</u> (**Tener**) cuidado …

B *El momento de la verdad*

GUARDIA 1   Señor, le pido que **pare** el motor.
GUARDIA 2   Y señora, le ruego que **baje** del coche.
GUARDIA 1   Insisto en que **se someta** usted, señor, a la prueba de alcohol.
MARILUZ   Quiero que **llamen** ustedes a mi familia. Son las doce ya.
GUARDIA 1   En un momento, señorita. Prefiero que **hagamos** nosotros la prueba en seguida.
GUARDIA 2   Señor, la prueba resulta positiva. Le digo que no **conduzca** el coche y que me **dé** usted las llaves.
MARILUZ   ¡Ay, qué vergüenza! Mamá nos va a matar …

C *En la comisaría*

1 Señores, les aconsejo **llevar** a su hija ahora a casa.
2 Le permitimos **pasar** la noche en casa, pero …
3 … le mando a ella **volver** aquí mañana para completar su declaración.
4 Les aconsejo no **hacerle** muchas preguntas. Está muy cansada.
5 Le recomiendo no **salir** con un chico que bebe tanto.
6 Bueno, les permitimos ahora **irse** a casa. Hasta mañana.

Chapter 26   Practice (page 119)

A *Creo en extraterrestres*
1 **Future time**: yo daré la bienvenida a los seres extraterrestres **cuando** los **vea**.
2 **Purpose**: vigilo el cielo cada noche **para que sea** yo el primero en verles.
3 **Emotion**: **no me sorprende** que **haya** más experiencias de encuentros cercanos.
4 **Future time**: **en cuanto llegue** el milenio, habrá más visitas de OVNIs.
5 **Emotion**: **me alegro** de que **visiten** la tierra, porque nos hace falta su inteligencia.
6 **Purpose**: nos ayudarán – **a menos de que** les **maten** las fuerzas armadas.

B *La hipnosis*
La hipnosis ha sido utilizada **por** ufólogos como un método **para** sacar a la luz la verdad sobre los contactos con extraterrestres. En muchos relatos de abducción **por** seres extraños, los abducidos experimentan una investigación. Algunos cambian esta invasión de su espacio físico y mental **por** un aumento en su capacidad intelectual. Pero **para** otros, la experiencia es desagradable. La hipnosis la reanima; pero precisamente **por** esta capacidad de despertar sentimientos, es peligrosa. No es que las víctimas están **por** exagerar; pero **para** ganar fama, el hipnotizador puede influir en los recuerdos o sugerir cosas – y estas 'sugerencias' pasan **por** verdaderas experiencias dentro de un OVNI.

C *Las abducciones imaginarias*
Hipnoticé 16 voluntarios, a **quienes** di la instrucción **que** tenían que imaginar una experiencia de abducción. Una 'víctima de una verdadera abducción', con **quien** hablé, describió lo que le pasó. Mi libro, en el **que** doy más detalles, explicará **que** los dos tipos de experiencia casi no diferían.

Chapter 27   Practice (page 122)

A *Antología del disparate*
El diamante: piedra preciosa, **cuyo** tamaño depende de su precio.
Gobierno: manera de arreglar las cosas, **cuyas** formas principales son dos – buenas y malas.
Examen: tres horas de tortura legal, **cuya** intención es demostrar la ignorancia.
Profesor: figura decorativa en un aula, **cuyo** rostro se parece al humano.
Deberes: el poner de tareas imaginarias, **cuya** función es tranquilizar a los padres.
Día escolar: período interminable, **cuyos** minutos son dos veces más largos que durante las vacaciones.

B *Las etapas de la vida*
1d El bebé empieza por salir con la suya.
2c El niño insiste en ir a lo suyo.
3a El adolescente sueña con ser adulto.
4e El adulto se cansa de ser adulto.
5b El anciano quiere ser niño otra vez.

C *Los skins*

Hoy, hablamos de los *skins*, detrás **de los cuales** andan adolescentes de sólo 14 años, atraídos por el halo de misteria y terror que inspiran. Tribu urbana, delante **de la cual** el público tiembla de miedo, sus miembros inician una campaña de terror en Castellón. Las plazas centrales, alrededor **de las cuales** se reunen grupos antagonistas, ya son zonas prohibidas para la mayoría de la población. La violencia del mes pasado – durante **el cual** murieron once jóvenes inocentes – se extiende más allá de Barcelona y Madrid. El odio tradicional (entre los *skins* y los homosexuales), **del cual** hablaremos más tarde, sigue provocando las agresiones.

Chapter 28   Practice (page 125)

A *Luisa y la droga*

Hace varios meses, la jovencita Luisa murió: cayó entre dos vagones de metro. La policía trata el caso como si **fuera/fuese** un accidente, pero la madre quiere que **investigue** los hechos. "En mi opinión, fue relacionado con la droga", dice. "Mi hija pertenecía a un grupo que tomaba drogas y a veces parecía como si **estuviera/estuviese** despistada, y no sabía lo que hacía. El líder es el culpable, en mi opinión: mandó a mi hija que se **pusiera/se** pusiese a robar cosas, y que **buscase/buscara** a otros para ayudarle. Luisa temia que los lideres la **matara/matase.** Le pidió a un amigo que se **uniese/se** uniera con el grupo para que ella **pudiese/pudiera** seguir viviendo". La madre de Luisa tiene dos mensajes. A los padres de jóvenes que viven así dice: 'Díganles que **abandonen** la droga y que **vuelvan** a casa. Y a los jóvenes dice "Un compañero o una compañera que se mete en la droga está en peligro. Os recomiendo que **habléis** con los padres de vuestro amigo o amiga. Es necesario que los padres **sepan** en que están metidos sus hijos".

B *La demolición de 20 apartamentos en Cala Blanca*

1 El complejo turístico fue construido por una compañía alemana hace diez años.
2 La propiedad fue vendida a una compañía británica poco después.
3 Los edificos fueron abandonados por el dueño actual hace tres años.
4 Las actuaciones de 'esponjamiento' fueron iniciadas por la Consellería de Turismo.
5 El año pasado, tres de los bloques fueron derribados.
6 Un solar de 1.500 metros fue recuperado por el Ayuntamiento.
7 La construcción de un parque público fue terminada la semana pasada.

Revision test 25–28 (page 126–128)

A *El pobre Andrés*

1 Cuando yo **practico** el snowboard, ¡siempre llevo la ropa adecuada, Mamá!
2 Vale – en cuanto **venga** Paco, él te mostrará el equipo.
3 Os ruego que no me **llaméis** por teléfono cada noche.
4 ¿Por qué? ¡Porque los demás me toman el pelo y no quiero que lo **hagan**!
5 Claro que os mandaré una postal. Siempre os escribo cuando **estoy** fuera.
6 Sí, me pondré una crema de sol. ¡Aunque no **salga** el sol, me la pondré!
7 ¡Mamá, por favor – no me **des** más consejos! ¡Ah, ya viene Paco!
8 Bueno, me alegro de que **estés** aquí, Paco. ¿Nos vamos ya?
9 Mamá, ¡insisto en que **te quedes** aquí! No necesito besos, abrazos y lágrimas delante de los demás. Bueno, adiós …

B *Nos aconsejan …*

1 Sus padres le mandan **ganar** dinero.
2 Sus resultados hacen imprescindible **repetir** el año.
3 Le aconseja **no ir a** la universidad.
4 Les permiten **posponer** el ingreso a la universidad.
5 Le recomienda **trabajar** o **viajar** durante un año.
6 Le aconsejan **vivir** un tiempo, o temporada en el extranjero.

C *Don Quijote*

La Mancha, **que** es un territorio de la parte central de España, está unida al nombre de Don Quijote, **cuyas** aventuras son ya cosas de leyenda. El autor del libro, Cervantes, a **quien** tantos admiran por su perspicacia y su ironía, describe lo que pasa a un señor **que** pierde el juicio a causa de dormir poco y leer demasiados libros de caballería. En la Plaza de España de Madrid está su estatua, al lado **de la cual** aparece su fiel escudero, Sancho Panza. La aventura de los molinos de viento, **que** confundió Don Quijote con gigantes y con **quienes** quería luchar, sigue siendo la más famosa de las historias.

D *Cruz y el fax*

CRUZ ¿A qué hora salimos **para** el centro comercial?
EVA ¿Si estamos listos **para** las diez y media?
CRUZ Vale. Oye, quiero mandar esta carta **por** fax.
¿Hay una oficina **por** allí donde me lo harían?
EVA Sí. Pero es caro. **Para** mandar un fax, te costará unas ochocientas pesetas. ¿Es **para** hoy?
CRUZ Sí, es urgente. ¡Pero ochocientas **por** un fax!
EVA Pues, mira. Voy abajo **por/a por** café. Si quieres, voy a casa de mi amiga al lado. Ella te lo hará.
CRUZ ¡Estupendo! Muchas gracias **por** tu ayuda.

E *Cosa de ancianas*

NURIA ¿Qué haces, tía? ¿Por qué te pones el abrigo?

SRA. **He decidido salir.**

NURIA Pero, ¿adónde vas? ¡Son las cinco de la tarde!

SRA. Voy a un merienda-baile. **Me encanta bailar.**

NURIA ¡Pero no puedes ir sola!

SRA. ¿Dónde está el teléfono? **Debo llamar un taxi.**

NURIA ¡Pero no vas a conocer a nadie!

SRA. Conozco a Federico. **Espero verle allí.**

NURIA Pero, tía, siéntate. Me parece que ponen una buena película …

SRA. **¡Odio ver la tele!** ¡Es cosa de ancianas! Bueno, me voy.

F *Mi mujer tiene la enfermedad de Alzheimer*

A veces, se olvida **de** cuidarse de sí misma, y yo necesito cuidarla físicamente.
Muchas veces insiste **en** hacer cosas que, físicamente, son muy difíciles. Empieza **a**
vestirse, por ejemplo, pero termina **por** no poder hacerlo. Tarda mucho **en** hacer
cosas que antes hacía rápidamente. Deja **de** hacer cosas de repente sin darse cuenta
de los peligros – por ejemplo, no se acuerda **de** que haya encendido el gas en la
cocina. Se decide **a** salir a horas imprevistas, o piensa **en** acostarse a las diez de la
mañana, porque no sabe qué hora es. Puede amenazarme **con** violencia porque no me
reconoce, y porque se siente frustrada y no entiende por qué. Pero es mi mujer, y
quiero ayudarla. Trato **de** ser positivo, y optimista, pero no es fácil.